"A dynamite look at the future for Christians! The problem is...she may be correct."

—Dr. J. C. Willke
President of Life Issues Institute
and the International Right to Life Federation

"Not all wars are fought with guns. America is under attack from those seeking to strip its citizens of their religious freedom. This book is a vital weapon in the arsenal to defeat anti-religious oppression."

—Oliver L. North, Lt. Col. USMC (Ret.)
Author of *New York Times* bestsellers *Mission Compromise*
and *War Stories: Operation Iraqi Freedom*

"Janet Folger understands our religious liberties are under assault and she is in the trenches fighting back, urging us all to join her. Her book is more than a passive cultural critique. It will inspire you to suit up for battle."

—David Limbaugh
Author of *New York Times* bestseller *Persecution*

"Janet Folger issues a no-holds-barred wake-up call and successfully conveys that unless we stand up and speak the truth *now*, we will not be allowed to do it later. Read this book!"

—Brad Dacus
President, Pacific Justice Institute

"A strong dose of truth and a plan to keep us out of jail."

—Dr. Jerry Falwell

"Facts that will scare you and solutions that will give you hope."

—Phyllis Schlafly

"The truth that cuts through political, national, and church boundaries. If you value your freedom, heed Janet's words."

—Father Frank Pavone, Priests for Life

THE
CRIMINALIZATION
OF
CHRISTIANITY

THE
CRIMINALIZATION
OF
CHRISTIANITY

JANET L. FOLGER

Multnomah® Publishers *Sisters, Oregon*

THE CRIMINALIZATION OF CHRISTIANITY
published by Multnomah Publishers, Inc.

Published in association with Loyal Arts Literary Agency, LoyalArts.com

© 2005 by Janet L. Folger

International Standard Book Number: 1-59052-468-3

Interior design and typeset by Katherine Lloyd, The DESK
Author photo credit: Kelly Rusin

Italics in quoted material are the author's emphasis.

Unless otherwise indicated, Scripture quotations are from:
The Holy Bible, New International Version © 1973, 1984 by International
Bible Society, used by permission of Zondervan Publishing House

Other Scripture quotations are from:
The Holy Bible, King James Version (KJV)
The Holy Bible, New King James Version (NKJV) © 1984 by Thomas Nelson, Inc.
Holy Bible, New Living Translation (NLT) © 1996.
Used by permission of Tyndale House Publishers, Inc. All rights reserved.
The Holy Bible, English Standard Version (ESV) © 2001 by Crossway Bibles,
a division of Good News Publishers.Used by permission. All rights reserved.

Multnomah is a trademark of Multnomah Publishers, Inc.,
and is registered in the U.S. Patent and Trademark Office.
The colophon is a trademark of Multnomah Publishers, Inc.

Printed in the United States of America

For information:
MULTNOMAH PUBLISHERS, INC.
POST OFFICE BOX 1720 • SISTERS, OREGON 97759

Library of Congress Cataloging-in-Publication Data
Folger, Janet L.
The criminalization of Christianity / by Janet Folger.
    p. cm.
Includes bibliographical references.
ISBN 1-59052-468-3
1. Religious fundamentalism--United States. 2. Church and state--United States.
3. Christianity and culture--United States. 4. Homosexuality--Religious aspects--
Christianity. I. Title.
BR115.C8F57 2005
261.7'2'0973--dc22
                                                        20050017751
        05 06 07 08 09 10—10 9 8 7 6 5 4 3 2 1 0

To all those with the courage to speak the truth in the face of ridicule, blame, assault, censorship, and the threat of being criminalized.

Including Anita Bryant, Bob Knight, Gary Glenn, Tony Verdugo, Guyla Mills, Phil Burress, Michael Schwartz— and the unnamed heroes of truth and freedom.

And to those who have faced imprisonment and persecution for their beliefs, including Swedish pastor Ake Green, the "Philadelphia Five," and our Canadian and European brothers and sisters who probably will not be legally permitted to purchase this book.

If they can silence the truth, they will silence the gospel.

Contents

Beyond Special Thanks...

To Jesus Christ, the way, the TRUTH, and the life.

My incredible parents, Jim and Beth Folger.

This book's MVPs, the FAITH Clarion Callers (www.FaithInt.org), who prayed an hour (or two) every day for four months until this book was birthed: Linda Swearingen, Amelda Thomas-Jones, Pastor Greg and Karen (and Caleb and Alicia) Fry, Jeannie Fuller, Fred Hammack, Pat Cerjan, and others including Sharon Wilson-Wheeler, Nancie Carmichael, Rita Robinson, Pastor Dennis, Sonja Decker, Tracy Campbell, and Beth Folger. There is no way I can possibly thank you for the prayers that sustained me.

Faith2Action prayer force and listeners, research associate Babsy Monaghen, F2A media director Wanda L. Sanchez, F2A communication director Ross Conley, Greg and Karen Darby of the Christian Interactive Network, Ray Smith, Don and Carol Van Curler, Lisa and A. J. Velazquez, Steve Crampton, Allison and Romeo DeMarco, Tom McMillin; John Jakubczyk, Bill Doran, Mat Staver, Peter Sprigg, John Herald, David Limbaugh, David Miller, Ken Ham, David Jolly, Jan LaRue, Alan Sears, Tim Austin, Canadian Member of Parliament Rob Anders, Karen Holgate of the California Family Council, Brad Dacus of the Pacific Justice Institute, Kevin McCoy of the West Virginia Family Association, Tom Hess, Tim Daily, Dr. and Lil Onstead, Jean Bulfin, Vic Elliason, Gordon Morris, Jim Schneider, Matt Lyons, Brother Lou Nordone, Leslie Stevens, Uri Katz, Lori Viars, Kathleen McGervey, Steve Galloway, Margie Moriarty, Deirdre O'Sullivan, Melva Perrish, Sarah Mishkin, Lynda Whitworth, Louise Bilotti, Sharon Stitely, Karen Puree, Lisa Frechette, Peyton Slagle, John Sullivan, Lexa Sutherland, Kathryn Walker, Cartoonist Jay Robere, Rich Westfall, Scott Ross, Betty

McGuire, Bill Runde, Philip and Bianca Nerenberg, Sharon Blakeney, Chris Gorbey, Marlene Rice, Mary Hammack, Matt Jacobson, Milton and Donna Buehner, and others too many to name who are so godly that they will keep praying for me even though they are not mentioned.

Chapter 1

THE WAR ON CHRISTIANITY

*The only thing necessary for evil to triumph
is for good men to do nothing.*

EDMUND BURKE, STATESMAN, ORATOR, AND POLITICAL THINKER

There is a war going on for the future of our country. Most people know that. What they may not know is that if Christians lose, the result won't be just public policy with which we disagree; it'll be a *prison sentence* for those who disagree.

We've all seen the attack coming. The year I was born, the Supreme Court said that kids can't pray in school—at least not out loud. Can't talk about God—at least not the *real one*—in school. If you want to use the name of Jesus, you'd better be taking it in vain or be in another country...like Russia.

My senior year, the Ten Commandments were ripped from classrooms for fear that unsuspecting students might read them...and actually obey them. Wouldn't want to discourage kids from lying and stealing and killing, after all. Then the Commandments were pulled from public buildings and courthouses from Alabama to Wyoming. And while we sit idly by, our enemies are warming up the sandblasters and taking aim at our national monuments and the Supreme Court, where the Ten Commandments are engraved.

Yes, we've all seen the attack coming. But I'm not sure we all see where it's going. After all, the Supreme Court said we're still allowed to say "one nation under God" in the Pledge of Allegiance. Maybe things are going to be okay after all.

Think so?

FAIR WARNING

In 1997, my friend Bob Knight, who directs the Culture and Family Institute at Concerned Women for America, gave a speech that opened my eyes and changed my life. He made a statement that, quite frankly, I didn't believe. He said, "The ultimate goal of the homosexual movement is the criminalization of Christianity." I immediately thought, *What an exaggeration! Come on, Bob. You can make your case without hyperbole.* I said nothing, but for the next several years I watched and listened. *And learned.*

After all, homosexuality wasn't *my* issue. I was the "pro-life girl." Helped pass the nation's first ban on partial-birth abortion and every other law the Supreme Court would allow to help women and restore protection to children—children who were real no matter what label was used to describe them and who through no action of their own had *someone else's* "choice" inflicted upon them.

About ten years ago, I was where you likely are right now: I knew the Bible had strong words against homosexuality, and I knew the health consequences were severe. For their own good, I hoped people didn't engage in it, but I didn't feel the need to speak to the matter. I knew some homosexuals, and, well, they were nice people. *Still are.* Christ Died for them, just like He died for me.

Then one night I was watching C-Span. It was airing a conference of the Human Rights Campaign, the largest homosexual lobby in the country. One of their directors, a lesbian, was pounding on the podium, screaming words I will never forget: "We must do away with words like *abomination!*"

My first thought was *I wonder where* that *word is found.* For those of you who don't know, it's in the *Bible* (Leviticus 18:22, KJV). God uses it to describe the practice the homosexual movement has built its identity around: homosexual sex.

I began reading everything I could get my hands on and talked often with the leaders on the allied side of the cultural war (that would be the side standing for life, liberty, and family). In one such conversation, Bob Knight predicted that homosexual activists would soon go after the Boy Scouts of America. *No way.* Why in the world would they want to go after a group as American as apple pie? One that teaches kids how to be prepared, tie knots, and help old ladies across the street?

But with the help of the ACLU and their network of activist judges, the homosexual lobby kicked the Boy Scouts out of city parks, public schools, and local meeting rooms. Next they took away their city, county, and United Way funding to mentor kids without fathers. They started calling them names like "discriminatory" and "bigoted." *Why?* Because the Boy Scouts didn't think it was in the best interest of young boys to let self-proclaimed homosexuals become scout leaders and go camping with them. The whole idea makes about as much sense as letting middle-aged men go camping with teenage girls.

Some time later, I had a conversation with a local representative of Intervarsity Christian Fellowship, which helps organize Christian clubs on college and university campuses. I was talking to her about the importance of speaking out on moral issues when she said something I'd heard hundreds of times: "Janet, we don't get involved in social issues. Our focus is *evangelism.*" I agreed that evangelism is *the* most important thing, but then I made a prediction.

"I hope I'm wrong," I told her, "but I don't think I am. I predict that if you don't get involved with the issues in our culture, *you will lose your right to evangelize.*" Less than a year later, Tufts University told Intervarsity Christian Fellowship that they were not permitted to meet on campus because they wouldn't allow homosexuals on their board of directors. (By the way, proabortion clubs don't let pro-lifers on their boards either, but they get to stay on campus.)

The campus crusade *against* Christ has since intensified, and "antidiscrimination policies" are trumping religious freedom on campuses across the country. In 2002, University of North Carolina-Chapel Hill attacked Intervarsity Christian Fellowship in the same way. As I write this, UNC has just revoked the charter of a Christian fraternity, Alpha Iota Omega, because they want the people who join to actually *agree* with the religious beliefs upon which the fraternity was founded.[1]

Threats to our freedoms are all around, but I believe there is *one issue* liberals are going to use to silence our churches. It's not the looming threat of losing their precious 501c(3) tax-exempt status that has kept churches quiet on critical moral issues like abortion. It's not all the nasty letters and threats about those "dangerous" nativity scenes.

The *greatest threat* to our freedoms comes from the homosexual agenda.

THE COMING PERSECUTION

Since the Bible says that persecution is coming anyway, some are of the opinion that we should just take it lying down. I've got news for you: It's already here.

In China, government agents can beat, imprison, or kill you for the crime of being a Christian. Christians in Sudan are being sold into slavery or killed. Muslims have wiped out entire villages in Indonesia and gunned down Christians in Iraq, Iran, Pakistan, Saudi Arabia, and Egypt—just to name a few. In 2004, missionaries were burned alive by a Hindu mob in India. And that's only the beginning. According to Freedom House, which tracks persecution worldwide, about 160,000 Christians are killed every year for their faith.[2]

I don't believe we have to take this lying down, especially while we still have the freedom to do something about it. I will undergo persecution if that's my *only* choice, but right now it's not. Paul appealed to Caesar because of his Roman citizenship, and we can do the same. We are Americans, endowed by our *Creator* with inalienable rights. We have freedom *of* religion, not freedom *from* it.

By the way, if this book is translated and/or smuggled into other countries like Canada, these freedoms apply to *you,* too, no matter what your government says. More on that later.

I know that the Bible says, "Blessed are you when they revile and persecute you, and say all kinds of evil against you falsely for My sake" (Matthew 5:11, NKJV). When persecution happens, we'll know we're on the right track. But that doesn't mean we have to usher it in. I will fight it with my last breath. But if it comes full-scale despite our prayers and best efforts, someone remind me to read that verse again, will you?

I know what many of you are thinking: *Who cares what the world does? As long as we can still do whatever we want in our churches, we'll be just fine. Our kids are in Christian schools, we listen to Christian radio, read Christian publications, go to church twice a week.*

All good things to do. But we've effectively withdrawn from society and built ourselves a nice little subculture that some have referred to as the Christian ghetto. *So much for being salt and light in a dark and decaying world.* Christians are the only group still in the closet. We'll just hold out in our holy bunkers until Jesus comes. I've heard it a million times: "Read 'the Book,' Janet. It's *going* to get worse. Let them do whatever they want in the world. We are not 'of the world.' We're still free to speak what we believe *in our church.*"

Really?

THOU SHALT NOT QUOTE THE BIBLE

I was prepared to make another prediction in this book that many of you wouldn't have believed. I had written it down as an unbelievable, outrageous possibility. I was going to say that if we remain silent in this battle, pastors will go to jail for speaking about homosexuality from their own pulpits in *their own churches.* But before I could finish the first chapter, it had already happened:

A Swedish court has sentenced a pastor belonging to the Pentecostal movement in Sweden, Ake Green, to a month in prison, under a law against incitement, after he was found guilty of *having offended homosexuals in a sermon.* Soren Andersson, the president of the Swedish federation for lesbian, gay, bisexual and transgender rights (RFSL), said on hearing the sentence that religious freedom could never be used as a reason to offend people. "Therefore," he told journalists, "I cannot regard the sentence as an act of interference with freedom of religion."[3]

Pastor Green is in his seventies. The prosecutor appealed the court decision, demanding that the pastor be sentenced to *six months* imprisonment. When a reporter asked, "What about the pastor's rights?" the prosecutor replied, "When he started reading Bible verses about homosexuality, he crossed the line."[4]

On July 13, 2004, Swedish Ambassador Cecilia Julin defended the sentence by saying, "Swedish law states that public addresses cannot be used to instigate hatred towards a certain group."

The ruling party of the central European nation of Slovakia has protested Pastor Green's prison sentence. According to the Slovak *Spectator,* Slovakian Interior Minister Vladimir Palko, who voiced the protest, said at a press conference that Sweden's actions were an example of how "left-wing liberal ideology was trying to introduce tyranny and misuse the [European Union]" to silence freedom of expression. He added, "In Europe people are starting to be jailed for saying what they think."[5]

Prison sentences for pastors who offend homosexuals in a sermon? Could've been worse. Sweden's law bans "all speech and materials opposing homosexual behavior and other alternative lifestyles" and calls for up to *four years* in jail for violating it.[6] That will be *next.*

The Anglican Bishop of Chester, England, Reverend Dr. Peter Forster, was under police investigation for saying, "Some people who are primarily homosexual can re-orientate themselves. I would encourage them to consider that as an option."[7] Police turned his case over for prosecution. I wonder what would have happened if an ex-homosexual had spoken about his life. Probably would've been arrested on the spot. If Reverend Forster can't talk about reorientation, I'm sure an ex-homosexual wouldn't even be allowed to exist.

What's the *next step?* Declare the Bible "hate literature" and censor its contents? *It's already been done.*

Hugh Owens, of Regina, Saskatchewan, Canada, took out an ad in response to all he was forced to observe during Homosexual Pride Week. Homosexuals had expressed their views in the streets; surely he could express his in a small newspaper ad. Forget about his views—he was just going to list some verses that expressed *God's view* on the matter. *Radical, huh?*

The ad listed four Scripture references (Romans 1, Leviticus 18:22, Leviticus 20:13, and 1 Corinthians 6:9–10) next to an equal sign and a drawing depicting two men holding hands. Superimposed on the line drawing was the universal red circle with a line through it, effectively summarizing the Scriptures listed. For that "crime," Owens was fined $4500. The newspaper

was also fined. Now merely *listing* Bible verses is a hate crime.

Owens was fined by the Court of Queen's Bench in Saskatchewan, which upheld a 2001 ruling by the province's human rights tribunal. The tribunal had said, "The slashed figures alone were not enough to communicate the hatred...but the addition of Bible references are more dangerous."[8] The Bench said that the tribunal "was correct in concluding that the advertisement can objectively be seen as exposing homosexuals to hatred or ridicule."[9]

Incidentally, Owens's fine was broken into three parts: $1500 Canadian for *each* of the three homosexual men who filed the complaint. Wow, if there's money in filing complaints, imagine the incentive for going after Christians who refuse to embrace, celebrate, and further the homosexual agenda!

THOU SHALT NOT TELL THE TRUTH ON RADIO OR VIDEO

Canada's Charter of Rights and Freedoms has a broad antidiscrimination provision that is interpreted to prohibit discrimination against sexual orientation. This provision has been used to silence religious organizations and pastors. Canada's Broadcast Standards Council rebuked Dr. Laura Schlessinger, an Orthodox Jew, for a speech she made on homosexuality, and stations were forced to make an announcement of the Council's ruling before the show was aired.[10] (In America, her television show was cancelled over the same issue.)

Dr. Jerry Falwell's *Old-Time Gospel Hour* and Dr. James Dobson's *Focus on the Family* must now edit their Canadian programs to remove anything that might be deemed critical of homosexuality, including Bible verses on the subject and information like the fact that according to the Centers for Disease Control, the majority of the cases of AIDS in the U.S. are men who engage in homosexual sex.[11] Wouldn't want *that* to get out. If people knew how dangerous homosexual sex is, they might actually *change* their behavior. Now it's illegal to tell them.

But maybe we could still get the word out if we made a video. *Great idea.* Some people in New Zealand tried. They made two Christian videos that questioned safe-sex slogans by exposing the link between AIDS and homosexual behavior. The New Zealand Parliament outlawed the videos for promoting "hate speech."[12]

THOU SHALT NOT POST BIBLE VERSES AT WORK

In the case of *Peterson v. Hewlett-Packard Co.*, a Christian worker exercised his right to free speech in response to a homosexual poster the company had placed near his cubicle. He posted Bible verses to express his beliefs on the matter. He was fired. Was he in Sweden? Canada? Try Boise, Idaho. The Ninth Circuit Court of Appeals wrote, "An employer need not accommodate an employee's religious beliefs if doing so would result in discrimination against his co-workers or deprive them of contractual or other statutory rights."[13]

The homosexual agenda trumps an employee's religious beliefs? Doesn't make me feel any better knowing that I bought my printer from them. But it might make that former employee feel a little bit better to know what I'm using it for.

When the California Department of Social Services didn't like the things an employee, retired Air Force Officer Enoch Lawrence, had posted in his cubicle, they ripped them from the walls. The items included a small sign that said "Jesus Spoken Here," several Bible verses, two published articles on current issues, and a bumper sticker that read "Marriage: One Man One Woman."[14]

I'm familiar with that bumper sticker. I just checked my records, and my organization, Faith2Action, printed it. *This is starting to hit close to home.*

The Department's policy states: "Each employee must exercise his or her own good judgement [sic] to avoid engaging in conduct that may be perceived by others as harassment and/or unprofessional, inappropriate behavior." According to Lawrence, although a Pagan Pride Festival flyer was posted in the break room, his pro-marriage bumper sticker, which reflected California (and U.S.) law, was forbidden.[15]

With the help of Faith2Action partner the Alliance Defense Fund, Lawrence filed a lawsuit, but not for money. "I just want them to stop violating my First Amendment rights and give me equal protection under the law." Lawrence added, "They should be protecting my rights, not persecuting me."[16]

THOU SHALT NOT BE TREATED EQUALLY

Sandia National Laboratories of Albuquerque, New Mexico, gave a homosexual employee group special rights, but when a Christian group asked for them, it was denied. According to Steve Crampton, representing counsel for the Christian group, the policy was in fact enacted for the purpose of giving homosexuals perks, but expressly stated that Sandia would not recognize groups "formed on the basis of religious beliefs." While homosexuals were allowed to hold events honoring their national "coming out day," Christians were prohibited from bringing in a speaker to discuss evolution and creation.

Even after grudgingly recognizing the Christian group in settlement of a federal lawsuit, Sandia censored the Christians' website by removing links to the Family Research Council and Exodus International—in the middle of "Gay Pride Month," which was widely advertised in Sandia's internal publications.[17]

For those of you keeping score at home, that's no Bible verses, no signs, no videos, no articles (with a conservative bent) on issues, no pro-marriage (if it's between a man and a woman) bumper stickers, no links, and no speakers. *Are you following this?*

THOU SHALT NOT WRITE LETTERS TO THE EDITOR

And then there's Chris Kempling. Nice guy. Upstanding citizen with a PhD in psychology. He's head of the Central British Columbia Public Health Board and a counselor at his local high school. He was also suspended from his teaching job for a month without pay for writing a letter to the editor of his local paper. The problem? The letter expressed his beliefs, which didn't agree with the homosexual agenda. He stated that homosexuality was not a genetic orientation, that homosexual sex was often unhealthy and promiscuous, and that homosexuals could become straight.[18] (All of which are true, but that's beside the point.)

Based on the letters alone, the judge found that there was "sufficient evidence" to pronounce Kempling a "bigot." Keep in mind, Kempling never said he wouldn't serve homosexual students objectively. In fact, he was never accused of any discriminatory act. He was accused of having the wrong thoughts.[19]

THOU SHALT "CELEBRATE" HOMOSEXUALITY

As long as you don't take out ads, turn down business, or preach about homosexuality from the pulpit, you're probably safe, right? Think again. Now you must "celebrate" homosexuality. Dianne Haskett, the mayor of London, Ontario, Canada, was fined $10,000 for refusing to proclaim a "Gay Pride Weekend." After she lost her case in Canada's courts, she resigned as mayor rather than be forced to proclaim the event. She even turned her mayoral duties over to her political opponent—just three weeks before election day. Incidentally, even though she left office and refused to campaign, she was reelected with 64 percent of the vote![20]

THOU SHALT NOT PRACTICE YOUR BELIEFS IN YOUR OWN OFFICE

When a lesbian approached two Christian doctors in San Diego County, California, to be artificially inseminated, the doctors refused. Rather than express tolerance toward the doctors' religious convictions and their right not to participate in her plan, she sued them. And a California appeals court found that the two doctors were wrong to refuse. Jennifer Pizer, the lesbian's attorney, clarified her legal position on the *Hannity and Colmes Show*: "When the doctor is in her church, she can do religion, but not in the medical office."[21]

When the doctor is in her church, she can do religion, but *not in the medical office*. Are you seeing the trend?

THOU SHALT PROMOTE HOMOSEXUALITY

In British Columbia, the Human Rights Tribunal was told that it wasn't enough for the provincial ministry of education to not say anything "negative" about homosexuality. No, it "discriminates against homosexual and bisexual students if it does not provide 'positive' messages of sexual orientation and gender identity in the classroom."[22]

So you can be driven from your business, forced out of office, fined for listing Bible verses or reading them on the air, and thrown in jail for what you say from your pulpit. At least you can practice your beliefs at home and in your Christian community. You can "do religion in church." You'd think that would include sending e-mails to your friends in your Christian community. That's true in Canada—*as long as no one finds out about it.*

THOU SHALT NOT SEND E-MAIL

If a complaint is filed, you may find yourself like Robert Jason, a retired law-abiding citizen of Fonthill, Ontario, who'd never had more than a traffic ticket. But get a load of his radical beliefs! This guy believes marriage should be between one man and one woman. Kinda like every nation, every culture, and every major religion for the last five thousand years of recorded history. So he sent an e-mail to that effect.[23]

The next thing you know, he gets a knock on his door from the local police, who interrogate him and his frightened wife and warn him not to threaten anyone—something he has never done or intended to do. But if merely expressing pro-marriage views threatened the homosexual activist who reported Jason, I have to think there will be more visits just like it—and perhaps result in more than a warning.

THOU SHALT NOT REFUSE, OR ELSE

Meet Scott Brockie, owner of Imaging Excellence, Inc. Want to put him out of business? That's easy enough. Just ask him to print stuff for the local homosexual and lesbian group, to which he's morally opposed. He'll turn you down. And when he does, rather than go to another printer, you can just file a complaint—and let the fun begin! That is, if you consider it fun to shut down the businesses of people who are philosophically opposed to your agenda.

Even though Brockie pointed out several other printers who would print their materials, the group sued. Brockie argued that his right to freedom of religion under section 2(a) of the Canadian Charter of Rights and Freedoms allowed him to exercise his religious beliefs. *So what?*

On February 24, 2000, the Ontario Human Rights Commission found Brockie guilty of discrimination and slapped him with a $5000 fine, which went to the plaintiff and his homosexual group. The Board ordered a payment of that magnitude because of the "seriousness of the breach that occurred." Brockie has since incurred a debt thirty-four times that amount. He now owes $170,000 for defending his Christian conscience through the various "Human Rights Commissions" and courts.[24]

THE CRIMINALIZATION OF CHRISTIANITY

The Ontario Human Rights Commission said, "Brockie remains free to hold his religious beliefs and practice them in his home and in his Christian community."[25] *Mighty nice of them.* Canadians are free to practice their beliefs at home. Just don't take them outside.

THOU SHALT NOT CARRY A SIGN

But at least we can still engage in old-fashioned protest—holding a sign that reflects our beliefs. No one can take that away, can they? If you live in England, they already have.

Harry Hammond, an elderly Englishman, was attacked on the street for holding a sign that read: "Stop immorality. Stop homosexuality. Stop lesbianism." After being heckled and ridiculed, Hammond was assaulted and knocked to the ground. At least somebody called the police. Too bad that when they showed up they arrested the wrong man: Mr. Hammond. He was prosecuted, and his conviction was upheld. Oh, and the "illegal" sign was "destroyed by order of the bench."[26]

THOU SHALT NOT AGREE WITH THE POPE

In Dublin, priests and bishops are being warned that if they distribute the Vatican's statement on homosexual marriage, they could be looking at the inside of a prison cell. The Vatican statement said that homosexuals should be treated with "respect, compassion and sensitivity."[27] But it added:

> There are absolutely no grounds for considering homosexual unions to be in any way similar or even remotely analogous to God's plan for marriage and family. Marriage is holy, while homosexual acts go against the natural moral law.... Those who would move from tolerance to the legitimization of specific rights for cohabiting homosexual persons need to be reminded that the approval or legalization of evil is something far different from the toleration of evil.[28]

It also states that "to vote in favor of a law so harmful to the common good is gravely immoral." Pope John Paul II has declared what Orthodox Christianity has taught throughout the centuries. Only now an anti-Catholic backlash is spreading around the world. Open hostility began with calling the statement everything from "homophobic" to "perverted." [29]

The *Chicago Sun-Times* ran a story about the Vatican statement with the headline "Pope Launches Global Campaign against Gays," prompting Cardinal Francis George to address the false accusation from the pulpit. He issued this warning:

> Divulging disinformation about the Pope [and] engaging in anti-papal propaganda...is usually, in history, a preparation for active persecution of the church. [30]

He was right. And it didn't take long. Aisling Reidy, director of the Irish Council for Civil Liberties, issued a warning to priests who quote, hand out, or send the Vatican's statement that they could be in violation of the 1989 Incitement to Hatred Act—and face up to *six months* in jail.[31]

Others who didn't like what Pope John Paul II said about their behavior sued him in a Dutch court. The court ruled that the pope's status as a leader of the Roman Catholic Church and the Vatican afforded him immunity from prosecution. As F2A partner Mathew D. Staver of Liberty Counsel points out in *Same-Sex Marriage*, a priest would not enjoy the same immunity.[32]

THOU SHALT NOT EXPRESS YOUR BELIEFS...IN AMERICA

But that's in England, the Netherlands, Sweden, and Canada, you say? They're persecuting Christians in communist and Muslim countries, too. But nothing like that could ever happen in America.

How about:

- A "reeducation class" to ensure that foster parents embrace the homosexual agenda (California)[33]

- Public schools with a mandated pro-homosexual ["antidiscrimination"] policy that sends objecting students to "appropriate counseling" without notifying their parents (California)[34]
- Being put out of business (with a $150,000 fine) for firing a man in a dress (California)[35]
- Being told by a judge that you can't teach your daughter anything "homophobic" (Colorado)[36]

These have all happened already. And it's getting worse.

Pastors in Pennsylvania are now seeking liability insurance to protect themselves from being prosecuted under the state's new Hate-Speech Law. That's right. They are reacting to the state's recent addition of "sexual orientation" to its hate crimes laws. Of particular concern is the expansion of the term *harassment* to include "harassment by communication," which means a person can be convicted on the basis of spoken words alone.[37]

Like the evangelical pastor who read from the Bible at a Lansdowne Borough Council meeting on July 21, 2004. The council president declared his Bible reading "hate speech" and forced the pastor to stand trial. On October 1, 2004, a *Wall Street Journal* editorial said, "For a government official to label this 'hate speech' suggests that that campaign flier warning about a Bible ban is less fanciful than it sounds."[38]

Their fear is a rational one. Hate crimes invariably lead to fines and jail time for those who "violate" them. Just ask Swedish Pastor Ake Green. Well, wait until he gets out of jail. *Then* you can ask him.

I believe that hate crimes bills are the single most dangerous legislation in America (I'll discuss this in greater depth in chapter 8). And it's not just in Pennsylvania. The "sexual orientation" clause was added to the Hate Crimes Statute in the U.S. Senate in June of 2004. It passed that body by a two-thirds vote: 65 to 33. Worried yet? Though as of this writing it still hasn't passed the House, take a look at how hate crimes laws are being applied beyond the homosexual issue.

THOU SHALT NOT PROTEST ISLAM

Maybe it had something to do with 9/11. Maybe it was the beheadings. Maybe it's what is written in the Koran. But Canadian Pastor Mark Harding doesn't believe the Muslim religion is one of *peace*. So when his local high school started handing out copies of the Koran and announced a policy of setting aside a room for Muslim students to pray in during school hours, Pastor Harding protested. Didn't think it was a good idea—especially since Christian, Jewish, and Buddhist kids weren't afforded the same opportunity.

After losing an appeal to Canada's Supreme Court on October 17, 2002, Mark Harding was said to have "willfully promoted hatred" in violation of Canadian law that had passed just six months earlier. He was then forced to undergo two years probation and 340 hours of "community service" at the Islamic Society of North America.

Pastor Harding, an evangelical Christian, says his evangelism is motivated by love for the Muslim people. In fact, in a phone call used as evidence against him, Harding says that he loves Muslims. He says he wants them to go to heaven. Yet he received more than three thousand hate-filled calls—many of them death threats. Some people in the courtroom motioned by running their finger across their neck from ear to ear.[39] Upon entering court for his trial, Harding required police protection from a large crowd of Muslims who were chanting, "Infidels, you will burn in hell."[40] Of course, *that* speech is loving.

Harding said, "I had a call from someone who said they were from [Louis] Farrakhan's [Nation of Islam] group, and they were going to break my legs." Another caller said he would rip out Harding's testicles.[41] Can't you just *feel the love?* Pastor Harding's punishment included Islam indoctrination under the direction of Mohammad Ashraf, the general secretary of the Islam center. To avoid going to jail, Harding was forced to go through Islamic reeducation.

Harding, forty-nine, has suffered four heart attacks since 1997 and is unable to work in his cabinet-making trade because of his poor health. Yet he must travel three hours to the Islamic Society of North America to complete his sentence. His attorney has entered a plea based on humanitarian grounds to allow him to complete his sentence at a local Islam center.[42] *Isn't that nice?* Perhaps if he's lucky, he can be indoctrinated closer to home.

PRO-LIFERS: AUTOMATIC SUSPECTS

The hate crimes bill SB 1234, which was signed into law by California Governor Arnold Schwarzenegger on September 22, 2004, creates a new requirement for law enforcement called "multimission criminal extremism" training. In addition to those categories already considered for special punishment under the term "hate crimes," the new training applies to *"anti-reproductive-rights crimes."*[43]

That means that if you're pro-life, you're an automatic suspect and that law enforcement is being specially trained to handle you. I wonder what they train officers to look for. Anti-reproductive-rights T-shirts? Those who've passed anti-reproductive-rights laws? Those who've debated the anti-reproductive-rights position? I have a feeling that if I lived in California, my picture would be found at the local post office. If you think that killing children is wrong, they're training people to deal with *you,* too.

This hate crimes law also expands the term *crimes* to include speech interpreted as "threats, intimidation, and coercion." As long as a victim claims the speech makes him or her feel "intimidated," violators are subject to penalties of $10,000 to $25,000 and a year in jail.[44]

This law could be used to criminalize expressions of biblical truth about homosexuality as "hate speech" and could very well target not just organizations that disagree with homosexuality, but bookstores that carry *this book.* Or maybe another book already ruled to contain "intimidating" beliefs: *the Bible.*

How in the world has our "free" and civilized society come to the place that Christians are singled out, labeled, fined, interrogated, humiliated, indoctrinated, fired, ordered to attend reeducation programs, and sent to jail for expressing biblical views? As Rabbi Daniel Lapin has said, "We are two nations occupying the same piece of real estate and engaged in a giant cultural tug-of-war."[45]

Yes, there is a war. But it's not just about policies that will be passed. Or about what our laws will look like. It's about whether we will be *free* to speak openly and exercise what we believe at our businesses, at our schools, at our churches, and over our airwaves. This battle is for truth and freedom. And we have been losing by default.

What are we called to do?

PUTTING YOUR FAITH TO ACTION

Many Christians believe that those who get involved in the cultural arena are off course. They say if we stay silent on controversial issues, like the slaughter of more than forty-five million American children who haven't yet fully passed through the birth canal, no one will be "offended." If we don't say anything upsetting, the seekers who visit our churches might just stick around long enough to get saved.

We work very hard to present a sensitive "positive Christianity" to seekers who don't like hearing about stuff like obedience and a place called hell. "All We Need Is Love" has replaced "Onward Christian Soldiers" as our anthem.

Love is critical, of course, but so is truth. The Bible says that God is love, but also that He is holy. If we're going to get into heaven, He requires a perfect score on the entrance exam—something we have already missed. *All* of us have sinned—that's why Christ died. But unless we embrace Him as Lord, we will face Him as Judge. Keep in mind that Jesus talked more about hell than He did about heaven. He wanted us to know about it so we could avoid going there. Kind of why He came. And if we make Him Lord, we have to actually do what He says.

But what of those who say that "issues don't matter"? I used to agree, but when I saw pictures of aborted babies in trash bags, I knew that all the rhetoric in the world couldn't make *that* right. As a fifteen-year-old, I knew that if I didn't do all I could to stop it, I could no longer point my finger at those who sat on the sidelines in Germany in the 1930s.

Turns out, God more than agrees. He *commanded* us: "Rescue those who are unjustly sentenced to death; don't stand back and let them die" (Proverbs

24:11, NLT). I knew I had to overcome my fear of public speaking when I read: "Open *your* mouth for the speechless, in the cause of all who are appointed to die" (Proverbs 31:8, NKJV). Add a commandment from the "top ten," and the case for pro-life involvement was made: "Thou shalt not kill" (Exodus 20:13, KJV), which, as it turns out, doesn't apply just to adults.

But maybe you don't feel called to obey these commands. Jesus said, "If you love me, you will keep my commandments" (John 14:15, ESV). We love God when we *do* what He says: "Faith by itself, if it is not accompanied by action, is dead" (James 2:17). You see, your actions *are* what you believe. Everything else is just religious talk. The Christian worldview encompasses every part of our lives—evangelism, issues, people, tasks. It penetrates everything, or it means nothing. That's why I formed Faith2Action: to turn people of faith into people of action, united to *win* the cultural war for life, liberty, and family.

I'm writing this book not to make the case for you to get involved in the issues of the day because I think it's a good idea, or even because God has commanded us to do so. I'm writing because I believe that if we don't speak up *now* on the issues in our culture, they will be used to silence us. You can stay in the closet if you'd like, but stay there much longer and you're going to wake up to find a padlock on the outside of the door.

If you want to be free to speak what you believe in your church, in your workplace, in your community, you're going to have to get off the sidelines and into the game. The battle for the Super Bowl championship is being waged, and our players are somewhere doing push-ups. But this is more than just a game. It's a battle for our freedom.

Yes, we have the *right* to remain silent, but if we use it much longer, we may hear those words being read to us just before we see the inside of a prison cell.

Chapter 2

THE BASICS

Before I answer the question of how we got where we are, I think it's necessary to start with a few basics—things that are fundamental to what Christians believe, but increasingly not what those who fight us espouse.

ABSOLUTE TRUTH EXISTS

Ready for an earth-shattering premise? Are you sitting down?

There is such a thing as truth. Absolute truth. *Absolutely.*

Don't believe me? *Doesn't matter.* Some things are true whether you believe them or not. Even if you've never heard of Sir Isaac Newton, the law of gravity still applies to you.

I can almost hear the liberal political pundits now: "How dare you declare that gravity is real? There are *entire cultures* that don't believe that. Who's to say *you're* right? Some tribal communities believe that we're held on earth by yearly human sacrifices. I'd rather depart from your white, Eurocentric belief system that depends on the so-called advances of people like Sir Isaac Newton and focus on the more inclusive and tolerant view that we don't really know whether gravity is real or not."

Today, expressing an absolute truth is considered "intolerance." For fear that those who disagree might be offended, those who actually believe something are increasingly silenced. Whether what they believe is true or not has become irrelevant. It's as if there's a right in the Constitution to be an unoffended listener (which, by the way, there's not). Tolerance is the highest virtue, and we must do away with things that stand in the way—even if one of them is truth.

You wouldn't believe how many Americans can't grasp the simple premise that there is such a thing as truth. In 1991, and again in 1994, pollster George Barna asked a random sampling of adults, and then a sample of Christians, whether they agreed with this statement: "There is no such thing as absolute truth; two people could define truth in totally conflicting ways, but both could still be correct." His results: In 1991, 67 percent of all Americans and 52 percent of Christians agreed. In 1994, those numbers had increased to 72 percent and 62 percent, respectively.[1]

In 2004 they asked teenagers the question as well. Here are the results:

In two national surveys conducted by Barna Research, one among adults and one among teenagers, people were asked if they believe that there are moral absolutes that are unchanging or that moral truth is relative to the circumstances. By a 3-to-1 margin (64% versus 22%) adults said truth is always relative to the person and their situation. The perspective was even more lopsided among teenagers, 83% of whom said moral truth depends on the circumstances, and only 6% of whom said moral truth is absolute.[2]

Two-thirds of adults and eight out of ten teens have bought into the lie that there is no absolute truth. There's a testimony to public schools for you: Only 6 percent of the next generation understand that there is such a thing as truth. Thankfully, the latest polling data doesn't affect the existence of truth.

great exercise to do! ✗

NORTH IS NORTH

Dr. James Dobson's son, Ryan, did a little experiment. In an arena full of students, he asked those in his audience to stand up, close their eyes, and point north. Pretty simple task. But when the students opened their eyes, people were pointing in every direction—including up. He then asked only those who were absolutely sure which way was north to remain standing and continue pointing. They did. And those "absolutely sure" people were *still* pointing in every direction.

Ryan then took out a compass. Holding it up and pointing to it, he proclaimed, "*This* is north. I don't care how sincere you are; I don't care what a good person you are, how much education you have, or how sure of yourself you are. If you are pointing in a different direction than *this* for north, you are… *wrong*."

EVIL IS REAL

Ready for another basic? Evil exists.

Don't believe me? *Doesn't matter.* Some things are true whether you believe them or not. If you question this, I gotta wonder if you ever read the paper. Ever watch the news? Were you around on September 11, 2001?

I rest my case.

But get a load of what the Sixth Circuit Court of Appeals had to say: "Adherents of all faiths are *equally valid* as religions."[3] That explains why in January 1999, CNN had a link on its web site to the Church of Satan.[4] And why U.S. Army posts have witch chaplains who have equal standing with Christian, Jewish, and Muslim chaplains. That's right, while Wicca chaplains are praying to Mother Earth, you're paying the tab with your hard-earned tax dollars.[5] I'm not sure if Halloween is an "official" paid holiday, or whether they're supplied with U.S. Army crystals, voodoo dolls, and goats just yet, but I'm looking into it.

All faiths or beliefs are "equally valid"? Would that include those of people who hijack airplanes and fly them into buildings? How about those who take Americans hostage and chop off their heads? How about the Nazis—were their beliefs equally valid?

A few years ago, professor Robert Simon said that while he had never had a student who didn't believe the Holocaust was real, he was shocked at what his students were saying about it. Between 10 and 20 percent believed what one student told him: "Of course I dislike the Nazis, but who is to say that they were morally wrong?"[6]

Up to 20 percent of students in universities can't even say that genocide is absolutely, always morally wrong. But regardless of what the next graduating class may think, there is good, and there is evil. And what the Nazis did was evil. If you're not grasping this, you need a book even more rudimentary than mine.

What about communists? Are their beliefs equally valid?

At the funeral services for former president Ronald Reagan, former Canadian Prime Minister Brian Mulroney said:

Some in the West, during the early 1980s believed communism and democracy were equally valid and viable. This was the school of moral equivalence. In contrast, Ronald Reagan saw Soviet Communism as a menace to be confronted in the genuine belief that its squalid underpinnings would fall swiftly to the gathering winds of freedom, provided, as he said, that NATO and the industrialized democracies stood firm and united. They did. And we know now who was right.[7]

And we know *now* who was right. It wasn't the school of "moral equivalence." It wasn't those who said communism and democracy were equally valid and viable. No. The Sixth Circuit Court notwithstanding, not *everything* is equally valid. There is good, and there is evil. For those who still don't get it: freedom good; communism bad. That's why when the Berlin Wall came down, the world celebrated.

I believe that this kind of thinking explains why so many people can say they are "personally opposed" to abortion but don't want to impose that belief on anyone to actually protect somebody.

It's a pretty strange position when you think about it. Abortion is murder, but if *you* don't think so, then go right ahead. What if this logic were used regarding rape? "I'm personally opposed to rape, but I don't want to impose my views on anyone else. Rapists should have the freedom to choose, after all. 'Who decides?' That's what I always say! It should be up to each individual, not the government. Men are perfectly capable of making decisions about their needs and their lives. We can't legislate morality and impose our views on them."

You can throw as many slogans at it as you'd like. Have a regular slogan-fest! Say them over and over, louder and louder. Paint them on banners. Doesn't make it right.

There is such a thing as truth. Gravity is real. North is north. And Ronald Reagan was right: Evil exists and must be opposed.

Let's try one for starters. See if this is elementary enough. Which of the following is good, and which is evil? The categories are God and terrorists. Which one's good, and which one's evil? Sorry, time's up. The answer: God = good; terrorists = bad. How'd you do? Well, if you're Robert Reich, former Secretary of Labor in the Clinton administration, you think it's the other way around. Terrorists aren't the greatest danger we face; it's those bad people who believe in God. In an article entitled "Bush's God," Reich wrote this:

> The great conflict of the 21st century will not be between the West and terrorism. Terrorism is a tactic, not a belief. The true battle will be between modern civilization and anti-modernists; between those who believe in the primacy of the individual and those who believe that human beings owe their allegiance and identity to a higher authority; between those who give priority to life in this world and those who believe that human life is mere preparation for an existence beyond life; between those who believe in science, reason, and logic and those who believe that truth is revealed through Scripture and religious dogma. Terrorism will disrupt and destroy lives. But terrorism itself is not the greatest danger we face.[8]

Terrorism isn't the greatest danger we face. *Of course not.* Those anti-modern Christians are the danger. If Reich had to choose between living next door to Mohamed Atta or to one of those Christians, it's clear who he would pick. After all, Mohamed Atta is far less dangerous. All he did was fly a plane into the World Trade Center.

The Bible has something to say about this backward thinking: "Woe to those who call evil good, and good evil" (Isaiah 5:20).

TRUTH VERSUS TOLERANCE

Imagine that you get a call one evening from a good friend in Arizona who's driving down the road in his new convertible. He's ecstatic as he describes the sound system and just how fast the car can go on the open road. He also reveals how good the beer he's currently drinking is, as were the five he just drank. He then points out how "much better the stars look" when he drives with the headlights off. You inquire as to his whereabouts and, being familiar with the road, realize that your friend is headed directly for the Grand Canyon. What do you do?

One approach is to "not impose your morality" and to be tolerant and supportive of your friend's actions. After all, if he's enjoying himself, who are *you* to ruin his good time? Who's to say it's wrong? Lots of people have driven drunk and are doing *just fine.*

Maybe you could make sure he practices "safe driving" and at least wears his seat belt. But he senses your disapproval and threatens to end the friendship if you continue to issue warnings. Do you give up?

No. If you *really* love someone, you will love him enough to tell him the truth. That's the difference between love and "tolerance."

Josh McDowell puts it this way:

True compassionate love that seeks to provide for and protect another person's health, happiness, and spiritual growth could not comply with the cultural call: "If you love me, you'll endorse my behavior." Because real love—true love—grieves over the inevitable results of wrong behavior.[9]

I've talked to people who call themselves pro-life but are so concerned about being "tolerant" and "accepting" that they have driven friends (and girl-friends) to abortion clinics so they could have their child killed. That kind of action is about as caring as driving them to the Grand Canyon so they can throw the baby off the edge themselves.

Here's how McDowell describes the difference:

> Tolerance seeks to be inoffensive; love takes risks.
> Tolerance is indifferent; love is active.
> Tolerance costs nothing; love costs everything.[10]

The Bible verse cited most by those who advocate tolerance is "He who is without sin among you, let him throw a stone at her first" (John 8:7, NKJV). The Bible verse cited least by those who advocate tolerance? "Neither do I condemn you; go and sin no more" (John 8:11, NKJV).

THERE IS A GOD OF TRUTH

Here's another basic: There is a God. Don't believe me? *Doesn't matter.* Some things are true whether you believe them or not.

By the way, there's a place you can find out about Him. He's got a book out now. Turns out, it's a bestseller—*the* bestseller of all time. It's available in bookstores everywhere…well, not *everywhere.* In some places, just asking for it can get you shot. But it's still available in the U.S. in an uncensored form, *for now.* So before the objectionable parts are blacked out, you might want to pick up a copy and see what it says about the issues of the day. Yes, even *our day*—*especially* our day.

It's the book that's going to tell you what side to be on, provided you'd like to be on the same side as the One who created you and win in the end and all. With everyone calling good evil and evil good, a lot of people are confused, and this book is going to tell you officially what is good and what is evil.

People talk about how narrow-minded and intolerant it is for us to say that Christ is the *only* way to heaven. Question: If there were only one exit out of a burning building, would I be intolerant and narrow-minded to tell you? I know I might offend those who think the basement door will get them out. Or those who seek an exit by opening the very hot door with the flaming inferno inside. I'm sorry, I may be insensitive by not affirming your beliefs, and I know I run the risk of hurting your feelings, but I would rather *save your life*. You see, I care more about *you* than I do about whether you like me.

Listen, it doesn't really matter what I say. The important thing is what *Christ Himself* said: "I am the way, the truth, and the life: no man cometh unto the Father, but by me" (John 14:6, KJV). Pretty clear stuff. If all roads really lead to heaven, why did Christ have to die? Doesn't make sense. If there are lots of roads, why not just choose a *much less costly* one? If God didn't have to send His Son to be tortured and crucified, I'm pretty sure He wouldn't have.

The bottom line is that when You create everything, You get to make the rules. And if You love me enough to give up Your life for me, You're the one I'm going to listen to. And whose rules I want to follow. Because we have a God who is *for* us, those rules are for our good.

Here's one that's not so hard to see: *Thou shalt not murder*. It's the rule our homicide laws are based on. I think we can all agree that, whether you like the source or not, it's a pretty good idea not to kill innocent people. The ACLU can see that when it comes to ax murderers on death row; they just don't seem to get it when it comes to innocent children who haven't completely passed through the birth canal yet.

Thou shalt not steal. If you don't agree with that one, let me know where you live so I can come over and take all your stuff. Don't agree with not committing adultery? I'm hoping that comes out on the first date, because if that's the case, I'm pretty sure you're not the man I've been waiting for. I know I can't speak for everyone—some women have written Scott Peterson love letters in jail—but that's just not what *I'm* looking for in a guy.

Don't agree with "Thou shalt not bear false witness"? I don't really *care* what you say, because chances are you're probably lying.

Even though there are a plethora of issues and a whole host of threats, there are really only two sides in the culture war: good and evil. Not as I define them, but as God does. Whether it's promoting the homosexual agenda, providing abortion on demand, publishing pornography, or preaching evolution, it's those pesky Christians who stand in the way of all that the liberals want to do.

Good versus evil. And worldviews collide. What are the issues of the cultural divide? Here's an "Introduction to Issues 101" that's a bit different than you'd get in most universities. They are what separate Christians and those who seek to silence them.

Abortion

As "controversial" as this one may seem, it's really as clear as "Thou shalt not kill." Once at a pro-life march, I read this on a teenager's sign: "Call me an extremist, but I think dismembering children is wrong." And sucking their brains out during delivery, as in a partial-birth abortion? Also something we're against.

You see, life is the prerequisite to every other right we have. Not just one issue, but the *priority* issue, because it doesn't really matter what a candidate's stand on education and health care is if you're dead. Abortion matters because it hurts women and kills children. The body count from America's 1973 abortion ruling is now over forty-five million and counting. No other issue has claimed as many human lives. Abortion has killed more than the casualties of all our wars combined.

Embryonic Stem Cell Research/Cloning

Semantics aside, this is creating new life for spare parts only to destroy it once we've finished. Destroying the donor. If we did that with blood drives, well, there wouldn't be a Red Cross. Adult stem cell research, unlike embryonic, has actually shown great promise—like for Hwang-Mi Soon, a South Korean woman who was paralyzed for twenty years but is now *walking* again thanks to stem cells from an umbilical cord.[11] And no one has to *die* for adult or umbilical-cord stem cells to help cure people. But the press (and the Democratic National Convention) would rather talk about what *doesn't* work.

Marriage

For the five thousand years of recorded history, marriage has been the sacred union of one man and one woman. Every social science indicator has shown that a family based on marriage between a man and a woman is the very best place for children, the safest place for women, and the healthiest place for men. After seeing my pro-marriage button, a man on the Metro in Washington, DC, put it this way: "The parts don't fit any other way." Men and women are uniquely designed not only to "fit," but to be able to procreate and to contribute to the rearing of children in distinct and unique ways. No, Mr. Judge, a woman is not a dad and never will be. Marriage matters because it is the foundation of our society. Without it, civilization crumbles.

Homosexuality

Doesn't matter how you claim you were born, your body was created with reproductive organs that work only with the *opposite* sex. Ever wonder about that? If you listen to the CDC instead of to what's PC, you'll know that the majority of the cases of AIDS in this country are among men who engage in homosexual sex. And independent research shows that, AIDS aside, homosexual sex is one of *the most dangerous* behaviors in which you can engage. It's likely to cut up to twenty years off your life.[12] Homosexuality is a significant issue not only because of the costs to society and the harm it does to those practicing it, but also because it threatens to silence all those who disagree with it.

Pornography

A multi-billion-dollar business that dominates the Internet and the minds of those who view it. God's plan is clear: for you to have all the sex you want—with someone who loves you for better or worse, richer or poorer, in sickness and health, till death do you part. Pornography is a cheap counterfeit. To look

THE CRIMINALIZATION OF CHRISTIANITY

at someone you can never have and who couldn't care less about you—what a rip-off! It consumes and entraps the mind, and users have called it "more addictive than cocaine." It is important not only because it destroys lives, relationships, marriages, and families, but also because it feeds the sinful drive of those who prey on women and children.

Assisted Suicide

Right to die? Statistics show that ten out of ten people die, and they don't need any special right to do it. Rather than talking desperate people down from the ledge, assisted suicide pushes them off. It turns doctors into executioners. Call me an extremist, but I also think that starving to death disabled people like Terri Shiavo is wrong. The attempt to kill Terri, and thousands like her, by this brutal method is legal and continues to threaten her life. Yet I would be arrested for starving a dog to death in protest.

Evolution

As Ken Ham of *Answers in Genesis* often points out, if the Bible's account of Creation is true, the fossil record should show evidence of a great flood. We would expect to find "billions of dead things, buried in rock layers, laid down by water, all over the earth." What the fossil record in fact reveals is billions of dead things, buried in rock layers, laid down by water, all over the earth. Ham also says we wouldn't see any transition fossils showing fish becoming reptiles and reptiles becoming birds. We don't. Just distinct fish, birds, reptiles, and mammals. None of which blend into or out of each other regardless of the unproven theories that have been written into science books as fact. Instead of learning that they are human beings made in the image of God, kids are taught that they are nothing more than complex food processors that came from the primordial slime. But which is more complex: a 747, a robot, a computer, or a worm? If you guessed worm, you're right. Its DNA structure, digestive system, and reproductive system are far more complex than those other things, which obviously had a designer. Maybe, just maybe, someone designed that worm, too.

Abstinence

I'll be the first to admit that this often runs counter to human emotions. But the consequences here speak for themselves: One in five Americans currently has an STD,[13] and two-thirds of all STDs occur in people younger than twenty-five years of age.[14] One in four sexually active teens has been afflicted.[15] Add to that millions of babies born out of wedlock (resulting in children growing up without dads), more than forty-five million aborted children, and all the failed marriages because of adultery. Then do a little survey inside today's prisons and see just how many inmates come from homes where the parents weren't married because of premature sex or adultery. The results will astound you.

Evangelism

This is sharing what God did in an effort to keep people out of hell. The objectionable message is that you can, in fact, go to heaven because someone else (namely Jesus Christ) paid the admission for you with His life. Unlike all other religions, which speak of how we can try to get to God, Christianity tells how God came *to us*. But telling people they have free admission to heaven is viewed negatively, of course. It's been renamed "proselytizing" by those who want to outlaw it.

FOLLOWING THE COMPASS

Yes, worldviews are colliding. One submits to the God who made us; another either pretends that what He says doesn't matter or denies that He even exists.

Those who deny Christ hate the fact that His words are chiseled on our national monuments and that Moses and the Ten Commandments are engraved in stone in our Supreme Court. God is mentioned in almost all state constitutions, mottoes, and seals—that's why just trying to remove them all is a full-time job for the ACLU. God and His principles are so embedded in our nation that they've been at it every day for the last forty years and still haven't gotten them all.

Reminders of God's existence are all around, and it makes the ACLU really, really angry. Reminders like today's date. Yeah, today's date. You see, God *divided* time and history for all mankind—that's where the BC and AD came from. Add the AD to the date sometime and watch their faces turn red. But whether they like it or not, there's a reason why the word *Christmas* bears a striking resemblance to His name. There was a time when your parents were allowed to see displays of Him in a manger. They even sang Christmas carols—before they were replaced with songs about snowmen.

The battle lines are drawn. You are either for God or against Him. You are either for good or for evil. Across the board—on every issue.

You see, we are commanded to be salt and light in a dark and decaying world. The Christian worldview is that we are to live out our faith in *every arena,* and that includes the schools, the legislatures, the courts, the media, Hollywood, the sciences, and the arts. It's not just about going to church and inviting people to go, too; we're supposed to be applying all we know to everything we do every single day. The Christian worldview must be expressed in the light of day, not just behind closed doors where nobody can see.

Because how will the two-thirds of adults and the eight out of ten teens who don't know that absolute truth exists find out if no one is bold enough to tell them? And how will they know God (who is the way, the *truth,* and the life) unless we tell them?

Chapter 3

STEP ONE: RIDICULE

The first step to silencing Christians goes all the way back to the sandbox. Good old-fashioned name-calling.

When you don't have a snappy comeback or a reasoned response, just call your opponent a name!

Want to know a liberal's definition of the word *bigot*?

> **big-ot:** 1. *n.* a conservative who is winning a debate with a liberal. See also: *Syn.* intolerant, extremist, homophobic, antichoice, Nazi.

That's right. Name-calling. Seen on playgrounds for centuries. Don't believe me? *Stupid head!* Yeah! *You remember.* And when you've got nothing else, just say it over and over. And *louder and louder.*

FINDING A VILLAIN

Have you ever wondered how so many people have bought into the lie of abortion? Same tactics, different decade. Let me take you back in time.

Imagine it's your job to sell to America, which protects children fully in nearly every state, the concept of tearing living children apart limb by limb. How would you go about it?

Well, let's ask the people who worked to make abortion legal. In *Aborting America*, former abortionist Bernard Nathanson, who founded NARAL (back when it stood for the National Association for Repeal of Abortion Laws), details the plan that paved the way for *Roe v. Wade*. Nathanson's partner Larry Lader explained how to go about it:

> [E]very revolution has to have its villain. It doesn't really matter whether it's a king, a dictator, or a tsar, but it has to be *someone,* a person to rebel against. It's easier for the people we want to persuade to perceive it this way.[1]

This is what Nathanson called a "good tactical strategy" for picking a villain: "A single person isn't quite what we want, since that might excite sympathy for him. Rather, a small group of shadowy, powerful people; too large a group would diffuse the focus, don't you see?"[2]

They wanted to appeal to the "liberal Catholic" crowd—you know, the ones that want the Catholic label but not what Catholics believe. Frankly, I've never really comprehended groups like Catholics for Free Choice. That's like saying I'm with Environmentalists for Littering or Gun Controllers for M-57s. Hey, if you don't like what they believe, quit. But I digress.

Nathanson and his proabortion allies picked their villain:

> [T]he Catholic hierarchy. That's a small enough group to come down on, and anonymous enough so that no names ever have to be mentioned, but everybody will have a fairly good idea whom we are talking about.[3]

Then he stirred up anti-Catholic prejudices and pontificated about the necessity for "separation of church and state." He also used the argument that abortion laws are a threat to American "pluralism," or that "one religious group" ought not to "impose" its views on others in our society."[4]

In other words, Nathanson and the other proaborts sought to demonize and silence the Christian opposition by using the old myth of separation of church and state. Nathanson now admits that "under the First Amendment... any group has a right to express its views and to try to persuade others of its stand on a moral issue."[5] By the way, NARAL's founder, Bernard Nathanson, is now pro-life.

They wanted abortion to appear to be purely a Catholic issue. And they did a good job. I remember that when I was speaking in the eighties, everyone assumed I was Catholic. To their credit, the Catholics stood firm, despite being demonized. They carried the ball on this issue when many wouldn't touch it. For that I am forever grateful.

Character assassination when they don't like what you say—you can just expect it. That is what I told Brenda Shafer. She was a nurse who assisted with partial-birth abortions in Ohio. We tracked her down, and I asked her to join in the fight to protect children from this brutal procedure.

When she and her husband agreed to testify before Congress, I gave her a warning. "Brenda, you're going to need to weigh the cost, because, make no mistake, you will become a target of the proabortion gang. The first thing they're going to do is call you a liar. They're going to assassinate your character, say you never worked there, and go after your family."

Just like clockwork. They said that she was a liar, that she never worked at the abortion facility. That was when she presented cancelled checks and pay stubs. Then they went after her character and her family. The name-calling, the intimidation, the threats.

Color me surprised.

But in spite of it all, Brenda spoke eloquently before Congress about what she had witnessed firsthand:

> I stood at the doctor's side and watched him perform this [partial-birth] abortion on a woman who was six months pregnant. The doctor delivered the baby's body and arms, everything but his little head. The baby's body was moving. His little fingers were clasping together. He was kicking his feet. The doctor took a pair of scissors

and inserted them into the back of the baby's head, and the baby's arms jerked out in a flinch, a "startle" reaction, like a baby does when he think that he might fall. Then the doctor opened the scissors up. He then stuck the high-powered suction tube into the hole and sucked the baby's brains out. Now the baby was completely limp. I never went back to the clinic. But I am still haunted by the face of that little boy. It was the most perfect, angelic face I have ever seen.[6]

IMAGINE IF THEY TARGETED...

I've been watching the assault against Christians for more than a decade. It's become so commonplace that many of us have become desensitized to it. Labeling, ridicule, demonization. It happens so often that most of the time we don't even recognize it. Because the labels "radical," "right-wing," and "extremist" appear everywhere we are quoted, it's as if they are part of our names. But imagine for a moment that you picked up the *Washington Post* and read this:

African-Americans are largely poor, uneducated, and easy to lead.

There would be outrage! Something like that would never be tolerated, nor should it be. However, if it's about Christians, it's completely acceptable. Here's what was really said:

Pat Robertson's and Jerry Falwell's followers are largely poor, uneducated, and easy to lead.[7]

By the way, this is from a "news article." The attack on Christians was so blatant that the following day the *Post* was forced to run a correction admitting there was no factual basis for the statement. However, no apology was forthcoming from the writer, Michael Weisskopf, because he "[tries] not to... attribute every point in the story if it appears to be universally true."[8]

What if something like *this* were said?

Jewish people are "bozos" and Judaism is a religion for losers.

Same reaction—universal outrage. The Anti-Defamation League would be calling for the job of anyone who said such a thing. The person whose job they'd be calling for would be Ted Turner, the former owner of CNN. But what he really said was:

Christians are "bozos" and *Christianity* is a religion for losers.[9]

Ridicule then moves to demonization. Imagine for a moment that Reverend Jesse Jackson said *this:*

The National Organization for Women was a strong force in [Nazi] Germany. It laid down a subtle scientific, theological rationale for the tragedy in Germany. NOW was very much in evidence there.

Now, you're probably looking at that ridiculous quote and thinking, *What a stretch—the National Organization for Women wasn't even around during the Third Reich, let alone a "force" there.* Neither was the Christian Coalition. Here's what Jesse Jackson really said:

The *Christian Coalition* was a strong force in [Nazi] Germany. It laid down a subtle scientific, theological rationale for the tragedy in Germany. The *Christian Coalition* was very much in evidence there.[10]

How about this one?

The Ohio Educational Association (a division of the National Educational Association) was conducting an official survey. Imagine that *this* was what they asked:

Are any of the school board members in your school district known or suspected to be communists?

McCarthyism! How dare you incite a witch hunt for communists? We'd have to turn in our college professors if such a policy were implemented. *Calm down.* Here's what they *really* asked:

Are any of the school board members in your school district known or suspected to be *proponents of the Radical Right?*[11]

At its annual convention, the National Education Association distributed flyers and packets decrying "the radical right." Why? Because Christians support freedom to choose where to send their children to school.[12] Screening out Christians—it's good to know NEA teacher union dues are being spent in such a worthwhile way, isn't it? Hey, at least they're not using *all* of it to elect liberal pro-abortion, pro-homosexual candidates!

And while we're on the subject of education, imagine former NEA president Bob Chase said this about what we should be teaching our children:

Schools cannot be neutral when we're dealing with [Ten Commandment] issues. I'm not talking about tolerance. I'm talking about acceptance. The Ten Commandments are a great resource for parents, teachers, and community leaders.

Did the NEA *really* want the Ten Commandments back in the classroom? No. *Duh.* He was talking about the *homosexual agenda:*

Schools cannot be neutral when we're dealing with *human dignity and human rights.* I'm not talking about tolerance. I'm talking about acceptance. [The film] *It's Elementary* is a great resource for parents, teachers, and community leaders.[13]

Here's another:

It's a real conflict for me when I go to a concert and find out somebody in the audience is a Democrat or fundamental Muslim. It can cloud my enjoyment. I'd rather not know.

No, of course *that* wouldn't fly. What Linda Ronstadt really said was:

It's a real conflict for me when I go to a concert and find out some-body in the audience is a *Republican or fundamental Christian*. It can cloud my enjoyment. I'd rather not know.[14]

I say let's not cloud her enjoyment anymore. Turns out, a lot of people at the Las Vegas casino, The Aladdin, felt that way. After Linda dedicated a song to Michael Moore, producer of the anti-Bush propaganda film *Fahrenheit 9/11*, the auditorium of the casino was filled with boos, and hundreds of people left. Others threw their drinks and caused such a ruckus that she was thrown out, and Aladdin Theatre for the Performing Arts President Bill Timmins asked her not to return.

While I can't support throwing drinks (I've long been an anti-drink-thrower), I have to say that this event gave me some hope. Maybe, just maybe, people are capable of standing up and fighting back.

Mel Gibson is one of Hollywood's leading men. Popular, handsome, revered, rich. Held in high regard by all. That is *until* he wanted to make a movie about Jesus. Nobody wanted to finance it. Nobody wanted to distribute it. If you are a Christian and want to express what you believe, brace yourself—you'll even get put in the same sentence with Pat Robertson.

Here's a portion of Andy Rooney's parody of a conversation between himself and God:

Rooney: "Pat Robertson and Mel Gibson strike me as wackos.... They're crazy… Mel is a real nut case."

God: What in the world was I thinking when I created him? Listen, we all make mistakes.[15]

Yes, if you spend all of your own money to tell the story about the excru-ciatingly high price God paid for our salvation, I'm sure that's what God would say.

By the way, as of July 2004, *The Passion of the Christ* had made $609 million.[16] And it's one of the top ten most successful movies of all time.

GETTING CHRISTIANS OUT OF AREAS OF INFLUENCE

Getting Christians out of areas of influence has been the goal of the name-callers for quite a while (many more examples can be found on www.F2A.org). This comment by Vic Fazio, Former Democratic Congressional Campaign Chairman, got my attention in September 1994, when the Democrats saw they were about to lose the majority in the Senate to Christian involvement in the Republican Party:

> The "fire-breathing Christian radical right"… is about to take over the Republican Party. They are what the American people fear the most.[17]

I thought Ralph Reed put Fazio's remark in perspective when he responded:

> Murder is the leading cause of death for African-American males aged eighteen to thirty-four, and a minority adolescent male living in our nation's capital has a higher likelihood of being killed than an American soldier did in Vietnam. Yet people of faith getting involved in public life is what the American people fear most.[18]

Saying that people fear them—that should keep them quiet. Maybe they could prevent a president's impeachment by name-calling, like Alan Dershowitz tried to do:

> A vote against impeachment is a vote against bigotry. It's a vote against fundamentalism, the right-to-life movement, and the radical right. And if this president is impeached, it will be a great victory for the forces of genuine evil, evil, genuine evil.[19]

Nope. Didn't work. Nice try though.

Not unlike 2004, when the homosexual lobby the Human Rights Campaign, which endorsed John Kerry for president, demanded that at the GOP convention the Republican Party forbid speeches and performances by people they didn't like. Like entertainer Donnie McClurkin, an accomplished gospel singer, author, and *former homosexual.*[20]

Can't have an ex-homosexual on stage! People might find out they exist. News like that could cast doubt on their false "born-that-way" argument. And *then* how would homosexual activists justify all those special rights they've been demanding?

Playgrounds are full of bullies calling kids names like "mean," "ugly," and "intolerant." So is the media. CNN *Crossfire* cohost Bill Press said this:

> It's just that their religion is so narrow, and it's so mean, and it's so ugly, and it's so intolerant, and it's so un-Christian.[21]

And here's what Roseanne Barr passes off for entertainment these days:

> You know what else I can't stand, is them [sic] people that are anti-abortion. F—them; I hate them. They're horrible; they're hideous people. They're ugly, old, geeky, hideous men....They just don't want nobody to have an abortion 'cause they want you to keep spitting out kids so they can f—ing molest them.[22]

Pro-lifers are child molesters—that's *hilarious.* Someone should ask her to sing the National Anthem at a ball game sometime. Oh yeah, that went over well as I recall.

In a conversation between syndicated radio host Howard Stern and a pro-life caller on November 11, 1999, Stern vehemently argued for abortion and partial-birth abortion in grotesque detail. At one point, he said, "You're an idiot. I can't stand dumb people. If I was president, I would have you gassed. I would march you into the ovens."

Howard Stern, heard across the nation on radio and TV, is suggesting that he would "march pro-lifers to the ovens." Go ahead and substitute the name of any other group of people. Insert the word *Muslims* and see what happens. Or *Jews*. Mention marching *them* to the ovens, and see how long you stay on the air.

According to Bill Johnson of the American Decency Association, over 9,700 advertisers have stopped advertising on Stern's show since 1996. Until 1999, he had added his show to between nine and twelve radio stations a year. But in 1999, he had "a net gain of negative one."[23]

That changed again in 2004 after Janet Jackson exposed herself at the Super Bowl. But, really, what woman *can't* relate to wardrobe malfunctions like that? It's as commonplace as having your slip show. But the FCC got some heat, so they started to enforce a few indecency laws. Clear Channel, which carried Howard Stern, was slapped with a $450,000 fine because of him. That's when they dropped Stern from six of their stations.[24]

But then Sirius satellite radio rewarded Stern for his appalling pro-life Christian bashing with a $500 million, five-year deal.[25] But if he said he would "march" *any* other group "into the ovens," he'd be lucky to be talking to a tin can on the end of a string.

And finally, a message of peace, love, and happiness from musician Bob Weir to a crowd of 30,000 at a May 1995 Grateful Dead concert:

Can I hear everybody say, "F—the Christian right?[26]

THE PLAYGROUND IS ONLY THE BEGINNING

If you are an active Christian, you are among those labeled politically incorrect, and you're fair game for ridicule. That's the first step in a movement to silence us. And, as in any campaign, if an accusation goes unanswered, it's assumed to be true. Once you take patriotic, law-abiding citizens and paint them as the scum of the earth—the kooks, the idiots—see how effective and well-received their message of salvation becomes. But in order to silence Christians entirely, labeling, name-calling, mocking, and ridicule quickly turn to blame.

Chapter 4

STEP TWO: BLAME

If they're Christians, you can hate them. You can ridicule them, and before you silence them, make sure you blame them for everything you don't like.

Pick a Christian, any Christian. And, hey, why not start at the top? There are now more than fifty books bashing Bush—by everyone from Michael Moore to Al Franken—including some that imply that President Bush is crazy. And communist dictator Fidel Castro has been reading them. In a speech on July 26, 2004, he quoted liberally from American sources, stating that Bush is a "mentally unstable religious fanatic."[1] *Nice.*

I recently interviewed Oliver North on my Faith2Action radio show, and I asked him why so many people hate President George W. Bush. "This president," he replied, "is despised by so many because he is a man of faith and is unashamed of it." He went on to say that in one of the presidential debates, Jim Lehrer asked the question "Who is your favorite philosopher?" Bush's answer was: "Jesus Christ, because he saved me and changed my life and changed my heart." North added, "I think they decided they hated him at that point."[2]

We don't have to go to the Middle East to see people burn pictures of our president (and our flag). People here hate President Bush as much as the

Muslim extremists do. We saw them line up in New York during the 2004 Republican National Convention. Here's how the *New York Post* described the event:

> Rachel Sammis is 14. The child from New Hampshire spent her first grown-up protest march carrying a huge picture of the president of the United States—decorated with a Hitler-style moustache scribbled in pen.... David Humphrey of Greenwich Village carried an NC-17-rated painting depicting Bush and Jesus in the buff. From the figures' private parts, airplanes flew into the World Trade Center.[3]

The anti-Bush fourteen-year-old informed the reporter that Hitler "killed, like, *hundreds* of Jews" before a friend stepped in to correct her with the word *thousands*.[4] What a great endorsement of the public school system! That's probably where they made their signs.

Former Vice President Al Gore compared President Bush's Christian faith with fundamentalist Islam, asserting that it emphasizes "vengeance" and "brimstone":

> It's a particular kind of religiosity. It's the American version of the same fundamentalist impulse that we see in Saudi Arabia, in Kashmir, in religions around the world: Hindu, Jewish, Christian, Muslim. They all have certain features in common.
>
> In a world of disconcerting change, when large and complex forces threaten familiar and comfortable guideposts, the natural impulse is to grab hold of the tree trunk that seems to have the deepest roots and hold on for dear life and never question the possibility that it's not going to be the source of your salvation. And the deepest roots are in philosophical and religious traditions that go way back.[5]

If you're looking for salvation in a tree trunk, that would be a good question to ask. But if your faith is in God, that's another matter altogether. If *anyone* knows about hugging trees, it would be Al Gore.

THE CRIMINALIZATION OF CHRISTIANITY

Gore went on to say:

The real distinction of this presidency is that, at its core, he is a very weak man.... I think [Bush] is a bully, and, like all bullies, he's a coward.[6]

Can you say *bitter*? I like grapes because they are sour.

And if you go on national television and expose yourself, whether you use a trench coat or a wardrobe that "malfunctions," make sure you place the blame where it properly belongs—on the president of the United States. Fallout from your behavior *has* to be his fault. He was just using Janet Jackson's unfortunate mishap to "distract people from the war in Iraq"![7] That's what she said.

Actress Sharon Stone said that Bush was to blame for the fact that the movie *Catwoman* didn't include a lesbian kiss. To be sure, the president took time away from running the country and overseeing the war in Iraq to interfere with her plans for a bigger and more lesbian part in the film. Stone proclaimed: "Halle's [Berry] so beautiful and I wanted to kiss her. How can you have us in the movie and not have us kiss? That's such a waste." Stone added, "That's what you get for having George Bush as president."[8]

Yeah, everyone thinks there should be a lesbian scene in a comic-book movie. Stone is right. Someone needs to be blamed for this travesty—and who better than the president?

At a Hollywood fund-raiser for John Kerry, Whoopie Goldberg joined in the Bush-bashing fun by making X-rated jokes about the president. In his closing remarks, Kerry said that Whoopie and her Hollywood pals conveyed "the heart and soul of our country."[9] After the event, Whoopie was cut from the Slim-Fast payroll. Almost makes me want to drink the stuff. Hey, if you don't like the taste, you know who to blame.

And of course, when former President Bill Clinton had sex with Monica Lewinski in the oval office and lied about it, there was really only one place to put the blame. Hillary Clinton went on national television to tell everyone just whose fault it was. It was a "vast right-wing conspiracy," of course.[10] Sure. Don't know how they maneuvered that blue-dress thing, but, rest assured, it was a right-wing conspiracy. *Had to be.*

After the Oklahoma City bombing, I started noticing that we were being blamed for terrorism:

The story of Oklahoma City [bombing] and the militias should not make us forget that the main form of political terrorism in the United States today is perpetrated by right-wing opponents of abortion.[11]

Syndicated columnist Ellen Goodman wrote that "radical anti-abortion groups like Operation Rescue and Rescue America have to be dealt with as *domestic terrorists as deadly as the ones who blew up the World Trade Center and as fanatic as the cultists in Waco.*"[12]

Pro-lifers are the main form of terrorism and have to be *dealt with* like the deadly terrorists who blew up the World Trade Center and the "cultists" in Waco? They burned the men, women, and children in Waco. Are we to be treated like that? Where do you buy good asbestos these days, anyway?

YOU'RE TO BLAME FOR LESBIANS' BAD HEALTH

The *Times-Picayune,* San Francisco, noted that lesbians have more health problems: "Compared with heterosexual women, lesbians appear to have higher rates of smoking, obesity and alcohol use." And apparently *heterosexuals* are to blame. The article states that "smoking and substance abuse, to the extent they are more prevalent among lesbians, may be linked to the stress of feeling targeted by prejudice."[13]

I actually think the blame should be placed on a combination of pro-life heterosexuals *and* President Bush. It's part of a vast right-wing conspiracy to get lesbians smoking, drunk, and overweight. Everyone knows that.

WHAT'S A SENSE OF HUMOR?

Knock Knock.
   Who's there?
   Sense of humor.
   What's a sense of humor?

THE CRIMINALIZATION OF CHRISTIANITY

Have you ever noticed how some people just can't take a joke? Feminists, for example. Question: How many feminists does it take to change a light-bulb? Answer: "That's not funny!" Question: How many lesbian activists does it take to change a lightbulb? Answer: "That's a hate crime!"

Governor Arnold Schwarzenegger, playing off a *Saturday Night Live* bodybuilding spoof, referred to the California legislature as "girlie men" for not passing his budget. Democrats protested that the remark was sexist and homophobic. Lesbian state senator Sheila Kuehl said the governor had resorted to "blatant homophobia."[14] Blah, blah, blah. *Enough already.* This constant victimhood is really getting old. Oops, better not say that in California—it's probably a hate crime there.

If I didn't think homosexual activists would try to make it sexual, I would stand up and proclaim that the emperor has no clothes. Homosexuals have played the victim card so much that they're on a new deck. That despite the reams of research showing that homosexual and lesbian income levels are "higher than the national averages"; that they "have more education" than heterosexuals; are "twice as likely to have household income over $60,000 than [the] general U.S. population"; and that they are among "the most economically advantaged people in the U.S."[15]

The unfounded finger-pointing has silenced many Christians who don't like being called "homophobic, bigoted extremists." But for those with courage enough to face the verbal assault with the truth on subjects like abortion and homosexuality, watch out—they're now blaming you for murder.

WE KILLED <u>WHO?</u>

Now abortion leaders are trying to prevent us from speaking the truth by calling us murderers. Kind of ironic, don't you think? Here's what Kate Michelman, former president of NARAL (National Abortion Rights Action League), had to say in 1998:

Those in the leadership of the other side must acknowledge and admit that their words drive unrestrained factions of their own movement to commit these horrific acts.... Denials and condemnations no longer suffice. They must stop referring to abortion as murder and to doctors who perform them as murderers.[16]

Truth doesn't kill. Abortion does. On January 22, 1995, the National Conference of Catholic Bishops ran a full-page ad in the *New York Times* that said it best: "Abortion policy must be debated. Without violence. But with truth."

Then Planned Parenthood joined NARAL in the movement to silence us by blaming people who speak the truth about abortion being murder. In 1998, their president, Gloria Feldt, said:

> That word game has turned deadly. It is time to point the finger where the blame belongs—at the doors of people who spew hate from radio and TV talk shows, Web sites, and pulpits.[17]

That's the way to keep the church quiet—call Christians murderers. Good one, Gloria.

Let's see, who's to blame for the death of Barnett Slepian and Matthew Shepard? If Polly Rothstein of the New York–based Westchester Coalition for Legal Abortion were playing a game of Clue, she would say that the pope did it, with his words, in the conservatory. No, no…make that *the church*. The pope's to blame. *Of course*. Rothstein said that the pope, the bishops, and the Protestant clergymen "didn't pull the trigger," but that the blood of Slepian and Shepard "is on the hands of religious leaders who have, with vitriolic language, incited zealous followers to murder abortion doctors and gays and lesbians."[18]

Think about this for a second: Christians who say: "Don't kill babies" should be silenced because some people may not follow their advice when it comes to adults?

Herblock, a political cartoonist, made a similar statement in a cartoon in the *Washington Post*. It showed a man with a gun standing behind a pro-life protester, complete with suit and tie and an "Abortion Is Murder" sign

reading "What, me, an accomplice?"[19] I didn't see a similar cartoon about environmentalists when Ted Kazinski, the "environmentalist" Unibomber, was caught. Did you?

TRUTH IN LOVE

Calling people who happen to disagree with you murderers isn't limited to the abortion debate. During the national Truth in Love Campaign, which expressed hope for change to those struggling with homosexuality, that approach became the latest fad.

I wouldn't even have gotten involved in the homosexual issue if extremists hadn't crossed the line into my freedom of speech. A lot of people have wondered how I, the pro-life girl, ended up coordinating the Truth in Love Campaign.

I knew something had to be done when former Clinton White House spokesperson Mike McCurry said that Senate Majority Leader Trent Lott [and *anyone* who believed what the Bible had to say about homosexuality] was "backward thinking." A spokesperson for the White House had just slapped millions of American families in the face. And in any campaign, if an attack goes unanswered, it is assumed to be true. That was when I called our nation's leading pro-family organizations and proposed the idea of responding in a full-page ad.

The ads (which you can see on the next few pages) appeared in all the country's major newspapers, as well as on television. Every major news outlet covered it, and *Newsweek* did a feature story with a picture of two ex-homosexuals on the cover. Even *Hard Copy* and *Extra* were lined up outside my office, not to mention members of the foreign press, who admitted that they "had never heard of such a thing as a 'former homosexual,'" let alone *thousands* of them.

Needless to say, lots of people didn't appreciate our point of view. That's why a Web search of my name reveals such lovely descriptions as "that evil Janet Folger." A verse I mentioned earlier comes to mind: "Woe to those who call good evil and evil good" (Isaiah 5:20).

One Truth in Love ad featured a picture of hundreds of ex-homosexuals with the headline "We're Standing for the Truth That Homosexuals Can Change." Brace yourself for the hateful, bigoted, intolerant speech in the ad that they claim is responsible for murder (Note: if you're under eighteen, you may want to ask your parents before reading it):

> We believe every human being is precious to God and is entitled to respect. But when we see great suffering among homosexuals, it's an inherent Christian calling to show compassion and concern.

Wow! I guess now you can see what all the fuss was about.

You can understand why the City of San Francisco Board of Supervisors would be prompted to accuse us of murder:

> It's not an exaggeration to say that there's a direct correlation between these acts of discrimination, like Matthew Shepard, such as when gays and lesbians are called sinful, and when major religious organizations say they can change if they try, and the horrible crimes committed against gays and lesbians.[20]

Look at what is being said here: A government body is saying that speech expressing hope for change for those struggling with homosexuality is what leads to "horrible crimes" and murder.

Forget the fact that I, as the coordinator of that campaign, never met Matthew Shepard. Forget that *no one* connected with the campaign ever met him. The very fact that we spoke a message of hope to the homosexual community was reason enough to blame his death on us. Our speech, the San Francisco Board of Supervisors says, must be silenced.

That, my friend, is why hate crimes laws are the most dangerous legislation in the country. It will lead to silencing our speech, just as the city of San Francisco tried to do.

Toward a new national discussion of homosexuality.

A recent gathering of Exodus, a nationwide ex-gay ministry, drew more than 850 former homosexuals to Seattle to proclaim that hope for change is possible for those still struggling with homosexuality.

We're standing for the truth that homosexuals can change.

Thousands of former homosexuals can celebrate a new life because someone cared enough to share with them the truth of God's healing love. Thank you Trent Lott, Reggie White, and recording artists Angie and Debbie Winans for having the courage to speak the truth about sexual sin.

If you love someone, you'll tell them the truth.

You might be shocked to know that most Christians who speak against homosexual behavior are motivated more by love than hate. Of course, "hate" gets all the headlines, but the truth still remains...We believe every human being is precious to God and is entitled to respect. But when we see great suffering among homosexuals, it's an inherent Christian calling to show compassion and concern. The truth we know is that God abhors any form of sexual sin, be it premarital sex, adultery, prostitution, or homosexuality. And if you were trapped in some self-destructive behavior, wouldn't you want someone to care?

Calling homosexual behavior sin is not anti-gay, it's pro-life.

We've seen the statistics...and they don't lie. Homosexual behavior is not healthy behavior when it accounts for a disproportionate number of sexually transmitted diseases (STD's) such as Gonorrhea, and Hepatitis A and B'; when 65% of all reported AIDS cases among males since 1981 have been men engaged in homosexual behavior'; and when homosexual youth are twenty-three times more likely to contract STD's than heterosexuals.' The cultural answer? More condoms! Yet its been proved that condoms don't protect against all contact STD's. In fact, they often fail...and they're also not designed to protect against the emotional damage done to your heart.

Homosexuality is not a sex issue...It's a heart issue.

There are problems for homosexuals even condoms can't fix. Studies also show a high degree of destructive behavior among homosexuals, including alcohol, drug abuse and emotional and physical violence.' And it occurs even in homosexual-affirming cities like San Francisco. So, it's not lack of acceptance... it's behavior – the visible response to a broken heart.

The truth may hurt before it can heal. But change is possible.

Thousands of stories from "ex-gays" (like those pictured above) confirm what counselors and pastors see every day. Homosexuals routinely describe deep-seated, almost unconscious desires that drive a same-sex urge. They also tell of rejection from early childhood and lack of

> **Senate Majority Leader Trent Lott**
> *when asked whether homosexuality was a sin, said:*
> *"Yes it is...*
> *In America right now there's an element that wants to make that alternative lifestyle acceptable...You still love that person and you should not try to mistreat them or treat them as outcasts. You should try to show them a way to deal with that."*

bonding to same-sex parents, sexual violence and rape, or mental and emotional abuse as critical elements in the formation of their gender-identity. But these life situations don't deny the choice each makes in yielding to temptation, no matter how strong the urge. Still, many have walked out of homosexuality...into sexual celibacy or even marriage. How? Often because someone cared enough to love them, despite where they went, and to confront the truth of their sexual sin. For the Christian, that love comes in the person of Jesus Christ and motivates our commitment to this issue.

We don't need to be perfect to talk about sin.

Quite the contrary. A sinner can spot sin a mile away. Just ask Trent Lott. Or Reggie White. They'd be the first to tell you they're far from perfect. The truth is we are all sinners. The critical difference in this debate is that some recognize their sin and repent, and others don't. That begs the larger question...if we can't talk about sin as a nation, just where is our moral compass pointed? And is there truth in a created moral order, or is truth anything we define it to be?

Taking a stand. Extending a hand.

For years Christians have taken a stand in the public square against aggressive homosexual activism. We've paid a heavy price, with sound-bite labels like "bigot," and "homophobe." But all along we've had a hand extended, something largely unreported in the media...an open hand that offers healing for homosexuals, not harassment. We want reason in this debate, not rhetoric. And we want to share the hope we have in Christ, for those who feel acceptance of homosexuality is their only hope.

You can make a difference.

We are a broad coalition representing millions of concerned families asking for an honest debate with our opponents. This is not a Republican issue...not a Democrat or Independent issue. It's a truth issue. We're asking you to reexamine the truth of homosexuality with ALL the facts in hand, apart from the half-truths and hostile name-calling. Ask us to explain our position on sin. Then ask the other side. But ask! Then let the real healing begin.

If you really love someone, you'll tell them the truth.

For information on contacting an ex-gay ministry in your area, please call 888-264-0877

In the public interest, this message was paid for by the following organizations, representing millions of American families:

Alliance for Traditional Marriage - Hawaii 808-523-8451	**Center for Reclaiming America** 877-INTRUTH	**Citizens for Community Values** 513-733-5775	**Coral Ridge Ministries** 877-466-7664	**Liberty Counsel** 800-671-1776
American Family Association 601-844-5036	**Christian Family Network** 937-236-5433	**Colorado For Family Values** 719-573-4319	**Family First** 303-471-8007	**National Legal Foundation** 757-424-4242
Americans for Truth About Homosexuality 703-491-7975	**Christian Coalition** 800-325-4746	**Concerned Women for America** 800-458-8797	**Family Research Council** 800-225-4008	**Korussu Ministries** 800-581-5030

(1) Mireya Navarro, "Federal Officials See Sharp Rise of Hepatitis Among Gay Men," The New York Times, March 6, 1992 (2) Centers for Disease Control, HIV/AIDS Surveillance Report, Vol.9, No.2, May, 1998 (3) American Adolescents: How Healthy Are They?, p. 31, American Medical Association, 1990 (4) Robert Garofalo and others, "The Association Between Health Risk Behaviors and Sexual Orientation Among a School-based Sample of Adolescents," Pediatrics, 101 pp 895-902, (1998).

During the campaign, Katie Couric said on the *Today Show* that claiming homosexuals can change prompts people to say: "If I met someone who was homosexual, I'm going to take action to try to convince them or try to harm them."[21]

I was on the *Today Show* the next day, when the homosexual lobby tried the same approach. I wish I had thought then to answer the way I did on a later radio show. I was accused of murder for holding to the traditional biblical view of homosexuality. The host said, "Well, if *you're* not responsible for the murder of [homosexual] Matthew Shepard, then *who* is?" My answer was, "How about the people who actually killed him?" It's kind of crazy, I know. I can see why it wouldn't readily occur to anyone.

And this just in: The people who killed Matthew Shepard have just confirmed that they didn't do it out of any animosity for his sexual behavior—they killed him for money for drugs. Both killers have now said their motive for attacking Shepard was robbery. It had nothing to do with his homosexuality.[22] Bet you didn't hear that.

SELECTIVE BLAME

While most have heard of the fabricated "hate crime" against Matthew Shepard, hardly anyone in America has ever heard of Jesse Dirkhising, a thirteen-year-old who was suffocated to death September 26, 1999, after being bound, gagged, and brutally sodomized by homosexual lovers Davis Don Carpenter, then thirty-eight, and Joshua Macabe Brown, then twenty-two, at the men's apartment in Rogers, Arkansas. The details of the five-hour assault are so horrific that I can't report them. Police found Jesse naked and near death on the bedroom floor. He was pronounced dead at St. Mary's hospital.

A Nexis media search reveals 13,500 stories on the name "Matthew Shepard," not including the massive TV coverage of the Shepard case, two major Hollywood specials, three TV movies, and a play. Meanwhile, Jesse Dirkhising, brutally murdered by homosexuals, was widely ignored by the media. A search for stories relating to Dirkhising revealed only 632.[23]

That's 12,868 *fewer stories* than appeared about Shepard, with placement and column lengths that likewise don't compare. Might an agenda have something to do with this skewed reporting?

You can bet that homosexuals weren't asked to appear on national television and questioned about whether homosexual preferences and behaviors were to blame for Jesse's death. They weren't questioned about such things as why they allow the pedophile organization the North American Man/Boy Love Association (NAMBLA) to march in their gay pride parades. They weren't grilled about the overwhelming results of research like that described in a recent article in the *Journal of Sex Research*. The study found that although heterosexuals outnumber homosexuals by a ratio of at least twenty to one, homosexual pedophiles commit about one-third of the total number of child sex offenses.[24] When you get a chance, ask the Catholic Church if it has noticed a connection between homosexuality and pedophilia.

Or how about the murder of Mary Stachowicz? Ever heard of her? *Didn't think so.* A fifty-one-year-old wife and mother of four, Mary Stachowicz was described by friends as soft-spoken, "concerned about the good of her parish, always seeking things for the poor as well as spiritual welfare for people."[25] She also believed what the Bible and the Catholic Church teach about homosexuality. She verbalized her belief, and for that "crime" she was murdered.

Mary was murdered by nineteen-year-old homosexual Nicholas Gutierrez for disagreeing with his lifestyle. According to police reports, she asked Gutierrez, who lived in an apartment above her, "Why do you [have sex with] boys instead of girls?" That was when he "punched, kicked, stabbed and strangled" her before stuffing her body into a crawl space under the floor of his apartment, where it remained for two days until he confessed to police.[26]

Chicago media reported these events, choosing headlines devoid of words like "gay" or "homosexual." While other pro-family leaders and I repeatedly went on national television to censure the death of Matthew Shepard, the homosexual community never condemned this horrific murder. Perhaps more telling was what they *did say:*

I really don't feel sorry for her. She paid a very steep price for being an arrogant religious fascist. Too bad for her. (posted on the ACLU Online Forum)

Quite frankly, if anyone in this case was being "persecuted" it was Mr. Gutierrez. Unfortunately for the victim this was a lesson that she learned too hard and too late. Maybe this will give pause to other people who similarly try to "help" homosexuals. (posted on ACLU Online Forum)

The woman who did such great evil is dead, but unfortunately the evil and the church and the society which creates it is not. (gay blogger)

Maybe [Stachowicz's murder] will strike fear in the hearts of a few fundamentalists....Where do I send a check for [Gutierrez's] defense fund?

The b— had it coming to her. I'm glad he killed her. Too bad he'll probably spend the rest of his life in prison getting his little butt pounded, but still, I'm glad he killed her. The b— deserved to die." (posted on Yahoo)[27]

Instead of condemning this horrific murder, homosexuals danced on Mary Stachowicz's grave.

May God help us.

EVEN MORE THAN BLAME

Do you see a trend here? Label them. Ridicule them. Blame them for everything you don't like. Even blame them for murder. But if rhetoric isn't giving you the desired results, you can always step up the *tactics*.

Chapter 5

MORE THAN JUST THREATS

The day my car burst into flames was the day I started taking the death threats seriously. I've seen *up close* what it's like to come under fire.

As spokesperson for Ohio Right to Life for nine years and national director for the Center for Reclaiming America for five years, I've had my share of hate mail. I never once thought about trying to make such correspondence illegal. People have their views, and if they want to kill children, I can understand why they don't think too highly of me. And they're free to say so. That's what the First Amendment is all about.

I've also had my share of death threats. Never paid much attention to them until 1994, when a noise woke me in the middle of the night. It was so distinct that I got up and looked out the window—something I had never done before. The next morning when I started my car, it burst into flames. (You can read the full story and see a picture in my first book, *True to Life*.) What made it worse was *that car was a Porsche*.

On Friday, May 13, 1994, the banner headline of Cleveland's *The Plain Dealer* read: "Right to Life Leader's Car Sabotaged. Odds Are, [the fire] Is Connected to Abortion Issue, Police Say." My bumper sticker read: "Abortion? Pick on Someone Your Own Size." Apparently, someone took that literally. At first the event shook me up a bit, but in the end I think it made me *more* pro-life—starting with *my own.*

JUST LIKE WILL AND GRACE

The protesters, the phone calls, the mail, the threats—I've seen a lot. I even had a stalker with a violent criminal record. But I have never seen anything like the threats and the tactics of the homosexual movement. *Ever.* Here's an example from ACT UP member Michael Petrelis:

> We should have shut down the subway and burned down city hall. I think rioting is a valid tactic and should be tried.... If someone took out [former congressmen] Jesse Helms or William Dannemeyer of California, I would be the first to stand up and applaud.[1]

I had never paid much attention to the homosexual agenda or their tactics until I heard about what ACT UP (AIDS Coalition to Unleash Power) did at St. Patrick's Cathedral. You know, when they stormed in, screamed obscenities, stomped on and desecrated the Communion bread, and urinated in the church. Typical posters outside St. Patrick's Cathedral included "Get over it, Mary," "Cardinal O'Killer," and "F— the church."[2] *Nice group of fellows.* Just like on *Will and Grace.*

    U. S. News & World Report columnist John Leo describes it further: "Savage mockery of Christianity is now a conventional part of the public gay culture." Not something you're likely to hear about in the conventional press. At an ordination ceremony in Boston, for example, the *Boston Globe* described the protest as "colorful, loud and peaceful." What they didn't write about was the simulated anal and oral sex, the parody of Communion using condoms instead of the eucharistic host, and the mocking depiction of Jesus' Sermon on the Mount as an endorsement of sodomy. They didn't report about how ACT UP protestors swarmed around a newly ordained priest and his elderly mother, pelting them with condoms, shouting, and intimidating them.[3]

Here's what Eric Pollard, the founder of that group, had to say about his tactics:

"I shall torture you during the daytime, and will keep you from a peaceful sleep at night."[4]

In Madison, Wisconsin, four hundred homosexual activists stormed the Trinity Evangelical Fellowship Church, where Scott Lively was speaking. While they shouted obscenities and slogans *inside* the church for nearly an hour, some of the protestors urinated and defecated on the floor. Hundreds of others banged on the outer walls and windows with rocks and trash-can lids, shouting, "Crush the Christians!" and "Bring back the lions!"[5]

FIRED FOR DISAGREEING

Former firefighter Ron Greer can relate. I say *former* because after serving eighteen years on the Madison Fire Department, Greer was fired by a lesbian fire chief for his stand against homosexuality. While pornography was perfectly acceptable, apparently biblical pamphlets were not—especially those that disagreed with the homosexual agenda. His pamphlet stated: "God is love. He is also Holy.... There is nothing loving about letting homosexuals slide into eternal damnation unresisted."[6]

Even though his eighteen-year service was exemplary, his Christian beliefs led to a pink slip, a vandalized house, and a yard filled with pink triangles. Pink triangle stickers, most with graphic sexual references, were pasted on the walls and windows of his home, signs were screwed into the porch and pounded into the yard, and a banner was stretched across his porch with slogans like: "Welcome to Fag City, USA," "Wisconsin Lesbians Against Greer," and "We want you, Ronnie."[7]

Greer is also very familiar with the "Bring back the lions!" shouts. That exhibition of "tolerance" took place at *his church,* where homosexual activists blocked the entrance (something that would have warranted federal intervention had it occurred at an abortion facility) and stormed the church. They outnumbered by ten to one the forty church members who were courageous enough to run the hostile gauntlet to get to a pew. [8]

BURN THEIR HOUSES

Chuck and Donna McIlhenny got a taste of such tactics after the San Francisco Presbyterian church he pastors fired a homosexual organist. In their book *When the Wicked Seize a City*, they describe what it is like to be the object of this kind of "tolerance":

> The harassment started. Rocks, beer bottles, beer cans were thrown through the church windows on many occasions. Swastikas were carved in the church doors and drawn on our house. A window in our car was smashed out. Graffiti was spray-painted all over the church, house and sidewalk. Anti-Christian, pro-homosexual leaflets were scattered around the neighborhood calling us Nazis, bigots, anti-gay, etc. Demonstrators would come into our Sunday services and disrupt the worship.... One time a man came pounding and spitting on our front door in the middle of the night, screaming, "We're going to get you McIlhenny—we're going to kill you politically!" We were verbally threatened outside the house on the way to the car. There were daily—24-hours-per-day—telephone calls. They began with screaming and obscenities. They graduated into phone calls describing our children—by name, appearance, where they attended school, when they got out of school, and what sexually deviant behavior was to be practiced on the children before killing them....Then on 31 May 1983 at 12:30 A.M., someone actually attempted to follow through with their threats to kill us [by firebombing the house while the children were asleep inside.[9]]

Burning the house while the family is inside. You'd be hard pressed to find another group as intolerant, intimidating, and violent. Except for maybe those Brownshirts in 1939. Before you bring a hate crimes charge against me,

I'm not the one who suggested that ACT UP members use *Mein Kampf* as a working model. Eric Pollard did. He's the guy who *founded* ACT-UP D.C. Unlike many of his colleagues, Pollard later regretted his tactics. In a letter to the homosexual newspaper the *Washington Blade* entitled "Time to Give Up Fascist Tactics," he said:

> This is very hard for me to write. It forces me to squarely confront my past actions and to accept responsibility for the damage I have had a part in causing. I sincerely apologize for my involvement in and my founding of the AIDS activist organization, ACT-UP D.C. I have helped to create a truly fascist organization.... The average Gay man or woman could not immediately relate to our subversive tactics, drawn largely from the voluminous *Mein Kamph,* which some of us studied as a working model.[10]

Mein Kampf as a working model. Tolerant stuff.

According to the Centers for Disease Control and Prevention, we spend ten times more money each year on AIDS than on cancer, heart disease, and stroke victims combined.[11] (Who says this issue doesn't affect anyone else?)

But if you feel that isn't enough money, here's one of Robert Schwab's tactics for you:

> If [AIDS] research money is not forthcoming at a certain level by a certain date, all gay males should give blood. Whatever action is required to get national attention is valid. If that includes blood terrorism, so be it.[12]

Blood terrorism. Are you following this? Purposely tainting the blood supply with AIDS-infected blood. Ask Doug Herman of Pure Revolution about it. He lost his wife and baby to "blood terrorism." Now he travels the country speaking about purity. And let me assure you, homosexual activists attack him. You'd think that killing his wife and daughter would have been enough.

DIAGNOSIS BY INTIMIDATION

Such intimidation is exactly the same kind of tactic that got the American Psychiatric Association to remove homosexuality from its list of mental disorders. That action was not the result of new research or even of a majority vote of APA members.

In 1963 the New York Academy of Medicine charged its Committee on Public Health to report on homosexuality because they feared it was on the increase. The committee reported:

> Homosexuality is indeed an illness. The homosexual is an emotionally disturbed individual who has not acquired the normal capacity to develop satisfying heterosexual relations.[13]

But just ten years later, everything changed. In 1973, the American Psychiatric Association voted to strike homosexuality from the official list of psychiatric illnesses. Why? Not because of any new revelations from research or any consensus within the scientific community, but because of *threats and intimidation.*

In *Homosexuality and the Politics of Truth,* Jeffrey Satinover, MD, (a board-certified psychiatrist with degrees from MIT and Harvard, as well as teaching awards from Yale) writes:

> Ronald Bayer, then a Fellow at the Hastings Institute in New York, reported that in 1970, homosexual activists within the APA planned a "systematic effort to disrupt the annual meetings of the American Psychiatric Association."[14]

Like bullies on the playground, homosexual activists didn't want to play by the rules. You know, the rules that say if you want to influence a body of science, you conduct properly designed studies and build scientific research that makes your case. No. There weren't any scientific studies like that (still aren't, as we'll discuss later). No problem, just harass and intimidate scientists who present studies you don't like. *Way easier.* Especially when there isn't any research to support your position. (Much more information on this is available at www.f2a.org.)

That's what they did to Dr. Irving Bieber, a prominent psychoanalyst and psychiatrist who presented a paper on "homosexuality and transsexualism" at the prestigious scientific setting of the APA convention in 1970. As Dr. Bieber began to present his research, homosexual attendees loudly mocked and laughed at him. They further disrupted his presentation by shouting and calling him names and making threats, suggesting that he deserved to be "drawn and quartered."[15]

On May 3, 1971, protesters broke into a meeting of distinguished APA members, grabbed the microphone, and gave it to an activist, who proclaimed:

> Psychiatry is the enemy incarnate. Psychiatry has waged a relentless war of extermination against us. You may take this as a declaration of war against you.... We're rejecting you all as our owners.[16]

"No one raised an objection," recounts Dr. Satinover. Their disruption resulted in more attempts at reconciliation and their appearance before the APA's Committee on Nomenclature. Further bullying and lobbying delivered the committee vote that maybe homosexual behavior was not a sign of psychiatric disorder after all.

The APA announced their new "finding" at the 1973 convention. Dissenters were allowed only fifteen minutes to discuss seventy years of psychiatric research that contradicted it before the hijacked vote was formally appealed to the full membership. The activists were ready. They already had a letter, drafted in part by their friends at the National Gay Task Force, urging for a vote to "retain the nomenclature change" and to send it to the thirty thousand members of APA, using money the NGTF had raised.

Of course, they didn't let the APA membership know that the letter came from homosexual activists, as "that would have been 'the kiss of death.'[17] The letter was able to secure a majority response from the third of the members who responded. But the vast majority was not behind the change. Four years later, the journal *Medical Aspects of Human Sexuality* reported the results of a survey they took showing that "69 percent of psychiatrists disagreed with the vote and still considered homosexuality a disorder."[18]

TREAT A HOMOSEXUAL, LOSE YOUR LICENSE?

Here's where it starts getting scary. Forget that fear, intimidation, disruption, coercion, name-calling, and threats overturned seventy years of scientific research. What matters is what homosexual activists did with the APA's "finding."

In 1994, they used it to try to make it *illegal* to give therapy aimed at helping homosexuals change—if you want to keep your license to practice, that is. The APA Board of Trustees proposed a little change: to make it "a violation of professional conduct" for a psychiatrist to help a homosexual patient transition to heterosexuality "even at the patient's request."[19] Had this been passed by the full APA assembly, any psychiatrist who treated homosexuals requesting treatment would not only be brought up for ethics violations, but would also lose his or her license to practice. *Nice, huh?*

It doesn't stop there. Just a few years ago, the APA published a study *favorable* to pedophilia—you know, child molestation. I guess if you call it "adult-child sex," it doesn't sound as bad.

Executive director Raymond Fowler wrote that despite publishing a study favoring pedophilia, the APA remains firmly opposed to child sexual abuse: "We believe that the sexual abuse of children is a criminal act and one that is reprehensible in any context."[20] *Really?* For how long? Then why was this trash published in the APA journal in the first place? Oh yeah, because they thought they could get away with that, too.

Shortly after that APA article appeared, I received my first hate letter for my stand against child molestation. I was called an "intolerant Nazi" for opposing child abuse because, after all, the APA said it was okay. I thought you might like a glimpse of what's coming. The tactic of using threats to subvert research may take us there again soon.

COMMITTED FOR HIS COMMITMENT

Meet Michael A. Marcavage. Deans List, White House intern with security clearance, founder and president of a ministry called Protect the Children, president of his own business, and volunteer for Campus Crusade for Christ. Oh yeah, he also went overseas with Feed the Children.

But while a junior at Temple University, Michael protested the blasphemous play "Corpus Christi," which depicts Jesus as a homosexual who has sex with his disciples. Michael posted flyers around campus and was planning a protest until he met William Bergman, vice president of campus safety, and Carl Bittenbender, director of campus safety, who talked him out of the protest in favor of a campus outreach. They said they would provide him with a stage, but when Michael went to the vice president's office to discuss it, they informed him that it wasn't a possibility. According to *WorldNetDaily*, this is what happened next:

> Exasperated, Marcavage said he then "excused himself, went to the bathroom, locked the door and prayed about what he should do next," AFA officials said.
>
> According to the student, Bergman followed him to the bathroom and began pounding on the door, demanding that he open it and resume the discussion about the stage. Marcavage said he opened the door and "told him that I believed our conversation was over."
>
> Next, according to Marcavage, Bergman "physically" forced him back into the vice president's office and "pushed me into a chair and held me with his arm." Fahling said Marcavage asked to leave but Bergman "allegedly refused to allow it."
>
> "Attempting to rise, [Marcavage] said the vice president tripped him to the floor," then was "manhandled" to a nearby couch by both men "where they held him down."
>
> Within moments, Marcavage said, a Temple University police officer arrived and handcuffed him. Then, "Marcavage was taken by police…to the Emergency Crisis Center at Temple University Hospital," AFA officials told *WorldNetDaily*.[21]

So now instead of homosexuality being on the list of mental disorders, those who oppose it are forcibly admitted to a mental ward.

PERSECUTED FOR PROTECTING

The Boy Scouts of America, a private organization with the constitutional right to freedom of association, has come under fire for not allowing self-described homosexual activists to become scout leaders.

Yes, there have been cases of abuse. It's not imagined. Check the files. Protecting the boys in their care may have a little something to do with why the Boy Scouts would like to keep their policy.

As a result of protecting the children who've been entrusted to them, the Boy Scouts have been kicked out of parks, schools, and public forums and denied funding by cities, counties, and the United Way. An *exemplary way* to treat a bunch of little boys learning honesty, courage, hard work, respect, patriotism, and positive values[22]—don't you think? With values like that, it's easy to see why they were booed at the 2000 Democratic National Convention. Come to think of it, I didn't see them at the 2004 convention. Did you?

As of this writing, the Boy Scouts have not caved in to the homosexual agenda. So far, despite being defunded, ostracized, thrown out, and left out, they've stood against the ridicule, the assault, the censorship, and the lawsuits. They have stood their ground like few others, but I have to wonder for how long.

In a similar vein, Father Buchanan, a Roman Catholic priest in St. Paul, interviewed candidates for the vacant position of an eighth-grade music teacher at Holy Childhood School. One candidate raised suspicions when he insisted he wanted to teach boys. Further research revealed that the candidate was homosexual and thus in disagreement with the school's policy of hiring people who agree with the school—and the Catholic Church and the Bible— on this and other issues.

The candidate sued Buchanan under the St. Paul "gay rights ordinance." The human rights agency made a preliminary judgment of discrimination and sent the file to the St. Paul city attorney for criminal prosecution—"with possible sanctions including a ninety-day jail sentence and a three hundred dollar fine." The good news is, before the priest could be sent to jail, the voters stood up and reversed the St. Paul ordinance—by a landslide.[23]

LESBIAN ROOMMATE OR LAWSUIT?

A similar ordinance in Madison was then used against Ann Hacklander and Maureen Rowe, who were looking for a roommate to help share expenses in their apartment. One of the candidates who applied was a lesbian. She wasn't chosen, so she immediately took the matter to the Madison Equal Opportunities Commission (MEOC), the enforcement agency of Madison gay rights law. The MEOC then forced Hacklander and Rowe to a four-and-a-half-hour "session" that drove them to tears. Hacklander said she "felt like [she] was in China," rather than the United States.

The outcome? The two women were ordered to pay the lesbian fifteen hundred dollars, attend "sensitivity training" taught by homosexuals, have their "housing situation monitored by the MEOC for two years, and write a formal letter of apology."[24] All for having a say in their choice of a roommate!

Speaking of roommates, the European Union has gone one step further. Now women in the EU are no longer permitted to advertise for a female roommate. That's right, the new EU equality law rulings "make it an offence for home-owners to stipulate whether they want men or women in their houses." Battered women's homes will apparently be forced to house men as well, and "widows, divorcees and groups of singles drop plans to take in lodgers."[25] If your daughter is studying abroad, she could be sued unless she agreed to share her dorm with Ted. Yes, Mr. Bundy would make a fine roommate, and he could now sue if denied.

TRICK OR TERRORISM?

Meet pastor and police chaplain Tom Hansen. He repeated what the Bible says about the activity being celebrated at the third city-sponsored Motor City Pride Fest in Ferndale, Michigan. That made him a target of the tactics of humiliation, intimidation, and the force of law. The pro-homosexual activists thought up a new way to ridicule those of us who disagree: They handed out candy on Halloween night with stickers that read: "Pastor Hansen is a bigot."[26]

Many in the community came to his defense, publicly expressing their support at a city council meeting. That's when *they* became targets, too. Those who expressed support were sent a threatening letter to make sure they never made the mistake of speaking up again. According to the *Ferndale Mirror,* the letter "urged them to beware if they should run into a gay person in a store or restaurant" and said that "some of us can be as mean spirited as you can…. We might just feel the need to publicly humiliate you, as you have done to us."[27]

Let's just take a minute and breathe in the tolerance. *Ahhhh.* That's great stuff. Yeah, we need more of that. The letter was signed: "the Greater Ferndale GLBT Community." Phillip Newton, who received one of the letters told the *Ferndale Mirror:* "I know some people who got the letter and are really afraid to go out in public."[28]

How in the world did we get here?

THEIR "DEMANDS"

You must understand: I'm not talking about homosexual *people* who are loved by God and free to live as they choose; I'm talking about a homosexual *agenda*. Here are the demands the homosexual movement made and distributed at their Gay Pride march in Washington, DC, on April 25, 1993:

1. That all sodomy laws be repealed and all forms of sexual expression (including pedophilia) be legalized
2. That defense budget funds be diverted to pay for AIDS patients' medical expenses and sex-change operations
3. That same-sex marriages and adoption, custody, and foster care within these structures be legalized
4. That homosexual education programs be offered at all levels of education, including elementary schools

5. That contraceptives and abortion services be made available to all persons, regardless of age

6. That taxpayer funding be made available for artificial insemination of lesbians and bisexuals

7. That expression of religious-based concerns regarding homosexuality be forbidden

8. That organizations like the Boy Scouts be required to accept homosexual scoutmasters[29]

Do any of these sound familiar? Just get out your pencil and check off the list. Number One: Sodomy laws repealed in the Supreme Court *Lawrence v. Texas* decision of June 26, 2003. About the only one they haven't already gotten is the one about forbidding the expression of religious-based concerns regarding homosexuality. That's the one that concerns me the most.

MOVE OVER ELIAN, STORM TROOPERS IN MIAMI

Ever since homosexual activists drove the steamroller over Anita Bryant, they've been vilifying anyone with the courage to speak out against them. In 1992, my friend Tony Verdugo came under fire for promoting a ballot initiative in Dade County, Florida. Claiming that groups like the Boy Scouts were "discriminating" against homosexuals by not allowing them to go camping with young boys, homosexual activists were using the words *sexual orientation* in the county human rights ordinance to deny those organizations access to funding. So Tony led a charge to remove the words.

We know about their assault on the Boy Scouts. Here's how they attack those who want to remedy the problem: If over the period of several months of gathering petitions, someone forgets that they have already signed and signs again, the homosexual activists come after them and start the intimidation process. Keep in mind that the reason groups gather more petitions than they need is because duplicate signing sometimes happens—any extras are tossed out. But in line with the bullying tactics of the homosexual activists, people who may have inadvertently signed twice or signed for a like-minded immediate relative are threatened.

They are told that if they committed either of these "offenses," they are in a whole lot of trouble, and if they didn't, of course, they're not. They are then asked, "Could it be that someone *else* signed your name?" Why, that would leave you free and clear of any dreadful duplicate petition-signing ramifications and allow us to place the blame on those nasty petition gatherers instead. *Forgery!*

Now, I've been involved with these petition drives. I know a little something about the rules. All the petition gatherer is required to ask a prospective signer is "Are you are a registered voter of the county/area?" No other proof is needed. They could be lying; they could be underage; they could be aliens. Verification responsibility falls *not* on the petition gatherer, but on the county, city, or state election supervisor. Someone can sign "Mickey Mouse," but the only thing the petition gatherer is responsible for is asking if Mickey is a registered voter in Miami-Dade County. (But upon verification, the petition would be thrown out since Mickey lives in Orlando—a different county altogether.)

I sent e-mails to my friends describing what happened next and asking for help. Here's the text from some of them:

Subject: Homosexual Assault Taken to New Level in Miami Dade—HELP SOUND THE ALARM!

August 16, 2002. I just got off the phone with Anthony Verdugo (of the Miami/Dade Christian [Family] Coalition & Take Back Miami Dade) with one of the most troubling incidents of political assault I have ever heard.

According to Anthony, he circulated more than five thousand petitions in the effort to give people the right to vote on the Miami/Dade Sexual Orientation amendment. And because of a charge by *one* person who couldn't remember his signature being "witnessed," police stormed his house at 6:00 A.M. today and placed him under arrest. Nearly breaking through the door in an Elian Gonzalez fashion, they arrested Tony (in front of his crying children) and held him for thirteen hours.

They also arrested a seventeen-year-old honor student who gathered over one thousand petitions, on a similar charge, and then a seventy-six-year-old man for a "notary mistake"—for inadvertently notarizing his own signature. I'm sure that with all the crime and drugs in Miami, people are sleeping more secure knowing that alleged mistake-making seventy-six-year-old notaries are off the streets and thrown behind bars. As Tony has said: *This is what happens when you oppose the homosexual agenda in this country.*

You can see the lengths to which some are willing to go to silence Christians.[30]

THE SO-CALLED STUDIES

But what of the study that touted the discovery of the "gay gene"? J. Michael-Bailey and Richard C. Pillard (who is openly gay) did a study on identical and fraternal twins. Of fifty-six pairs of identical twins, they found that twenty-nine of them (52 percent) were both homosexual.[31] Now think about that for a minute: If homosexuality *were* genetic, given the fact identical twins have "identical genes," for their premise to be true, *all* identical twins would have to be either both homosexual, or both heterosexual.

Again, to support the premise that homosexuality is genetic, 100 percent of homosexual identical twins would have to be homosexual! There's really no room to debate this. If eye color is genetic, and one identical twin has blue eyes, then the other does, as well. Or else they are not *identical* twins.

This study, widely reported in the media, was used to make the case that homosexuals are "born that way," but it actually *proves the opposite.* (Much more on these studies can be found at www.f2a.org.)

LIKE IT OR NOT, EX-HOMOSEXUALS EXIST

Perhaps the most compelling argument that homosexuality is *not genetic* are *former* homosexuals—the most politically incorrect and ignored individuals around.

We know there's hope for change for homosexuals because thousands *already have changed*. As far as we know, with the possible exception of Michael Jackson, people are unable to change their race. Martin Luther King Jr.'s niece, Alveta Scott King put it this way: "While I have met many former homosexuals, I have yet to meet a former black."

Unlike homosexuality, race *is* genetic and unchangeable. The existence of ex-homosexuals negates the "born-that-way" paradigm activists have used to pave the way for demanding special protections and quotas. Quotas like the ones my friend Gary Bauer discovered were used at the 2004 Democratic National Convention:

> Democrat parties in at least 15 states set numerical "goals" for the number of homosexuals that must be in their state delegations for the Democratic National Convention. California, for example, set the "goal" of 22 homosexual men and 22 lesbians in their 440-member delegation. Maine Democrats want to be sure at least 3 of their 35 delegates are homosexuals, but being broadminded they are willing to accept bisexuals and transgendered delegates as sub-stitutes.[32]

I'm sure cross-dressers are feeling discriminated against. Don't worry. They'll probably have their own quotas by 2008. Who knows? By then *pedophiles* may have their own delegation.

Do we really want sexual behavior to be the criteria for qualifying as a delegate to nominate candidates for president? By the way, I didn't see any quotas for *ex*-homosexuals in that list.

Robert Spitzer, who helped lead the charge to take homosexuality off the American Psychiatric Association's list of mental disorders (DSM) in 1973, conducted a study to see if ex-homosexuals had really changed their orientations. His conclusion: "Like most psychiatrists, I thought that homosexual behavior could be resisted—but that no one could really change their sexual orientation. I now believe that's untrue—some people can and do change."[33]

I recently interviewed my friend Mike Haley, of Focus on the Family, on my Faith2Action radio show. Mike is a former homosexual activist. He was molested as a boy and spent twelve years in homosexuality before leaving it. He has been married to his wife for ten years, and they have two adorable sons. I asked him about that process. He told me it wasn't easy. At first he couldn't stand Christians because he felt judged. He said he would have loved to hear from someone in church who had left homosexuality—to know it could be done and not just hear that it is wrong. (His story, and much more information on this, can be found at www.f2a.org.) Like the song played at every Billy Graham crusade says, "Just As I Am." But once the power of God transforms our lives, we don't stay the way we came.

I don't believe the church has done a very good job reaching out to homosexuals. Frankly, we've done a lousy one. Concerned about not softening God's stand against homosexuality, many Christians have not adopted Christ's attitude toward sinners—of all types. God loves sinners and doesn't need them to get perfect before He takes them in.

Whenever I feel as though this entire battle really isn't worth it, I think about "Robert," a man who used to picket me. He came up to me one day after a talk I gave and introduced himself as a former protester… and *former* homosexual. "I thought you all hated us, but now I know differently," he said. "Thank you for having the courage to keep telling the truth long enough for me to hear it."

If the Christian position is criminalized, people like Robert will be the true victims. They'll go on believing that there is no escape from unwanted feelings of homosexual attraction.

Do you see a trend here? Label them. Ridicule them. Blame them for everything you don't like. Even blame them for murder.

When that doesn't work, step up the tactics. *Assault them.* Disrupt and intimidate. Taint their blood supply to kill their children. Even though all the research is against you, force scientists and everyone else to comply with your demands anyway. If they protest you on campus, throw them in the mental ward. If you run out of ideas, read *Mein Kampf.* Bully, threaten, attack, and vandalize. If they still won't submit to your agenda, storm their homes and set them on fire. If none of those things work, show just how reasonable you are and pee on their carpets and poop in their church. Who can deny the logic and rationale of an argument like that? *Really.*

But what if they still won't keep quiet? The next logical step is to *make them.*

Chapter 6

CENSORSHIP AT HOME AND ABROAD

Five-year-old Antonio Peck was told to make a poster on how to "save the world." So little Antonio drew a picture of Jesus and printed the words: "The only way to save our world." When he showed his picture to the teacher, he was told that it was "unacceptable." It was supposed to be about the environment. So he drew another poster of people taking out trash and put Jesus on the side, praying. When Antonio's picture was displayed on the bulletin board, the teacher folded over that part. After all, Jesus is not someone you are allowed to see in school. He must be censored.[1]

Then there's Greg Cunningham, who came to a university in Miami with his Genocide Awareness Project (GAP), which places huge posters depicting forms of genocide throughout history next to pictures of another set of victims—unborn babies. He had to put barricades around his displays because students have tried to cut, mangle, and destroy them. Here's a quote from the school paper the day I visisted: "Whoever these people are, they should be shot."[2]

It's good to see that a university campus is still about the free exchange of ideas. Imagine something like that being said about a homosexual group on campus. That would be a hate crime!

And you've heard of being sent to the back of the bus? Two Christians in the state of Washington would have liked to be treated that well. Michelle Shocks of Seattle was riding home on a bus one day when another passenger boarded saying, "Praise the Lord!" He was happy to be out of the pouring rain. Michelle asked the passenger where he went to church, and they started to privately discuss religion across the aisle. But then the driver ordered them to refrain from their discussion because it might "offend" the other passengers. Michelle moved to a seat next to the other passenger, and they continued their discussion in hushed tones so as not to offend anyone. The driver pulled to the side of the road and demanded that both passengers leave the bus. Michelle, who was twenty-five years old and five months pregnant, was forced to walk her last mile home—in the rain![3]

Are Christians being told to go to the back of the bus? No, they're being *thrown off* the bus.

As ridicule moves to blame, blame moves to censorship. Now that you've felt the tolerance for our diverse viewpoints and the warmth from the outside world, take a look at some other attempts to silence us.

NO ROOM IN THE PARK

San José, California, spent $500,000 of scarce public resources to construct a statue of the Aztec god Quetzalcoatl. Mayor Blanca Alvarado said the Aztec religion contained "those elements that seek to elevate the human consciousness to a higher plane."[4] The Aztec religion takes us to a "higher plane"? If the practice of ripping open countless victims' chests with flint knives and pulling out their still-beating hearts takes us to a "higher plane," thanks all the same, but I'll stay on *lower ground*.

At the same time the tax-funded bloodthirsty Aztec deity "was held to be a cultural symbol by a federal judge," the San José Parks Board decided to remove a nativity scene from the park where the Aztec statue stands. The board's decision was reversed due to a flood of protests to city hall.

The American Atheists had organized a protest of sixteen "courageous atheists" to ask for the removal of the nativity scene from public property and to call on the City of San José to cease funding the sponsoring organization.[5] Sixteen atheists versus one ceramic baby Jesus—what bravery, what valor, what *courage!*

CYBERSPACE AND JAIL SPACE

The Web search engine Google has now censored ads from a Christian group, denying them the ability to express the biblical view of homosexuality. According to an article by Ron Strom, "Google recently banned an advertisement from a Christian organization, Stand to Reason, because the group's website contains articles opposing homosexuality that were determined by Google to be 'hate speech.'" What kinds of ads aren't censored by Google? I can't print most of what is listed, but these direct quotes should give you an idea: "full length hardcore gay movies," "XXX oral & anal sex live 100+ cams," "ultimate gay male mega site, hardcore XXX action."[6] Google will take ads for these kinds of things—they just censor what the Bible has to say about them.

John Reyes and 150 other college students held a peaceful, pro-life demonstration in front of a high school in Lynchburg, Virginia. But school officials called the police. When asked to leave, John promptly complied, but that wasn't good enough. He was later indicted for trespassing and sentenced to six months in jail. The judge who sentenced John has allowed criminals convicted of grand larceny, possession of cocaine, and assault and battery to serve no jail time at all. The prosecutors said that John's six-month jail sentence sent the "correct message" to future protestors. And what might they have meant by "correct message"? Sell deadly cocaine or hurt others and you receive a "get out of jail free" card; share a pro-life message and you "go directly to jail."

NO EVANGELIZING IN... CHICAGO

Maybe the Baptists shouldn't be allowed to evangelize. A communist idea? No. This one came from the Council of Religious Leaders of Metropolitan

Chicago. In 1999, the Southern Baptist Convention, representing 15.8 million members, held its annual conference in Chicago. It was estimated that more than one hundred thousand people participated in an outreach to the city through evangelism, housing rehabilitation, work in medical clinics, and church planting.

But the Council of Religious Leaders tried to prevent it, saying, "A campaign of the nature and scope you envision could contribute to a climate conducive to hate crimes."[7] So now the Baptists should be silenced because of what they believe. *Interesting.*

Want to know where this is going?

In France, where only one-half of one percent of the population is evangelical Protestant, the government has now defined evangelicals as "representing extreme factions of the traditional Reformed church." One man seeking appointment to a high office was told by government officials that he would not get the post as long as his children remained in a Christian school.[8]

Have a desire to keep your children? In Quebec, anti-Christian bigotry has now reached into homes. A government employee removed a child from her Baptist family there because she thinks Baptists "might have unusual beliefs regarding child rearing."[9]

THE BATTLE FOR THE BENCH

That kind of discrimination has come to the United States judicial process. Back in April of 2003, President George W. Bush nominated Claude Alexander Allen to the United States Court Fourth Circuit of Appeals. His nomination was blocked. Surprise, surprise. But get a load of why. The lovely ladies at the National Organization of (some) Women submitted a reason their obstructionist-minded Democratic supporters considered valid enough to keep Allen off the bench: His children are homeschooled.[10]

I am also confident that senate Democrats would never confirm our Founding Fathers to the bench! They believed in God and what the Bible says—and they were homeschooled, too!

THE CRIMINALIZATION OF CHRISTIANITY

There was another important reason to keep Allen off the bench. As the self-described Alliance for Justice pointed out, he has worked to advance an "only-abstinence-until-marriage agenda." They said, "Everything about Allen's record suggests that…he would be unable to separate his personal extremist views from what the law requires."[11]

Can you imagine parents wanting their children to wait until marriage before having sex? *Extremists!* No wonder they're keeping him from serving as a judge.

And now the highly esteemed, yet proabortion, pro-homosexual American Bar Association, which pretends to be mainstream when giving its coveted "stamp of approval" to left-wing judicial candidates, has taken yet another step of censorship. According to a proposed change in the ABA's ethics rules in August 2004, they think judges should be forced to quit groups like the Boy Scouts or be removed from the bench.[12] Have to make sure no one who doesn't march in lockstep with the homosexual agenda slips through the filibustered confirmation process. We're talking about the *Boy Scouts* here. How long before they demand that members of orthodox Christian religions step down based on the same rationale?

Think I've overstated matters? Consider this. You know the long line of judges Democrats in the Senate are blocking? They have something in common that might shed some light on the problem. Yes, they all graduated from fine law schools. All did well in their class. All are qualified candidates. Yet all were filibustered. What would keep them from even being allowed to be voted on? What did they all have in common? Judges Priscilla Owen, Katheryn Kuhl, William Pryor, and Charles Pickering all *taught Sunday school.*[13] Wow, that's worse than belonging to the Boy Scouts!

Kay Daly, president of the Coalition for a Fair Judiciary said, "In a recent confirmation hearing for [Attorney General William] Pryor, a nominee to the Eleventh U.S. Circuit Court of Appeals, Senator Charles Schumer (D-NY) said plainly that Mr. Pryor's deeply held personal convictions as a pro-life Catholic simply would not be left at the courthouse door. In other words, being a Catholic is just fine if you are Senator Leahy or Kennedy and selectively follow the doctrines of the faith. But if you *actually practice*

Catholic teaching, you need not apply for a federal judgeship."[14]

Regarding Leon Holmes, Daly said, "the main complaint of the extreme Left against Mr. Holmes's nomination seems to be centered upon his embrace of biblical tenets of traditional marriage."[15]

In the debate to confirm Leon Holmes for the U.S. District Court in the Eastern District of Arkansas in July 2004, Senator Jeff Sessions pointed out that members of other faiths would never have been treated in a like manner. "Are we going to demand that they come before the Senate Judiciary Committee and renounce their faith before they become a federal judge?"[16]

TAMING THE FUNDAMENTALISTS

But can't we all just get along? Can't we, as the Sixth Circuit said, all just agree that "all faiths are *equally valid* as religions"?

Robert Muller is a UN member who, as Under–Secretary General of the United Nations for more than thirty years, was the right-hand man to past UN Secretaries General U Thant, Kurt Waldheim, and Javier Pérez de Cuellar. Muller is now working on a project of his own—a one-world church. "My dream," he says, "is to get a tremendous alliance between all the major religions and the UN."[17] There's just one little problem standing in the way of his dream—those darned Christians. In *New Genesis,* Muller points out that "Peace will only be possible through the taming of fundamentalism."[18] The bottom line is that fundamentalism must be "tamed" to make way for tolerance. If you believe the Bible, that "taming" is aimed at you.

Fundamentalist has become a cliché for *radical extremists.* We hear it used all the time to describe terrorists. If your "fundamental" belief is that Christians and Jews are "infidels" who should be killed and that doing so secures you a place in heaven, that word may be interchangeable. If, however, your "fundamental" belief is in a loving God who sent His Son to die in your place, you may find that belief tamed, silenced, and criminalized internationally.

The United Religions Initiative (URI), founded by California Episcopal Bishop William Swing in 1997, culminated with the signing of the United

Religions Initiative Charter in 2000. The URI "Principles" listed include this little gem:

21. Members of the URI shall not be coerced to participate in any ritual or be proselytized.[19]

Babsy Monaghen, my research assistant, just asked what they mean by *proselytize*. Here's how I defined it for her in an e-mail:

Proselytize: A negative way to say "evangelize" or "spread the gospel" when your goal is to prevent it.

Actually, I just looked it up. Here's the *exact response* I sent her:

Yeah, proselytize is the negative code word used to prevent us from spreading the gospel. They use it to silence Christians and penalize anyone with the audacity to tell them how to keep from going to hell. When you see it, know that they are evil.

The word is one of the favorites of those who want to criminalize Christianity. But using the negative label doesn't change our constitutional rights of freedom of speech and freedom of religion.

The Parliament of the World's Religions met in Barcelona, Spain, from July 7 to 13, 2004. When you read the program, you can play a little game of count the times the words *tolerance, diversity,* and *pluralism* are used. Do a little digging and find out about the "development of a global consciousness" and "global unity." Hear "world peace" uttered more times than at all the beauty pageants combined. Their world religion goals read like a *Left Behind* novel—except they're less entertaining and a lot scarier.

Labeled the UN's "Prophet of Hope," Robert Muller believes that "world unity cannot be achieved without a one-world government and a one-world religion."[20] Ponder these excerpts from UNESCO's Declaration of Principles on Tolerance:

- *Tolerance is respect,* acceptance and *appreciation* of the rich diversity of our world's cultures.... It is not only a moral duty, it is also a *political and legal requirement.*
- Tolerance...upholds human rights, *pluralism....* It involves the *rejection of dogmatism and absolutism.*
- [T]olerance does not mean toleration of social injustice.... It also means that *one's views are not to be imposed on others.*
- [I]ntolerance...is a global threat.
- *Tolerance promotion* and the *shaping of attitudes* of openness, mutual listening and solidarity *should take place in schools* and universities and through non-formal education, at *home* and in the *workplace.* The communication *media* are in a position to play a constructive role...and *highlighting the dangers of indifference* towards the rise in intolerant groups and ideologies.
- [P]romote systematic and rational tolerance teaching methods that will address the cultural, social, economic, political and *religious sources of intolerance*—major roots of violence and exclusion.[21]

The problem for the UN United Religions Initiative is that Christians aren't going to go along with their dream of a "one-world religion." They want to "tame us" because Christians simply won't pretend that southbound roads head north. We're not going to follow a UN commandment to worship the watered-down, lowest-common-denominator god of "tolerance" and "pluralism" over the real one. *Sorry.* We won't comply with their nightmare of a dream.

And when that happens? We could be sent to the World Court for violations. What kind of violations might they get us on? There's one that you would never in a million years think could possibly apply to you, but if you take a stand as I have against an agenda aimed at denying truth and silencing us, you could be headed to the World Court.

One such violation might include "mental" genocide, believe it or not:

In the present Convention, genocide means any of the following acts committed with intent to destroy, in whole part, a national ethnic, racial or religious group, as such:

A) Killing members of the group
B) Causing serious bodily or *mental harm* to members of the
   group
C) Deliberately inflicting on the group conditions of life calculated
   to bring about its physical destruction in whole or in part.[22]

We're not going to do the first one, of course. We even think "Thou shalt not kill" should be posted in public. But take a look at the second one: "Causing...*mental harm* to members of the group." If you read above the fourth-grade level, you've probably picked up a dangerous trend by now. If homosexual activists can claim "mental harm" because employees display Bible verses and bumper stickers, and if they are fining businessmen in Canada and trying to throw Swedish pastors in jail for reading from the Bible, how much of a stretch is it to see those same practices applied *internationally?*

FREEDOM: AN ENDANGERED SPECIES

As I write this, I am praying to God for the reelection of President Bush, for a hundred reasons including this one, expressed by President Bush in the presidential debate September 30, 2004:

My opponent talks about me not signing certain treaties. Let me tell you one thing I didn't sign, and I think it shows the difference of our opinion—the difference of opinions.

And that is, I wouldn't join the International Criminal Court. It's a body based in The Hague where unaccountable judges and prose-cutors can pull our troops or diplomats up for trial.

And I wouldn't join it. And I understand that in certain capitals around the world that that wasn't a popular move. But it's the right move not to join a foreign court that could—where our people could be prosecuted.

My opponent is for joining the International Criminal Court. I just think trying to be popular, kind of, in the global sense, if it's not in our best interest makes no sense.

I'm interested in working with other nations and do a lot of it. But I'm not going to make decisions that I think are wrong for America.[23]

The eventual consequences of noncompliance? Read the book of Revelation. It might help keep you from reading about it in the paper—or experiencing it firsthand. Yes, it will happen, but it doesn't *have* to happen on our watch. If Christians, Americans, and all people who love liberty will stand up and fight the movement toward a world church and a world government—complete with world enforcement—our children can still know this freedom. That goes for the censorship and assault here at home, as well.

Ronald Reagan said it this way:

Freedom is never more than one generation away from extinction. We didn't pass it to our children in the bloodstream. It must be fought for, protected, and handed on for them to do the same, or one day we will spend our sunset years telling our children and our children's children what it was once like in the United States where men were free.[24]

Chapter 7

CHRISTIAN BASHING FROM THE BENCH

*It used to be that men of God were considered men of principle,
that presidents could confidently nominate them, that it was
an indicator of integrity, of character, or decency—
now it's a one way ticket to a filibuster.*

KAY DALY, PRESIDENT OF THE COALITION FOR A FAIR JUDICIARY

The trend toward silencing Christians is real. Label them. Ridicule them. Even blame them for murder. And if they still won't keep quiet? The next logical step is *make them* keep quiet through the court, the best friend of the anti-Christian movement.

SUPERPOWER ROBES

If I were to name the number one problem in America, it would be…men in black robes. Women, too. Not college graduates—I mean judges. They're the ones who rule this country. The president and Congress have almost become window dressing. They can go through motions, pretend to pass laws, but the judges are the ones who decide which ones to keep, which ones to strike down, and which ones to rewrite entirely. The other two branches have become kind of like the royal family in England—there to cut ribbons and pose for photo ops, but without ultimate power. Sure, the president can sign bills into law. But with judges standing by to strike them down before the ink dries—like they did with the ban on partial-birth abortion—what's the point? Oh yeah, he gets to *appoint* those judges. And the Senate gets to confirm them—or to block their right to be voted on.

The three branches of government are supposed to be equal. At least that's what *I* learned in civics class. Then again, I went to *public* schools. And I thought the legislature was supposed to be the branch that passes laws. That's why I spent a decade of my life lobbying *them*. If I had known that judges get to write the laws, veto ones that other people write, and strike down on a whim the initiatives on which the people voted, I would have made a career change.

The best deal is to get appointed to the Supreme Court. Then you get an *S* on your robe and get to override *everybody*—for life. Like a foreign law or constitution better? *So what* that you were "sworn" to uphold ours? There's nothing anyone can do about it!

State courts have superpowers, too. In Massachusetts a court unraveled five thousand years of law and recorded history by a one-judge margin. *Not bad,* unless you happen to like families that are best for children. That was for one state, but all they need is for their buddies in the other states to agree with them. And don't you know it, they've already started. A judge in Washington State has already unraveled marriage there, striking down the state's Defense of Marriage Law. Let's see if he has any like-minded friends on the higher courts. Yes, defense of marriage laws in Washington and thirty-seven other states don't mean a thing. Law *schmaw.* They have the robes.

Alexander Hamilton made the Founding Fathers' intentions clear in the Federalist Papers: The judiciary was to be the "least dangerous branch" of government.[1] You know something's wrong when one activist judge can undermine the will of 290,000,000 Americans, every state law, every state ballot initiative, and the other two branches of government.

Of course, if *I* had a black superpower robe, I would use my powers for good. But the point is this: Judges, or any branch of government for that matter, shouldn't *have* that kind of power.

Judges' disregard for the law has become legendary. Can't you just see them in their chambers laughing about the laws that took ten years to pass that they strike down before they order lunch? Like the bad guys in cartoons, the black-robed villains scheme behind their chamber doors. "Sure, people may not like the new law we've written, but our next ruling will be to *silence them!* In fact, we can silence *all the people* we don't like! We can and we *will! Ah, Ha-Ha-Ha, Ha!* Impeachment? *They wouldn't dare!"*

Exaggerated? Maybe just a tad. But here's something that's not: Give people absolute power to do evil, and some of them will use it. *Duh.* Unchallenged, some judges have done great evil. And here's how they've been silencing, ostracizing, and criminalizing those with whom they disagree.

No Prayer

- Verbal prayer offered in a school is unconstitutional, even if that prayer is both voluntary and denominationally neutral. (*Engel v. Vitale*, 1962; *Abington v. Schempp*, 1963; *Commissioner of Education v. School Committee of Leyden*, 1971)
- If a student prays over his lunch, it is unconstitutional for him to pray out loud. (*Reed v. Van Hoven*, 1965)
- When a student addresses an assembly of his peers, he effectively becomes a government representative; it is therefore unconstitutional for that student to engage in prayer. (*Harris v. Joint School District*, 1994)[2]

No Jesus

- A city council meeting can pray, as long as they don't say the name of Jesus. (*Rubin v. City of Burbank*, 1999)[3]
- The ACLU of San Diego and Imperial Counties sent a letter to the mayor of La Mesa and city council officials demanding that they end the practice of opening council meetings with "sectarian prayers that make specific references to Christianity." They are threatening to take them to court if they continue to allow prayer to the Christian God.[4]

No Bible

- In Omaha, Nebraska, a student was prohibited from reading his Bible silently during his free time, or even to open his Bible at school. (*Gierke v. Blotzer*, 1989)[5]
- It is unconstitutional for a classroom library to contain books that deal with Christianity, or for a teacher to be seen with a personal copy of the Bible at school. (*Roberts v. Madigan*, 1990)[6]

No Christmas

- A Frederick County, Maryland, school employee was prohibited from handing out Christmas cards on a public-school campus.[7]
- Red poinsettias were banned from the Ramsey Court House in St. Paul, Minnesota, because they offended one person who believes the flowers to be a symbol of Christianity.[8]
- In Worthington, Ohio, students were prohibited from bringing in Christmas cookies with the colors red and green or in the shapes of stars or bells.[9]

No Crosses

- It is unconstitutional for a war memorial to be erected in the shape of a cross. (*Lowe v. City of Eugene*, 1969)[10]

- It is unconstitutional for a public cemetery to have a planter in the shape of a cross, for if someone were to view that cross, it could cause "emotional distress" and thus constitute an "injury in-fact." (*Warsaw v. Tehachapi*, 1990)[11]
- In June 2004, the Los Angeles County Supervisors voted three to two to remove a tiny cross from the official county seal rather than face a potential lawsuit from the ACLU. The cross had been there for forty-seven years.[12]

A receptionist for Florida Governor Jeb Bush's office came under fire for posting at her desk a greeting card showing a flag with a cross on it. A lawsuit was filed, and though the purpose of the card was to honor those who lost their lives on September 11, state senator Debbie Wasserman Schultz (D-Weston) declared, "To me, it's offensive and hurtful."[13]

She needs to stay out of cemeteries, then, because there are lots of crosses there. Perhaps she should sue—they're so hurtful and offensive. Churches, too. They have those offensive symbols where everyone can see them.

ANNOUNCEMENTS AND APPEARANCE

I first noticed the dangerous trend toward silencing pro-life Christians in April 1994, when I heard about a judge in San Diego. This judge had ordered pro-life pregnancy center workers to "announce themselves" to callers and identify themselves as "pro-life." They were also ordered to inform everyone that they give their information from a "biblical perspective."[14] Think about this. The judge didn't order any workers at the abortion center to "announce themselves" to all their callers or inform them that their information came from a "proabortion, secular perspective."

Pro-lifers having to announce themselves. It's like lepers shouting "unclean!" What's next? Here's a time-saving idea: Perhaps we should sew little yellow crosses on our sleeves so people will know just by looking at us that we're pro-life Christians. That should eliminate the need to announce it.

A few years ago, a judge ruled that a statue of Jesus in a Wisconsin public park violated the so-called separation of church and state. So a group of concerned Christians bought the area around the statue for more than $21,000. That way the statue could stay in the park, right? *Wrong.* The Seventh Circuit Court of Appeals ruled that since the statue *appeared* to be on public property, it still violated the Constitution.[15] By that logic, if you live in Minnesota right on the border with Wisconsin, it may appear that you live in Wisconsin. If appearance is what matters, this judge *just might* let you vote in both states!

STUDENT'S CAN'T

Judge orders prayer police to roam the halls....

I already know what you're thinking. "Prayer police" is just an exaggerated way to summarize the 1962 Supreme Court ruling that took prayer out of school. Kids can still pray on their own, right? Not according to U.S. District Judge Ira DeMent. He actually ordered that a "monitor" roam the halls of high schools to listen in on conversations to make sure no one is praying.

On October 30, 1997, Judge DeMent issued a ruling you're not going to believe:

> The Defendants... are permanently enjoined from...permitting... including, but not limited to: vocal prayer, Bible and religious devotional or scriptural readings; distribution of religious materials, texts, or announcements; and discussions of a devotional/inspirational nature, *regardless of whether the activity is initiated, led by, or engaged in by students.* (Section 6 [a])

Here's what the injunction was intended to do:

- **Prohibit praying during a crisis:** "No exception to this provision shall be permitted during times of perceived crisis or exigent circumstances." (section 6 [c])

- **Discipline violators:** "When the enjoined activity by students occurs... school officials... are hereby ordered to take appropriate disciplinary action as they would for any violation of school disciplinary rules." (section 6 [c])

- **Reeducate school officials:** "It is ordered that defendant Dekalb County Board of Education shall...conduct a mandatory in-service training session for faculty and administrators in Dekalb County public schools that is reasonably designed to familiarize these school officials with the provisions of this permanent injunction...[which] shall occur during the 1997–98 school year." (section 7 [c])

- **Appoint monitors:** "It is...ordered that defendant Dekalb County Board of Education shall: nominate...three...persons with a description of qualifications to serve as a monitor for the purpose of insuring compliance with this permanent injunction." [section 7 (g)]

- **Assign monitors' duties:** "The monitor shall have the power and authority to: enter any classroom or public school property, school assembly, sporting event, commencement exercise, or school-sponsored or school-initiated event for the purpose of observing and reporting on compliance for the duration of this permanent injunction...and collect complaints regarding any violation of any provision of this permanent injunction for the purpose of investigating violations and if warranted, reporting them immediately to the court." (section 7 [ii])

- **Charge taxpayers:** "The monitor shall be paid by the Dekalb County Board of Education." (section 7 [v])[16]

Believe it...government-ordered Prayer Police in our public schools!

A GOVERNMENT CRACKDOWN ON RELIGION MIGHT BE EXPECTED IN BEIJING. BUT IN ALABAMA?

Incredibly, Judge Ira DeMent of the United States District Court for the middle District of Alabama's Northern Division has ordered Federal monitors into Alabama schools to report on and cite, under penalty of law, any incidence of religious activity. The following are verbatim excerpts from his permanent injunction. Please read the following very carefully:

Students are not allowed to discuss God:
"The Defendants...are PERMANENTLY ENJOINED from...permitting...including, but not limited to: Vocal prayer; Bible and religious devotional or scriptural readings; distribution of religious materials, texts, or announcements; and discussions of a devotional/inspirational nature, regardless of whether the activity is initiated, led by, or engaged in by students." [section 6(c)]

Students can not pray during a crisis:
"No exception to this provision shall be permitted during times of perceived crisis or exigent circumstances." [section 6(c)i]

Monitors will be watching:
"IT IS...ORDERED THAT DEFENDANT DEKALB COUNTY BOARD OF EDUCATION SHALL: Nominate...three... persons with a description of qualifications, to serve as a monitor for the purpose of insuring compliance with this PERMANENT INJUNCTION." [section 7(c)]

Monitors will be reporting:
"...Monitor shall have the power and authority to: Enter any classroom or public school property, school assembly, sporting event, commencement exercise, or school-sponsored or school initiated event for the purpose of observing and reporting on compliance for the duration of this PERMANENT INJUNCTION; and collect complaints regarding any violation of any provision of this PERMANENT INJUNCTION for the purpose of investigating violations and if warranted, reporting them immediately to the court." [section 7(c)(i)i]

Tax monies will pay for surveillance:
"The monitor shall be paid by the Dekalb County Board of Education..." [section 7(e)]

Teachers must also turn in their students:
"When the enjoined activity by students occurs...SCHOOL OFFICIALS....are hereby ORDERED to take appropriate disciplinary action as they would for any violation of school disciplinary rules." [section 6(c)]

Re-education will ensure obedience:
"IT IS...ORDERED THAT DEFENDANT DEKALB COUNTY BOARD OF EDUCATION SHALL....Conduct a mandatory in-service training session for faculty and administrators in Dekalb County public schools that is reasonably designed to familiarize these school officials with the provision of this PERMANENT INJUNCTION...(which) shall occur during the 1997-98 school year." [section 7(c)]

Who ever thought it could come to this? With the pound of his gavel a single Federal Judge has ordered government monitors into Alabama public schools to seek out and report any signs of religious activity, from individual prayer to Bible reading to even inspirational discussions! The establishment of this new Federal "Prayer Police" has moved us one more step away from democracy and ever closer to the state police policies of Beijing and the former Soviet Union. Anyone who doesn't believe this is happening should read the quotes from Judge Dement's ruling above.

This permanent injunction on religious activity of any kind, at any time, and for any reason is a full-frontal assault on religious liberty. It signals a sharp escalation in the battle over the religious freedoms on which this country was founded, despite studies that show how religious faith has traditionally benefited society. In fact,

youth who identify with a strong faith practice have lower teen pregnancy rates, lower rates of sexually transmitted disease, lower incidence of drug use, and less involvement with vandalism or youth violence. Adherence to religious faith is not the problem with public schools. In many ways, the moral framework it provides is the solution to much of what ails public education today. It's enough to make you wonder just whose side these judges are on.

It's time to draw attention to judges who abuse their authority by stealing our freedoms one ruling at a time. Please join us in our efforts to expose, and if necessary call for the impeachment, of judges who legislate from the bench. We're working hard for America's faithful. **1-800-582-4794**

CENTER FOR
RECLAIMING
AMERICA

In America, there's still just one word for judicial tyranny:

IMPEACHMENT!

The Center for Reclaiming America An outreach of Coral Ridge Ministries P.O. Box 552, Ft. Lauderdale. 33302 www.coralridge.org/ctra/

Thankfully, DeMent and his "prayer police" were overruled—or, as they say in cartoon talk, "foiled again!"

NO KIDDING!

Samuel Kent is another robe-wearer. He's a federal judge. So his orders can be mean, and nobody's going to do anything about it. Even though they can. In 1995, Kent ruled that if American students prayed in the name of Jesus, they would be sentenced to a six-month jail term. Now, you can take Jesus' name in vain. You can soak His cross in urine for your art project as practice for when you get funded by the National Endowment of the Arts.[17] But you'd better not pray. And he means it. He's *not* kidding.

> And make no mistake, the Court is going to have a United States marshal in attendance at the graduation. If any student offends this Court, that student will be summarily arrested and will face up to six months incarceration in the Galveston County Jail for contempt of Court. Anyone who thinks I'm kidding about this better think again....
>
> Anyone who violates these orders, no kidding, is going to wish that he or she had died as a child when this Court gets through with it.[18]

You see, this is a Christian kid that didn't get aborted. Bummer. Well, the next best thing is if we catch him or her praying. Then we can "*make* him wish he or she had died as a child"!

Where'd they get this guy? China? The Gestapo? The former Soviet Union? No, he's from Texas. He's just trying to make America *resemble* those other places.

THE SLIM MASSACHUSETTS MARRIAGE MARGIN

A one-judge margin in one state—Massachusetts—overruled the will of 290,000,000 Americans, every state law, and every state ballot initiative. And now marriage is in jeopardy everywhere.

What you may not know is that in a speech at the Massachusetts Lesbian and Gay Bar Association in 1999, the judge who wrote that opinion, Chief Justice Margaret Marshall, actually praised sexual orientation protections and the "growing body of gay-friendly international jurisprudence."[19] Can you say *conflict of interest*? This blatant ethics violation went unanswered. How can you raise money for a homosexual activist group and claim to be objective? That's the kind of people who are writing law from the bench and unraveling five thousand years of recorded marriage law.

Remember when Supreme Court Justice Scalia gave a speech in favor of the phrase "one nation under God" in the Pledge? Because of that, he recused himself from the Pledge decision before the Court. But then again, he's honorable.

THOU SHALT NOT TEACH ANYTHING "HOMOPHOBIC"

Meet Dr. Cheryl Clark. She used to be a lesbian. Isn't anymore. That's right. She became a Christian and experienced that "hope for change" we've been talking about. She doesn't live with her lesbian domestic partner anymore. Doesn't go to gay pride rallies. Now she goes to *church*—and she takes her little daughter "Jenny" with her.

But Elsey McLeod, the lesbian she used to live with, didn't like that much. So she sued Clark for joint custody of Jenny, even though she's not related to her in any way. McLeod also told the judge that some things were hanging on the bulletin board of the church that she didn't particularly like Jenny looking at, like stuff from Focus on the Family and Promise Keepers. Apparently she didn't think Jenny's mom should have the right to direct the religious upbringing of her own child.

Now a judge agrees with her. Denver District Court Judge John W. Coughlin awarded visitation and joint parenting responsibilities to McLeod. Then he ordered a restriction on the religious instruction of Jenny and forbade her mother from exposing her daughter to anything "homophobic."[20]

Did you hear that, parents? Now judges are deciding what you can and cannot teach your kids regarding homosexuality! Does that mean Clark can't read her daughter certain sections of the Bible, like Romans 1? Does she need to cover Jenny's ears during the sermon in church and cover her eyes when they walk past the church bulletin board? Is Clark forbidden to give her testimony about leaving the lesbian lifestyle if her daughter is present?

What happens if Cheryl Clark meets a member of the dreaded Promise Keepers and marries him? Will the judge remove Jenny from the house because of her step-dad's potential influence on her? If she can't be exposed to the "homophobic" literature of the Promise Keepers, will she be allowed to be exposed to one if its members?

Just so you know, here are three of the "outrageous" and "potentially harmful" things Promise Keepers believe:

- A Promise Keeper is committed to honoring Jesus Christ through worship, prayer, and obedience to God's Word in the power of the Holy Spirit.
- A Promise Keeper is committed to practicing spiritual, moral, ethical, and sexual purity.
- A Promise Keeper is committed to building strong marriages and families through love, protection, and biblical values.

You can see why the judge wouldn't want Jenny seeing stuff like that on a bulletin board. Mat Staver, president of Faith2Action partner Liberty Counsel, who filed an amicus brief in the case said: "Forbidding the raising of children in the parent's Christian beliefs is anathema to parental rights and religious freedom.... Courts may not give parents a no-win decision of either abandoning their Christian beliefs or abandoning their children."[21] Yet that is exactly what they are trying to do.

SOLUTIONS

We have a system of liberal law schools churning out liberal lawyers who become liberal judges making liberal laws from the bench. In order to move up, they are endorsed by the liberal, proabortion, pro-homosexual American Bar Association.

I'm as sick of writing about this stuff as you must be of reading it. I'm sick of the assault from the men in black. The good news is that something can be done.

Our Founding Fathers provided some remedies. Impeachment is one. But it takes a two-thirds vote in the Senate to do that. It also takes men and women of courage in Congress to suggest such a thing. But legislators who went through those same liberal law schools pledge allegiance to the liberal judges they've created and are too terrified to challenge them. They've been taught from the first day of law school about the magnificence and splendor of men (and women) in black. They are to be revered, as their knowledge and brilliance comes from on high. To use the word *impeach* is tantamount to blasphemy. *Hardly.*

How do we get back the system of checks and balances?

I got a call one morning from Faith2Action partner Phyllis Schlafly, a heroine in the pro-family movement if ever there was one. Single-handedly stopped the Equal Rights Amendment. She called with an idea about how to stop the judicial tyranny. Guess what? It turns out that *Congress has the power to limit the jurisdiction of judges.* Did you know that? I didn't.

As Phyllis explains in *The Supremacists: The Tyranny of Judges and How to Stop It,* all of the federal courts, with the exception of the Supreme Court, were created by Congress. And what Congress creates, Congress can restrain, regulate, or abolish altogether.

You see, Article I Section 8 of the Constitution states: "The Congress shall have power…to constitute tribunals inferior to the Supreme Court." Article III Section 1 and Article I Section 2 add some clarification. The former says, "The judicial power of the United States shall be vested in one Supreme Court, and in such inferior courts as the Congress may from time to time ordain and establish"; while the latter states: "The Supreme Court shall have appellate jurisdiction, both as to law and fact, with such exceptions, and under such regulations as the Congress shall make." This means Congress can "make exceptions" to the kinds of cases that even the Supreme Court can hear.[22]

Cool, huh?

And we're not just dusting off something in the Constitution that hasn't been used since the 1800s. It's been used before—recently. In 2002, Senator Tom Daschle (D-SD) led the fight to pass a law to prohibit all federal courts from hearing cases about brush clearing in his home state. *Brush fires in South Dakota.* Perhaps there are some other issues that reach *at least* that level on the priority scale.

Turns out some others have the same idea as Schlafly—and they've already had their first victory in limiting federal jurisdiction. On July 22, 2004, the U.S. House, by a vote of 233 to 194, approved Representative John Hostettler's (R-IN) H.R. 3313, the "Marriage Protection Act," which removes from federal courts the right to tamper with the 1996 Defense of Marriage Act (DOMA).

House Judiciary Committee Chairman F. James Sensenbrenner Jr. (R-WI) said:

> This legislation ensures the people and the States will have a say in marriage policy. The American people will be protected from a single federal judge or a few federal judges attempting to impose same-sex marriage upon this Nation. Any challenges to DOMA will be heard in state courts, which the U.S. Supreme Court says are just as competent to decide federal constitutional questions as are federal courts.[23]

Remember, it was the *state* court in Massachusetts that went against state law and five thousand years of historical marriage to redefine marriage for the entire state. But keeping *federal* judges from imposing that terrible ruling on the rest of us is a good start. The cases are already before them challenging state Defense of Marriage Laws.

In a press release following the vote, Sensenbrenner said:

> H.R. 3313 defends the Constitution by using one of the very "checks and balances" provided in the Constitution. Thomas Jefferson wrote that leaving federal courts as the ultimate arbiter of all constitutional

questions is, "a very dangerous doctrine indeed and one which would place us under the despotism of an oligarchy," and that "[T]he constitution, on this hypothesis, is a mere thing of wax in the hands of the judiciary, which they may twist and shape into any form they please." This legislation heeds Jefferson's wise words.[24]

Then on September 22, 2004, the House approved by a vote of 247 to 173 a bill sponsored by Todd Akin (R-MO) that would prevent federal courts, including the Supreme Court, from hearing cases challenging the words *under God.* Now we just need action in the Senate.

"Far from violating the 'separation of powers,'" House Judiciary Committee Chairman Sensenbrenner reiterated, "legislation that leaves state courts with jurisdiction to decide certain classes of cases would be an exercise of one of the very checks and balances provided for in the Constitution."[25]

Right after he was kicked off the Alabama Supreme Court, Judge Roy Moore said, "Under the Constitution of the United States, federal courts had no jurisdiction over the acknowledgment of God by the individual states. In recent years, federal judges have usurped state power with regard to the acknowledgment of God." Then he began work on a bill of his own "about whether or not we can acknowledge God as the source of our law and our liberty."[26]

Moore is backing the "Constitution Restoration Act." Sponsored in the House by Robert Aderholt (R-AL) and in the Senate by Richard Shelby R-AL), the act would prohibit federal courts from ruling in cases involving government officials who acknowledge God "as the sovereign source of law, liberty or government."[27]

Good idea.

A GLIMPSE INTO THE ACTION PLAN

How are we going to take back the courts? Limiting their jurisdiction is just a fire wall. The first thing we need is for the right judges to be nominated and confirmed. Here's a glimpse of the strategy I laid out for my own organization.

I formed Faith2Action to *win* the cultural war by working together. It's the first organization I'm aware of in our history that links to nearly every major national pro-family organization from one place: www.f2a.org. (Links to state groups are coming next, then international groups!) The idea is that if we are to win the cultural war, we must first know what our allies are doing. Then we have to find where the battle is the hottest—where our focus is critical for victory. I am convinced that if we are to win, the primary focus must be on the Supreme Court.

Phase I: Supreme Court Nominations

To win the cultural war, we must fill *every* vacancy with a pro-life, pro-family justice who will interpret the Constitution rather than legislate from the bench. This is the most critical battle in our lifetime and the only way to protect our freedoms and marriage and restore protection to unborn children.

We are now approaching what may be one of the most pivotal points in our history, as one to four vacancies on the U.S. Supreme Court will likely be announced in the next presidential term. That's why Faith2Action provided a means for people to support the president in this effort in a unique and positive way. We provided a customized button to our linking partners that allowed them to send the president a red rose—the symbol of life! It came in a bud vase with the following message urging him to appoint pro-life judges:

> Dear Mr. President:
> Please be encouraged that I share your "goal that says the unborn ought to be protected in law and welcomed to life."
> "And you,...in accordance with the wisdom of your God, which you possess, appoint magistrates judges to administer justice to all the people...who know the laws of your God." —Ezra 7:25

In about three weeks, more than four thousand rose orders came in—enough to fill the National Press Club room floor to ceiling and then spill out and fill two additional hallways. The video was exquisite! The message was

delivered in a unique, positive, and beautiful way. Here's part of what Tim Russert said about it on *Meet the Press:*

> Ms. Folger said other conservatives haven't forgotten that the last Republican appointee to the court was Justice David H. Souter, nominated by Mr. Bush's father—who most often sides with the liberal wing of the court. "There can never be another David Souter again," Ms. Folger said.

Phase II: Supreme Court Confirmations

In January 2003, in yet another effort, Faith2Action commissioned Wirthlin International, a respected polling firm, to ask the American people:

> Would you favor judicial nominees to the U.S. Supreme Court who would uphold laws that restore legal protection for unborn children?

Sixty-six percent—a full two-thirds—said *yes!* A lot of people were worried about the question. They strongly advised me against using the word *restore* and insisted that we say *increase* legal protection for unborn children. No. I wanted to know how many people wanted judicial nominees who would uphold laws that *restore* legal protection for unborn children. Two-thirds. *Glad I asked.*

This message needs to be delivered to the president and the Senate. Knowing the American people are standing behind judges who would uphold laws that restore legal protection for unborn children may make them bold enough to aggressively fight for those judges.

PARTIAL REFEREES

When he addressed the Harvard University's Kennedy School of Government in September 2004, Supreme Court Justice Antonin Scalia questioned "abstract moralizing" from the bench. "What I am questioning," he said, "is

the propriety, indeed the sanity, of having value-laden decisions such as these made for the entire society…by judges." He added, "The court has taken sides in the culture war.[28]

He's right. And the side they've taken isn't ours.

Chapter 8

JUSTICE FOR ALL?

Discrimination leads to legislation. It has to be enforced, after all. That's how what we believe becomes criminalized.

And it's the Hate Crimes Bill they'll use to do it if we let them. This is the most dangerous legislation in America. It's what is being used around the world to persecute Christians in places you would never—

I interrupt this sentence to bring you breaking news. Another pastor in Sweden has come under attack. *This just in:* Pastor Ulf Ekman, high-profile founder of the Uppsala Word of Life Church, was hit with a lawsuit for "hate speech against homosexuals."

Just how many pastors need to be thrown in jail for Americans to see the agenda to criminalize Christianity and the danger of hate crimes laws? Pastor Ekman can see it: "There is a deliberate political move in all of Europe toward restricting the freedom of religion, with Sweden serving as a sort of European Union pilot project."

"Unless we now claim the freedom to preach the gospel in all of its facets and consequences, we soon will not be allowed to preach it at all," Ekman added. "The freedom of religion and of speech are interrelated. We must stand up for the right of all citizens to believe and speak without government censorship." Sound familiar?

Ekman urged the European church to "lay aside its timidity, its policies of silence and compromise, and raise its voice now, or [believers] will soon be facing very dangerous times indeed. The agenda of the political left in Europe—socialists and liberals—is by no means secretive. The church must get involved politically, too, forming a counter-lobby."

After a few days of statements like this, authorities decided that maybe they had picked on the wrong guy. He was doing more harm than good to their agenda of criminalizing Christianity, and they decided not to prosecute him after all.[1]

BULLDOZED AT THE BOROUGH

You've already read about Michael Marcavage, the student at Temple University who was thrown in a mental ward for protesting a blasphemous play that featured Jesus Christ as a homosexual (see chapter 5).

But no one in Delaware County, Pennsylvania, had heard about him until July 21, 2004, when he read from the Bible at the Lansdowne Borough Council meeting. Marcavage is president of Repent America. More importantly, he is an American. But you wouldn't know that by how he was treated.

Here's what happened at the council meeting. Remember, this is not occurring in China. Not Sweden. Not Canada. This is America. *But not the one I know.* Marcavage's statement says:

> Several people spoke during the public comment/question period, in which I then followed. I addressed the council by saying [on camera] "Good Evening. I just wanted to express a couple of things this evening. First being at the direction that the council is leading our community…. I would like to share from the Scripture concerning homosexuality. It was apparent that Mr. [Norman] Council, [president of the Borough council] was angry, as he informed me that "we are not going to have this discussion." I then told him that "I would

just like to read the Scripture verse, and then I'll sit down." He prevented me from reading from the Bible through interruption, referring to the Scripture I was about to read as being "hate speech" and that I twist Scripture. I then informed him that I will "read it as it is." Mr. Council replied, "I understand, but we're not gonna have it. It's not gonna happen." I told Mr. Council that he may be able to limit my time, but could not change the content of my speech. He said, "Ok well, what I'm going to do is limit your time. It's up!" I then stated, "That's just an unfair practice.... You have to stay consistent with the other speakers." Mr. Council continued, "I am not going to allow you to come before this council and use it as a forum to engage in hate speech, it's simply not going to happen." I then said, "Mr. Council the Bible is not hate speech." ...I respectfully petitioned him to allow me to proceed as motions were made to adjourn the meeting. The motion to adjourn passed as I began to read from Romans 1, although the council left the room completely, residents of the borough still remained.[2]

According to Marcavage's account, while he was still reading, Police Chief Kortan forcibly removed him from the room, and in the hallway one of the council members hit him on the arm. Kortan then threw Marcavage into an elevator, pushed him against the back wall, and showered him with nonstop verbal abuse.

Marcavage says he was first told that "no charges" were going to be brought against him, but then things changed. "Chief Kortan called me the next day stating that he 'thought about it overnight and decided to charge me' with 'Disrupting Meetings and Processions' and 'Disorderly Conduct.'"[3] And the guy Marcavage accused of punching him in the arm? Oh yeah, *his charge* of "disorderly conduct" was dismissed.[4]

I'm not a lawyer, but since when is punching someone disorderly conduct? I was under the mistaken impression that that's assault. And while we're asking, *since when* is reading from the Bible within the specified time frame for public comment "disrupting meetings and processions" and "disorderly conduct"?

Assistant District Attorney Alyssa Kusturiss said, "Council perceived what he was reading as hate speech. It would be homophobic today. They couldn't let him go on. You can't go up to the podium and start reading from the Bible."[5]

"You can't go up to the podium and start reading from the Bible"? *Really?* Really. Michael Marcavage faces up to fifteen months in jail and a $2,800 fine.

WHICH IS WORSE? NAME-CALLING OR ROBBERY?

I have a question: Which is worse? Robbing people or calling them a mean name?

Which one deserves the *greater* penalty?

Before you answer, let's say the name was *really* mean—like "Four-Eyes!" I used to wear glasses, and I personally have been victimized on the public school playground by such horrific verbal assaults. They hurt my feelings. And there ought to be stiff penalties for things like that.

How stiff? You decide. If you're the one setting the penalties for both of these terrible wrongs—robbery and name-calling—and one offense will get you three and a half to seven years in the state prison, and the other twenty-three to twenty-six and a half years in the same cell, which gets you three and which gets you twenty-three years behind bars?

Some think being called four-eyes is so mean that the perpetrator of this hate crime against the visually impaired should serve twenty-three years behind bars. The state of New Hampshire agrees.

I know what you're thinking. *Can't be.* We can't criminalize name-calling. Public schools would be empty—kids would be behind bars until their thirties. Oh, I left something out. The mean name wasn't "Four-Eyes." Nor "Fatso," thus shamelessly targeting lovers of cheesecake. The only people a twenty-three-year jail sentence protects from mean names are homosexuals.

In New Hampshire, robbing someone outside a convenience store is a Class B felony that typically carries a sentence of three and a half to seven years in a state prison and a four-thousand-dollar fine. But according to Assistant County Attorney Roger Chadwick, if you are also convicted of a

THE CRIMINALIZATION OF CHRISTIANITY

"hate crime" (shouting an anti-gay name), the sentence becomes "enhanced" by twenty-three to twenty-six and a half years—bringing your grand total behind bars to a whopping thirty years.

Oh, and it's not a hypothetical case. According to the New Hampshire *Union Leader*, twenty-three-year-old John Guimond is facing those charges. He's charged with stealing a cell phone, keys, and a shopping bag from a twenty-four-year-old homosexual man and his seventeen-year-old minor "male partner" after approaching them in a parking lot and putting the victim in a "head lock."[6]

That's a bad thing to do. And a three and a half to seven year sentence and a four-thousand-dollar fine sounds fair. I'm not sure my cell phone is worth a four-thousand-dollar fine and three and a half to seven years in prison, but I think that sentence is a nice deterrent to robbery.

But keep in mind, no weapon was used, no injury sustained. Just that mean name—something far, far worse. Something that may land him *thirty years* behind bars.

Think about this for a minute. If saying a mean antihomosexual word adds an additional twenty-three to twenty-six and a half years to a sentence, and if you live to be eighty, the penalty for the words you say is one-fourth of your life. And while this was in addition to a robbery penalty, how much of a jump would it really be to penalize the "speech infraction" alone? And just what constitutes an "antigay epithet"? Would it be saying, "Homosexuality is a sin," or "Homosexuals should repent"? What if you told someone, "Homosexuality is harmful to your health"? If I were you, I wouldn't try it in New Hampshire.

SOME PEOPLE ARE MORE EQUAL

How in the world did we get to the place where a twenty-three-year sentence can be imposed for the words we say? Well, there's a basic principle we had to violate. It's called equal justice under the law.

By setting up a hierarchy of victims, some immediately become more valuable than others—like victim affirmative action. That way cold-blooded murder of one class of people somehow isn't as bad as when the exact same crime is perpetrated against a specially protected minority group. The goal is to target thoughts. But murder is murder, whether it's done to a child like Jesse Dirkhising or a grown man like Matthew Shepard.

By the way, the suspects in the killing of homosexual Matthew Shepard were charged with first-degree murder and found guilty. Under Wyoming law, where Shepard was killed, first-degree murder is subject to the death penalty. What happened to Shepard was heinous. But tell me, how do you toughen the sentence of the death penalty?

It's interesting that when I appeared on the *Today Show* with Elizabeth Birch, then spokesperson for the homosexual lobby group the Human Rights Campaign, I was actually for a tougher sentence for the killers of Matthew Shepard than they were. Birch went on and on about the details of the case, which I find as offensive as she does, but the HRC was not for the death penalty for the killers, as *I was*. Instead, they wanted to silence the message of dissent. They used the murder to say that those of us who disagree with behavior responsible for the majority of the cases of AIDS in this country are somehow to blame when people do things we vehemently oppose. They are really about creating "thought crimes."

Hate crimes legislation is the cornerstone for the criminalization of Christianity. And here's where the homosexual strategists say it starts:

It is strategically advantageous to be recognized as disadvantaged and victimized...the greater a group's victimization, the stronger its moral claim on the rest of society.[7]

In any campaign to win over the public, gays must be portrayed as victims in need of protection so that straights will be inclined by reflex to adopt the role of protector.... Gays should be portrayed as victims of prejudice.[8]

You have to agree, they've gotten pretty far riding the victim train.

Just what are these "crimes" that are being reported? A disagreement?

THE CRIMINALIZATION OF CHRISTIANITY

A statement of politically incorrect principle? How about reading the Bible? Or posting verses? If you think these are a stretch, go back and read chapter 1 again.

The goal of hate crimes legislation is to silence all those who disagree. Plain and simple. And who disagrees with homosexuality enough to actually speak up? Oh yeah, Christians. They aren't going to be browbeaten into submission when they fear God more than man.

THE TRUTH ABOUT "HATE"

At the height of the post–Matthew Shepard "hate crime" media frenzy, here's what the facts reveal:

> According to the FBI, of 18,000+ murders nationwide, only 8 were found to be "hate crimes," and only 3 of them were "antigay." Such murders are horrible, but they are not epidemic.
>
> The FBI "hate crimes" report (1997) showed that crimes based on race, religion, sexual orientation or other biases were *rare* and on the *decrease*.
>
> According to the FBI, of 13.2 million criminal offenses, so-called hate crimes" account for under 1/10 of 1 percent. The report also showed the most "bias" offenses were low-level crimes, including speech perceived as threatening. The most common offense was "intimidation."
>
> The vast majority of American communities reported no "hate crimes" incidents at all, even though activists claim that America is undergoing a "hate crime" epidemic.[9]

In the last reported period, 2002, hate crimes reached an all-time low.[10] The church burnings, shootings, and vandalism that have occurred and the death threats I've experienced, all of which were accompanied by an "anti-Christian" epithet, aren't among them, of course. The 1999 shooting in which a gunman opened fire during a prayer service at a Baptist church in southwest Fort Worth, killing eight people, wasn't reported as a hate crime, of course.[11] Apparently, those bullets were *loving*. If it had happened at a homosexual meeting, that's *all* you would have heard.

In addition to underreporting crimes against religious people, apparently there is also a trend of faking hate crimes. Before you accuse me of a hate crime for saying that, take a peek at the facts:

- In Houston, a homosexual mugging victim was left for dead in a traditionally "straight" section of town. The press initially covered it as a hate crime, but investigators found that the man had been assaulted elsewhere and transported there, "to make it look like a hate crime."[12]
- In Salt Lake City, a homosexual teacher at first thought biased offenders had put signs in her yard to intimidate her, but some of her own homosexual students later confessed to doing it.[13]
- In South Carolina, a lesbian was charged with giving false information to a police officer for reporting that she was beaten. Police contend she hired a man to beat her and then she reported it as a hate crime.[14]

John Leo of *U. S. News & World Report* describes numerous incidents, including a homosexual man at the University of Georgia who reported that he had been victimized in nine hate crimes, including three arsons. Under questioning, the man admitted to setting the fires himself. Leo also pointed to the lesbian at a Minnesota university who slashed her own face and then claimed that two men had shouted antihomosexual remarks before attacking her. The woman later confessed to the lie.[15]

HATE-LESS RAPE?

And what about rape? Is that a hate crime? Not according to Senator Ted Kennedy, the biggest proponent of hate crimes legislation in Congress. Here's what he had to say in the Senate Judiciary Committee hearing:

THE CRIMINALIZATION OF CHRISTIANITY

What we're really talking about are these types of crimes that are so horrific in terms of the nature, are really not just directed at an individual, but really are directed at a whole community, and really the society.... You have to be able to show the gender animus that is there.

So this doesn't apply to every rape case. You've got to be able to demonstrate that this is a mindset that individuals, in terms of individuals, who are going to have, on the basis of race or in terms of sexual orientation or in terms of whatever these criteria.[16]

Later, Robert Knight said:

I'm amazed at Senator Kennedy. He's not here to defend his remark. But, he said that, and I think I'm correct in saying this—he said that not every rape involves gender animus....

I cannot imagine, if a woman were here who had been raped, she could take the Senator seriously. Every rape is a crime against all women. It's a crime against the community. It sends communities into sheer panic. When a child is snatched and abducted, and molested... that's a crime against the whole community. Yet, that wouldn't be covered under this.

The whole concept of hate crimes is flawed, because it sets up special classes of victims afforded a higher level of government protection than others victimized by similar crimes. That violates the concept of equal protection. It politicizes criminal prosecutions.[17]

Former lesbian Yvette Schneider explained it to me this way: "Why should I receive *less protection* now that I am no longer a lesbian?" If I am targeted because I'm five foot two and easy to overpower, the crime is every bit as bad as if I were targeted for any other reason. The bottom line is that *all crimes are hate crimes*—not just those against specially protected groups.

Faith2Action's communication director Ross Conley designed a coupon that helps explain it. As long as you're fighting this dangerous bill, you're free to use it any way you'd like:

ATTENTION VIOLENT CRIMINALS!

Target the "right victim" and get a discounted jail sentence!

Under a special discount offered by the U.S. Senate, violent criminals who target Grandma because she's old and vulnerable may serve *less time* than those who target a grown man who engages in homosexual behavior. Forget fair and equal justice, that's a thing of the past!

Just tell Grandma her life isn't worth as much as a homosexual's. I'm sure she'll understand — some victims' lives are more important than others.

HATE CRIMES DISCOUNT COUPON | NO EXPIRATION DATE

30% OFF* JAIL TIME

For assaulting Grandma or other non-homosexuals

CRIMINAL: Present this Sentence 'Saving' Coupon along with the "Hate Crimes Prevention Act" for a reduced penalty just for targeting Grandma, a small child, or an innocent bystander rather than a homosexual. **HOMOSEXUAL:** The Senate says that your sexual activity gives you special protection under the law. If the U.S. House agrees, present this coupon (and homosexual sex verification) to receive more protection than a Grandma assaulted in the exact same way! **GRANDMA:** Tough luck!

* Actual sentence discount may vary

THIS COUPON VOID IF PROHIBITED BY THE U.S. HOUSE

Let's look at that for just a minute. If I say homosexuality is a sin or read from the Bible, which calls the practice an "abomination," all someone has to do is say that it's hateful, and I'm looking at "a term not exceeding two years." Hey, at least I still get to communicate my beliefs in "private conversation"... *as long as no one else hears.*

Yes, that's the definition of *genocide* we're all familiar with. I wonder if our Founding Fathers would have worked as hard as they did to protect the freedom to voice dissenting opinions if they knew what used to be called freedom of speech was really a form of genocide.

"APPROPRIATE" COUNSELING

What happens if a child in the California public school system disagrees with the homosexual lobby in school? Why, he or she is sent for "appropriate counseling," of course. According to Assembly Bill 1785, now law, the School Safety and Violence Prevention Act establishes "an in-service training program for school staff to learn to identify at-risk pupils, to communicate effectively with those pupils, and to refer those pupils to appropriate counseling."[25] This law clearly states that its intent is to train school personnel to detect children who may have the "potential" of someday displaying discriminatory or prejudicial attitudes and to instruct teachers to refer those children for reeducation, or "appropriate counseling" (a more acceptable phrase).

The bill also added to the list of "hate crimes" and/or "hate-motivated incidents" that must be reported on standard school crime reporting forms and listed "demeaning jokes" as a "hate-motivated incident."[26] It does specify, however, that "sexual orientation shall not include pedophilia." Very nice of them. Students are still allowed to disagree with that. *For now.*

In 1999, the California legislature enacted the Carl Washington School Safety and Violence Prevention Act and appropriated $100 million to collect data on "hate-motivated incidents," while the education code was amended to "adopt policies directed toward creating a school environment in kindergarten and grades one to twelve, inclusive, that is free from discriminatory attitudes and practices and acts of hate violence."[27]

Teachers and administrators go through the indoctrination first, in in-service training programs that teach them how to target the Christian kids or "at risk pupils" who disagree with the homosexual agenda.

How can you know who these potential suspects might be? Well, when you force the homosexual agenda on these children from kindergarten, you can spot who might like the homosexual propaganda of the day. When the teacher reads them *King and King,* for example, where a king meets the "man of his dreams" and lives "happily ever after," check out little Johnnie's reaction. If he doesn't readily embrace the homosexual agenda, there's your potential hater. Send him to be reeducated with all that money, and whatever you do, don't tell his parents.

HEY, MISTER, NICE DRESS

And now the thought police are coming after Americans who think a man in a dress isn't in compliance with their office dress code. The "Hey, Mister, Nice Dress" law, AB 196, which passed the California legislature, hits business owners with a $150,000 fine if they fire a cross-dresser—even if he oversees small children or works in a private Christian bookstore.

And two years ago, the California legislature passed a law that mandated "sensitivity training" for foster parents, complete with a toll-free hotline for children to call should their foster parents discourage them from pursuing a homosexual lifestyle.[28]

And if you don't like the gender on your birth certificate, you can now legally rewrite history. That's right, at least twenty-one Iowans have obtained new birth certificates after undergoing sex-change operations.[29] Sex-change recipients are now able to change historical fact and pretend that they were born the way their surgically altered bodies reflect. Forget about facts. Forget about full disclosure. History is what we say it is!

THE UGLY FACE OF FACE

I first noticed thought crimes in the pro-life movement with the so-called Freedom of Access to Clinic Entrances (FACE) legislation targeting peaceful pro-life demonstrations. While I have always believed in fighting abortion within legal means, peaceful civil disobedience has long played a part in our country's battle for civil rights. I'm told that the restaurant where Martin Luther King Jr. held his first sit-in has been made into a museum. Yet pro-lifers who wish to use the exact same means to stand for the civil rights of the unborn are declared felons.

To get an idea of how this law specifically targets the *thoughts* of a pro-life protester, imagine three people sitting in front of the door of a medical building where they perform abortions *and* do animal research. The first pro-testor is an employee of the abortion clinic who's upset because she doesn't make enough money. The second protester is engaging in civil disobedience because rabbits are being used for cancer research down the hall. And the third protester is a pro-lifer. She is upset about the fact that they are per-forming partial-birth abortions inside the building and, *like the others,* she's trespassing to make her point.

All three are blocking the building's entrance, and under equal justice laws prior to FACE, all three would be equally in violation of the trespass law. FACE, however, makes one of them a felon. Guess which one?

The first one is involved in a labor dispute. She'll probably be asked to leave, and if she doesn't, she'll likely get a slap on the wrist for trespassing before getting her raise. The animal rights activist? Most likely the news media will come out and film the action—especially if a Hollywood star is involved—and the cameras will zoom in on the mean police officer carrying away this noble defender of rabbits.

The third protester? She's a felon. Not because of her actions—she was doing the exact thing as the other two—but because of her belief that it is wrong to pull a living infant four-fifths of the way out of the womb before sucking the child's brains out. That's right. FACE says she will now lose her right to vote, her right to bear arms and run for office...and she will spend hard time in a *federal* penitentiary (one year for the first offense, three years for repeat offenses). That's called a *thought crime,* and it targets the pro-lifer not for his or her actions, but for having a *pro-life motivation.*

How are we going to stop this steamroller? I don't know about you, but

I am sick of responding, reacting, and defending. I believe that we not only need to stop hate crimes laws and the other freedom-stripping laws that silence those of us who refuse to bow to the homosexual agenda, but that we need to do so proactively. Liberty Counsel proposed a sample ordinance for cities and states wishing to make a stand proactively. What Mat Staver did was describe the characteristics necessary to receive special standing as a protected minority. They include:

1. longstanding history of widespread discrimination
2. economic disadvantage
3. immutable characteristics

All of these apply to African-Americans; *none* of them apply to homosexuals. See the difference? If you already have protection for a minority based on sexual orientation, you can get it removed on these grounds. If your city or state doesn't have anything on the books regarding sexual orientation, I strongly recommend passing a proactive ordinance that describes what is necessary to receive special legislated protection.

MARRIAGE IN THE BALANCE

I began to write this book on the morning of May 17, 2004—the day that, by a one-vote majority, the Supreme Judicial Court in Massachusetts redefined marriage for that state and all those who exported their newly acquired "marriage licenses" elsewhere. Forget about the three-day waiting period (rules don't apply when it comes to the homosexual agenda). News programs celebrated this event, tying it into the fiftieth anniversary of the Supreme Court's decision in *Brown v. Board of Education,* claiming this redefinition of marriage as a "civil right" and accusing all those who oppose it of bigotry.

The four judges who undermined and redefined marriage against the will of the people of Massachusetts put marriage in jeopardy everywhere else. While judges may have given us this mess, the law can fix it. You see, the only thing we have that trumps judges (besides impeaching them, that is) is amending the Constitution. Because the nearly forty states that have Defense of Marriage Acts—or DOMAs—aren't secure. One activist judge can strike those acts down, as we're already seeing in Washington State and elsewhere.

The Federal Marriage Amendment—which was voted on in Congress in 2004 but fell short of the two-thirds needed to send it to the states—is one way to prevent judges from striking down state laws. But until we have a Federal Marriage Amendment, the answer is to amend your *state constitution.* Hawaii, Alaska, Nebraska, Nevada, Missouri, and Louisiana have done it, as eleven more did on November 2, 2004 (all of which won by a landslide). The time to act is now—before a judge in *your* state destroys marriage.

Why does it matter? Society embraces marriage because it is the foundation of the family, the building block of our civilization. More than ten thousand studies confirm that marriage between one man and one woman is the very best place for children.[30] Every bit of real-world evidence and social science research also confirms that marriage is not only the very best place to raise children, but also the safest place for women and the healthiest place for men. It's the foundation for the family on which our society is built. Marriage is between one man and one woman and always has been. It's the law for a reason.

WHAT'S AHEAD?

We don't have to imagine the future. The results of embracing the homosexual agenda are already evident in Scandinavia.

In 1989, Sweden became the first country in Europe to legalize homosexual unions, with Denmark and Norway following closely behind. Stanley Kurtz, a research fellow at the Hoover Institution, published "The End of Marriage in Scandinavia," an article stating that the issue is not "marriage for homosexuals," but rather, according to homosexual activists themselves, "social approval for homosexuality." After four years, only 749 homosexual Swedes and 674 homosexual Norwegians bothered to "get married." After nine years, only 2,372 homosexual couples had taken advantage of the Danish law. The issue is acceptance, and the outcome is the destruction of traditional marriage.

European statistics show that a majority of children in Sweden, Denmark, and Norway are now born out of wedlock. Sixty percent of firstborn children in Denmark are born out of wedlock, and in some areas of Norway, *80 percent* of firstborn children are conceived out of wedlock, as are 60 percent of subsequent births.[31] Southern Seminary president Al Mohler reports that in Sweden, while older couples tend to get married after having more than one child, young couples dispense with marriage altogether. The younger couples that do get married often do not like to admit it—it is so far out of "the norm" that they feel embarrassed.

What's behind this? It's really not as much about "marriage" for same-sex couples as it is about furthering the homosexual agenda. But don't take my word for it, take a look at what same-sex marriage proponents have to say:

A middle ground might be to fight for same-sex marriage and its benefits and then, once granted, *redefine the institution of marriage completely,* to demand the right to marry not as a way of adhering to society's moral codes but rather to debunk a myth and *radically alter an archaic institution.*[32] —Michelangelo Signorile

Enlarging the concept to embrace same-sex couples would necessarily *transform it into something new....* Extending the right to marry to gay people—that is, abolishing the traditional gender requirements of marriage—can be one of the means, perhaps the principal one, through which the institution divests itself of the sexist trappings of the past.[33] —Tom Stoddard

It is also a chance to *wholly transform the definition of family in American culture.* It is the *final tool with which to dismantle* all sodomy statutes, get education about homosexuality and AIDS into public schools, and, in short, usher in a sea change in how society views and treats us.[34] —Michelangelo Signorile

Being queer is more than setting up house, sleeping with a person of the same gender, and seeking state approval to do so.... Being queer means pushing the parameters of sex, sexuality, and family, and in the process, *transforming the very fabric of society....* As a lesbian, I am fundamentally different from non-lesbian women.... In arguing for the right to legal marriage, lesbians and gay men who would be forced to claim that we are just like heterosexual couples, have the same goals and purposes, and vow to structure our lives similarly.... We must keep our eyes on the goals of providing true alternatives to marriage and *radically reordering society's view* of reality.[35] —Paula Ettelbrick

And there's this from pro-homosexual author Judith Levine:

Because American marriage is inextricable from Christianity, it admits participants as Noah let animals onto the ark. But it doesn't have to be that way. *In 1972 the National Coalition of Gay Organizations demanded the "repeal of all legislative provisions that restrict the sex or number of persons entering into a marriage unit;* and the extension of legal benefits to all persons who cohabit regardless of sex or numbers." Would polygamy invite abuse of child brides, as feminists in Muslim countries and prosecutors in Mormon Utah charge? No. *Group marriage could comprise any combinations of genders.*[36]

Levine left out the part about the 1972 Gay Rights Platform calling for abolishing age-of-consent laws. Interesting omission given that in *Harmful to Minors: The Perils of Protecting Children from Sex,* Levine describes a Dutch Law that reduced the statutory age of consent to twelve (under certain circumstances) as being a "good model of reasonable legislation."[37]

On May 17, 2004, Tony Perkins, Gary Bauer, Dr. James Dobson, and other pro-family leaders spoke out about where this so-called same-sex "marriage" disaster would head—to polygamy and beyond. Everyone I heard responded with the same reaction. The homosexual activists denounced us for even suggesting that same-sex "marriage" would open the door to polygamy. "Those are scare tactics! No one will use this decision to legalize polygamy!" *Really?*

The lawsuit has already been filed.

The lawyers argued before U.S. District Judge Ted Stewart that three Utahans should be able to live together legally as husband and wife *and wife.* They claimed that the antibigamy and antipolygamy laws are unconstitutional based on the U.S. Supreme Court's *Lawrence v. Texas* ruling, which declared that the "right to privacy" included sodomy.[38]

JUST THE BENEFITS, PLEASE

Hey, I have an idea. Let's just compromise. Don't like homosexual "marriage"? Let's just give them domestic partner benefits! Sure, the homosexual lobby says that allowing everyone to bring their partner to their health-care provider won't cost much.

The National Gay and Lesbian Task Force's *public* position on so-called domestic partner benefits, published on the NGLTF Web site in answer to the "It will cost too much" objection, states:

> The most common reason cited by companies who do not implement DP benefits is the perception that to do so would be cost prohibitive.... *These concerns are baseless.*[39]

Five words come to mind: Liar, liar, pants on fire. Strong words? Listen to what that *same group* had to say in the homosexual newspaper the *Washington Blade* on March 7, 2003, when it came to providing domestic partnership benefits for their *own* members:

NATIONAL HOMOSEXUAL LOBBY CUT SAME-SEX BENEFITS
FOR ITS OWN EMPLOYEES "GLARING HYPOCRISY,"
CHARGES CRITIC AFTER REVELATION

WASHINGTON, D.C.—The stunning revelation Friday that the nation's leading homosexual advocacy group had *cut* domestic partner benefits for its own employees, reportedly saying the costs were "prohibitively expensive," drew charges of dishonesty and hypocrisy from opponents of the group's efforts to pressure employers nationwide to offer such benefits.

"Based on its own experience, the National Gay and Lesbian Task Force has been knowingly dishonest in public about the increased cost to employers of extending insurance coverage to individuals whose homosexual activity puts them at dramatically higher risk of domestic violence, mental illness, substance abuse, life-threatening disease, and premature death," said Gary Glenn, president of the American Family Association of Michigan.[40]

Think about this for a minute. This is the group telling corporate sponsors throughout the country that they *must* give domestic partnership benefits because they're so doggone cheap—but they couldn't afford to do it themselves. Can you say *hypocrisy*? What might homosexual marriage—or even civil unions—do to the bank? According to Dr. James Dobson in *Marriage Under Fire,* granting same-sex "marriage" benefits threatens to break it:

The health care system will stagger and perhaps collapse. This could be the straw that breaks the back of the insurance industry in Western nations, as millions of new dependents become eligible for coverage. Every HIV positive patient needs only to find a partner to receive the same coverage as offered to an employee. It is estimated…that drastic increases in premiums can be anticipated and that it may not be profitable for companies to stay in business.[41]

GOD SPEAKS…SO SHOULD YOU

You've heard it said that Jesus didn't say anything about homosexuality or same-sex marriage. *Really?*

"Haven't you read," [Jesus] replied…'For this reason a man will leave his father and mother and be united to his wife, and the two will become one flesh?' So they are no longer two, but one. Therefore what God has joined together, let man not separate." (Matthew 19:4–6)

God's design for marriage was spelled out in His very first book. (Don't worry, I'm not going to say "Adam and Eve, not Adam and Steve.") Read this:

A man will leave his father and mother and be united to his wife, and they will become one flesh. (Genesis 2:24)

That's what Jesus affirmed and reaffirmed in Matthew 19:4–6 and Mark 10:7. Paul did the same thing in Ephesians 5:31.

Marriage matters because civilization matters. A change in the law will impact us all. It will affect what teachers must force your children to learn in school, what businesses must provide, what taxpayers must subsidize. It will alter adoption law, forcing agencies to place children with homosexual couples in order not to discriminate, leaving children as the victims without the hope of having both a mother *and* father—what more than ten thousand studies show is best for them. The law will determine our future on this.

Your involvement is necessary to pass state marriage amendments and the Federal Marriage Amendment, to repeal domestic partnerships and civil unions, and to stop the so-called Hate Crimes Bill that paves the way for the criminalization of Christianity. The number of the U.S. Capitol is 202-224-3121. It reaches your two U.S. Senators and your Congressional representative. I recommend you use it every week.

If you care about your freedom, that is.

Chapter 9

THE BATTLE FOR THE NEXT GENERATIONS

W e've come a long way from the first American textbook—the New England primer, published in 1690—used to teach reading for the next nearly two hundred years. First-graders learned the alphabet and the Bible at the same time: For the letter *A,* they learned, "In Adam's Fall, we sinned all." For the letter *C,* they recited, "Christ crucified, for sinners died." Instead of being told that they were an "accident," one of the more complex animals to rise from the primordial slime, students learned about Creation and that Jesus, the Son of God, "for sinners died." Oh, and they also used another textbook: the Bible.

"Should not the Bible regain the place it once held as a school book?" someone once asked. "Its morals are pure, its examples captivating and noble." Who would say such an outrageous thing? Jerry Falwell? It had to be someone with no clue about what the First Amendment really means. *Right?* The guy who said that was Fisher Ames. Who was he? Only the *author* of the First Amendment. I'm pretty sure he had a clue about what it meant.

We've listened to those who have expelled God from school. And where has it gotten us? Take a look at how far we've come in the last forty years. David Barton has often talked about the survey conducted forty years ago in which teachers were asked to name their biggest problems. Prior to 1962, when prayer was taken out of school, here's what the answers were: "talking, chewing gum, making noise," and the dreaded "running in the halls." After prayer was taken out, the problems were rape, robbery, assault, burglary, arson, bombing, and murder.

We've certainly come a long way. *In the wrong direction.*

WHAT YOU TEACH AFFECTS WHAT THEY BELIEVE

The textbooks in Massachusetts are already written to teach our children that homosexual "marriage" is just another option that we should accept, subsidize, and celebrate.

Why does this matter? That's what I was asked by Alan Colmes on *Hannity and Colmes.* He asked me if there was anything a teacher could say that would change my sexual orientation. I answered no, but then again I'm an adult. We're talking about impressionable kids who are still forming their beliefs.

As I pointed out on the show, the numbers speak for themselves: According to *Time* magazine, 18 percent of teens in San Francisco either claim to be homosexual or are "questioning" their sexual orientation. In the most pro-homosexual area of the country, nearly one in five claim to be homosexual or "questioning," compared to the national average, which is as low as 1–3 percent of all teens. What you teach children impacts what they think.

Right now, there are more than seventeen hundred Gay, Lesbian and Straight Education Network (GLSEN) clubs in high schools across the country. More than one thousand high school Gay-Straight Education Alliances have formed and are now making inroads into middle schools. Coproducer of *It's Elementary: Talking About Gay Issues in School* Debra Chasnoff stated, "What's clear in the film is that the younger the kids, the more open they were. If we could start doing this kind of education in kindergarten, first grade, second grade, we'd have a better education."[1] Better homosexual indoctrination, that is.

The latest buzzwords to get homosexuality in the door of your child's school are *safety, tolerance,* and, the favorite, *diversity.* The latest tool homosexual activists are using to indoctrinate elementary school children is a book called *Cootie Shots: Theatrical Inoculations Against Bigotry for Children, Parents and Teachers.*[2] Designed for kindergarten through second grade, it features skits like "Play Wedding," in which "[t]wo little girls play dolls and talk about a wedding between two men one of them attended."[3] Another skit features a girl saying the line: "The one I love she wears a dress." The title character in a skit promoting cross-dressing responds to the question "What's with the dress, Jack?" with "It shows off my legs."[4]

And while homosexual activists would never permit anything that hints at insulting their behavior, take a look at the violence in this little ditty, "In Mommy's High Heels," sung by a "cross-dressing boy":

> *Let them say I'm like a girl!*
> *What's wrong with being like a girl?!*
> *And let them jump and jeer and whirl*
> *They are the swine, I am the pearl....*
> *Let them laugh, let them scream,*
> *They'll all be beheaded when I'm queen."*[5]

What do you do with those "swine" who disagree with you? Why, behead them, of course. If we had written that about what to do with cross-dressers, we'd all be in jail.

HEATHER, HER TWO MOMS, AND THE GANG

We've all heard about *Heather Has Two Mommies,* a children's book supposedly written to engender tolerance of homosexuality. But as John Leo writes, "Surely schools can generate respect for Catholic children, let's say, without putting *Heather Finds Peace as a Nun* on the reading list."[6] But try to have a say in what your children are reading, and you'll find yourself under vicious attack.

Journalist Richard Vigilante takes issue with schools undermining parents' values: "If Americans do not have the right to maintain, for themselves and their families, moral beliefs taught for millennia by the religions to which between 70–90 percent of the population subscribe, then a lot of us are living in the wrong country."[7] Or maybe our fellow citizens have been asleep while those who want to undermine our beliefs, values, and institutions have taken over.

But now the junior brainwashing books have moved beyond *Heather Has Two Mommies, Daddy's Roommate,* and *Gloria Goes to Gay Pride.* Now there are more than a hundred such books, ranging literally from A (*Amy Asks a Question: Grandma, What's a Lesbian?*) to Z (*Zack's Story: Growing up with Same-Sex Parents*). The Gay, Lesbian and Straight Education Network of Colorado recommends *ninety-one* of them.[8]

In British Columbia, some people weren't fond of their children being indoctrinated with such propaganda as *Asha's Mums; One Dad, Two Dads, Brown Dads, Blue Dads;* and *Belinda's Bouquet* (by the same author who brought you Heather and her two mommies), so they tried to get them removed. The BC Teachers' Federation, who recommended these lovely books to indoctrinate kindergartners and first graders, didn't care for the idea of parents having something to say about it. When the school board responded, David Dhudnovsky, president of the BC Teacher's Federation Board, accused the board of imposing a "private religious agenda on the public school system."[9]

And the Court of Appeals agreed. They denied Surrey School Board the right to remove homosexual propaganda from first-grade classrooms. According to the Court, the board's earlier decision to remove the pro-homosexual literature was found to be illegitimate because it was "influenced" by the religious beliefs of parents in that school district.[10] You see, only the homosexual activists and atheists are allowed to do that.

JUNIOR THOUGHT POLICE

Now it's not just what your kids are being taught; it's that those beliefs are now being enforced by junior "thought police" trained to roam the school hallways looking for verbal offenses. *No kidding.* Spearheaded by former U.S.

Attorney General Janet Reno and the National Association of Attorneys General, a program of training students to police the halls for "violators" has already been implemented in Maine, Massachusetts, and West Virginia. Other states with representatives on that task force included Tennessee, Pennsylvania, Florida, Mississippi, and New Jersey.

The West Virginia Office of Civil Rights has organized teams of middle and high school students and teachers—three students per grade plus one or two faculty advisers—who are to report harassment, which in their definition includes "homophobic slurs," to law enforcement officers.

Claiming that the 1990 federal FBI Hate Crime Statistics Act gives them authorization, the police curriculum instructs officers about "homophobia" and how to identify "bias" crimes. Throwing the First Amendment by the wayside, the manual provides sample scenarios that illustrate how a "victim" may rightfully feel threatened (which would constitute a crime) if the alleged perpetrator is perceived as more powerful, has a hostile tone of voice, or stands too close.[11]

Imagine that two students have a disagreement that escalates into a close-standing, hostile-sounding argument of sorts. One is a homosexual and one is a Christian who opposes his views on homosexuality. Both have done the same thing, but *only one is a criminal.* Yeah, that would be the Christian kid. If the Christian kid happens to be tall, he's got a triple violation going for him. He's a "close-standing," "hostile sounding" *and* "more powerful" opponent of the homosexual agenda. You can be sure he'll be sent for more than "appropriate counseling."

THE "ENFORCERS" ROAMING THE STREETS

The West Virginia Hate Crimes Task Force uses the National Hate Crimes Training Curricula in police training centers at selected colleges and universities receiving grants from COPS, Community Oriented Policing Services, a division of the U.S. Department of Justice. The federal grants fund faculty and staff to conduct these "hate crimes classes" and refer to the state-based training functions as Regional Community Policing Institutes (RCPIs).

Even more disturbing are the descriptions of typical offenders in the training manual. Types of perpetrators of bias crimes that police are to watch for include the "mission" offender. This person believes he has received his instructions from a higher order, like God or the Führer. Of course those who believe in God and a "higher order" are just as suspect as those who put their faith in a führer. *You can see why they would be the same kind of suspects.* (That, again, would be sarcasm.)

The manual also identifies "homophobia" as one of the identifying characteristics by which to spot "hate groups." These suspect groups include Christians whose ideology is apocalyptic and who believe we are in, or approaching, the period of violence and social turmoil that will precede the Second Coming of Christ.[12] If you're a Christian who believes what the Bible has to say about homosexual behavior, you're a suspect. If you've noticed that reading the paper is strikingly similar to reading the book of Revelation, you are also on a police "most wanted list" of potential criminals.

To get further insight into the kind of speech they're trying to outlaw, we can take a look at a recent state bill before the West Virginia legislature that proposes adding "sexual orientation" to the state's student harassment code. The wording would redefine sexual harassment to include "unwelcome behavior, verbal or written words or symbols directed at an individual because of gender or sexual orientation."[13]

Words, verbal or written, and symbols are now harassment. Teen thought police roam the halls in schools and police roam the streets, looking for anyone who trusts in a "higher authority" they can accuse of such verbal, written, or symbolic violations. Would a cross be a symbolic violation? All it has to do is offend someone. How about a T-shirt? Wonder no more.

"YOU NAZI!"

Sixteen-year-old Tyler Chase Harper attended Poway High School in an upper-middle-class suburb north of San Diego. One day he wore a T-shirt to school that "violated school policy."

Tyler had had the shirt specially made in response to a school-sponsored day designated to promote "tolerance" for homosexuals and lesbians. The T-shirt didn't say "Gay Pride." That would have been allowed, of course. His shirt reflected his now illegal views. It read: "Homosexuality Is Shameful" and "Our School Embraced What God Has Condemned." It also cited the Bible passage Romans 1:27.

Administrators told Tyler he would be suspended if he wore the shirt on campus, and the school district likened it to wearing a swastika or derogatory racial reference. Students hung a banner across from the school with the words: "Chase Rocks." And printed T-shirts that said: "We Support Chase."[14] No word yet on whether those students were also threatened with suspension.

FREE CIGARETTES, BOYS AND GIRLS!

Imagine I work in the PR department of R. J. Reynolds and that I want more people to smoke. Here's an idea I ripped off that could earn me real points at the board meeting and a big fat salary:

Mr. Chairman and members of the board,

I believe that if our goal is to increase cigarette sales, we must do whatever we can to get more people smoking at younger and younger ages. With that in mind, I have developed a curriculum for ages K through 12 that will put us in a more positive light. It begins with the children's book *Heather Has Two Cigarettes.*

I also believe there is an increasing intolerance and hostility toward smoking and that there need to be school programs to engender acceptance of the smoker's orientation. Mean-spirited students, administrators, and even teachers have often harassed students who smoke, adversely affecting their self-esteem. This hate speech must be stopped. Evidence shows that citing the dangers of smoking and attempting to persuade young smokers to 'change' into nonsmokers may actually cause them irreparable harm and even lead to suicide. In fact, many in our school-club pilot program—GLSEN or Glad Little Smokers Enlist Now—have testified that becoming a 'nonsmoker' violates how they were made. They have tried to change and have failed, proving the impossibility of such a preposterous notion. Those who say they've become nonsmokers are just living a lie.

Smokeaphobic groups like the American Cancer Society and the bigoted Surgeon General like to point out 'supposed dangers.' But as we all know, many people who smoke *never* develop lung cancer or suffer adverse consequences of any kind. We can also point to the great figures in history who were smokers, like Abraham Lincoln and that chain-smoking Michelangelo. In fact, I understand the vice president's daughter is a smoker.

SPEAKING OF SMOKING...

Let's talk health. Why don't high school cafeterias have smoking sections? Why don't elementary schools have students read books defending smoking, like *Heather Has Two Cigarettes*? Because everyone knows smoking is downright bad for you. What people don't seem to grasp is that homosexual behavior is even *worse*—up to *three times* more dangerous than smoking.

According to the *New England Journal of Medicine*, smoking reduces your life expectancy by "7.3 years for men and 6.0 years for women." On the other hand, studies show that "among gay and bisexual men in Vancouver, the HIV/AIDS epidemic has reduced life expectancy by up to 20 years."[15]

There you have it: *Homosexuality is three times more dangerous than smoking.* Think about that when they insist on teaching it to your children. And that number doesn't even *touch* the other life-threatening risks that studies show are associated with homosexual behavior:

- A twenty-five to thirty-year decrease in life expectancy
- Chronic, potentially fatal liver disease—infectious hepatitis, which increases the risk of liver cancer
- Inevitably fatal immune disease including associated cancers
- Frequently fatal rectal cancer

- Multiple bowel and other infectious diseases
- A much higher than usual incidence of suicide[16]

Apparently it's having a somewhat negative impact abroad, as well. We just sent $15 *billion* of our tax dollars to Africa to fight HIV and AIDS.[17] Yep, what we need is *more* behavior that leads to this kind of widespread disease. I wonder if they'll reveal to the kindergartners that Daddy's roommate has AIDS.

I could write a book solely on the negative consequences of homosexuality, but several have already been written, including *Getting It Straight: What the Research Shows about Homosexuality,* by Peter Sprigg and Timothy Daily of the Family Research Council. In it you can read all the research about the outbreaks of Hepatitis A, B, and C, gonorrhea, syphilis, Gay Bowel Syndrome, anal cancer, and anal and genital warts, just to name a few.

I know what you're thinking: *Yuck.* Really bad stuff happens to the body when you go against its design. And yet we promote this to our kids in school. Another Bible verse comes to mind: "It would be better for him to be thrown into the sea with a millstone tied around his neck than for him to cause one of these little ones to sin" (Luke 17:2).

THE DANGEROUS DUO: PRAYER AND THE BIBLE

According to a *New York Post* editorial, Mildred Rosario, a junior high teacher in the Bronx, talked to her students about God. When a student asked her if a friend who had recently died went to heaven, Mildred comforted the students and led them in prayer. Peter Melzer, a high school teacher in the Bronx, was a member of the pedophile group North American Man/Boy Love Association (NAMBLA). One prays to God and one preys on boys. Guess which one got fired? If you guessed the pedophile, you're wrong. Thanks for playing. The answer is: Mildred Rosario.[18] *You can't pray to God in school, silly.*

Back in 1980, the Supreme Court ordered the public schools to take down the Ten Commandments because kids might "read, venerate [respect], and perhaps obey them." Now a public school teacher near Houston has called the Ten Commandments "hate speech" that might offend other students and ordered a student to throw away his Ten Commandment book covers. Another teacher at the same school sent two girls to the principal for bringing their Bibles to school. The principal then threw the Bibles in the trash and said, "This is garbage."[19]

Public schools have become more than just religion-free zones; now they are religion-hostile zones. In the spring of 2005, the U.S. Supreme Court will hear a Ten Commandments case argued by Attorney General Greg Abbot and Mat Staver of Liberty Counsel. When they hear the case, I wonder if they will glance up to see Moses holding the Ten Commandments engraved above them in their own courtroom.

DO YOU KNOW WHAT YOUR CHILDREN ARE DOING?

A survey released by the Society for Adolescent Medicine indicates that "about 84 percent of parents do not believe that their teenage children have ever had sex, but CDC data show that almost 50 percent of ninth- through 12th-graders ages 14 to 18 are sexually active."[20] And is it any wonder with what they're being taught? Listen to this:

TEACHER HAS KIDS TASTING CONDOMS, NEW MEXICO AUTHORITIES STAND BEHIND HIM

Parent Lisa Gallegos said that when her 15-year-old daughter balked at putting a condom in her mouth, instructor Tony Escudero told her, "Come on, sweetie, have a little fun."

The New Mexico Health Department is standing behind a sex-education teacher in Santa Fe who encouraged ninth-graders to taste flavored condoms.... Also, Gallegos quotes her daughter as saying when a male student expressed his disgust with homosexual activity, Escudero said, "Never say never, because you never know. Someday you might like it that way."[21]

What does the president have to say?

To encourage right choices, we must be willing to confront the dangers young people face—even when they're difficult to talk about. Each year, about 3 million teenagers contract sexually-transmitted diseases that can harm them, or kill them, or prevent them from ever becoming parents. In my budget, I propose a grassroots campaign to help inform families about these medical risks. We will double federal funding for abstinence programs, so schools can teach this fact of life: Abstinence for young people is the…only certain way to avoid sexually-transmitted diseases.[22]

But far from supporting abstinence training, Dr. Mary Calderone, the first president of the Tennessee Sexuality Information and Education Council of the United States (SIECUS), called on educators to prepare children to step into a new world: "To do this, they must pry children away from old views and values, especially from biblical and other traditional forms of sexual morality."[23]

If you don't believe there is a culture war going on, you need to take a look at a taxpayer-funded sex-ed program from the Centers for Disease Control. They produced a nifty little book for the public schools with a very nice-sounding name—*Reducing the Risk.* They're really good at coming up with nice-sounding names. Too bad they usually mean the opposite. Just listen to how they present the option of abstaining from sex:

You could become a hermit, or so unpleasant that everyone stays clear of you. Or you could never become involved in a romantic relationship.[24]

Am I the only one who sees this stuff? The *Reducing the Risk* program teaches your children that the only way to abstain from sex is to become unpleasant hermits—so that everyone stays clear of them! This is what passes for "abstinence education" now. I wonder who does their campaign? Could they create some public service announcements for drug prevention in their free time? "Hey, boys and girls, if you don't want to take drugs, become a hermit! Or so unpleasant that everyone stays clear of you—and never offers you a joint." I think in their off time they're actually busy writing Christian characters for sitcoms and movies.

Here's Planned Parenthood's big complaint:

Abstinence-only programs force-feed students religious ideology that condemns homosexuality, masturbation, abortion, and contraception. In doing so, they endanger students' sexual health.[25]

And what's easier than confronting young people when they engage in harmful behavior? "Support them" in whatever decision they make! This is what actress Sharon Stone said at a United Nations Conference on AIDS and teenage sexuality:

No matter how much we guide our children within our families and within our churches, we are no stronger than the power of sexuality.

The solution is to have parents of teens buy a box of 200 condoms, and put them at a little-used location of the house...but where the teens can find them. That way the kids won't be afraid to ask, and the parents won't know![26]

Their method of throwing condoms at the problem of teen pregnancy has failed miserably. If you want a peek at where that flawed logic will get you, take a look at the same logic at the next level:

Social workers in Winnipeg have begun handing out "high-quality" crack pipes and instructions to addicts on the city's streets, part of a harm-reduction strategy put in place by local health officials.... The kits are not handed out to just anyone who asks, she stressed, but are given to crack cocaine users who have been assessed by trained social workers, who in many cases have had multiple interactions with those users.... Winnipeg's new harm reduction strategy—dubbed the "safer crack use kit."[27]

That's right, boys and girls! Get your free "Safer Crack Use Kit." According to the story, the pipes come with a kit that "includes metal screens, alcohol swabs (for those users who do end up sharing), pipe cleaners, matches, lip balm, at least one condom, and information about where addicts can get help. It also includes instructions on how to use the kit."[28] Yes, smoking crack is illegal and dangerous. But some people are going to do it anyway...so why not *help them* commit illegal, self-destructive acts? *That's what I always say.* I can't believe I'm not making this up. It's actually being done.

"HOW TO BE GAY 101"

If your children manage to make it through high school unscathed, they can always be indoctrinated in college. The University of Michigan offered an English course called "How to Be Gay: Male Homosexuality and Initiation."[29] The course description says, "Just because you happen to be a gay man doesn't mean that you don't have to learn how to become one." It explains that students "will examine a number of cultural artifacts and activities" including "camp, diva-worship, drag, muscle culture, taste, style and political activism."[30] The class also spends time teaching students how to be gay by an in-depth study of interior design, cross-dressing, and Broadway musicals!

A college recruitment class subsidized with your tax dollars and tuition money. Imagine what would happen if the class were "How to Be a Christian 101" or "How to Be Pro-Life 101."

I don't know if they have a lab or not, whether drag study requires cross-dressing participation, or if field trips to gay bars are mandatory, but it seems like a pretty good incentive to pull tax money and children from the University of Michigan.

WANT A DEGREE IN JOURNALISM?
HOMOSEXUAL ACTIVISM REQUIRED

Want to be a journalist? Now you may have to promote homosexuality in order to receive accreditation. The Accrediting Council on Education in Journalism and Mass Communications (ACEJMC), which accredits journalism departments at 104 colleges, is adding sexual orientation to the diversity standard, according to Susanne Shaw, ACEJMC Executive Director.

Not surprisingly, the Lesbian and Gay Journalists Association became a member of the council last year, and according to James Bruce, a professor at an accredited school in Tennessee, a "splinter group" of homosexual activists within the council pushed for the changes. What will happen to those schools that refuse to bow to the homosexual agenda for their accreditation? Shaw said, "I am a little premature when I say that they won't lose their accreditation."[31]

You betcha they'll lose it! That's why the standards were altered—to make everyone comply *or else.* You think the news is biased now, just wait until the mandatory bias shows up in your hometown paper. And it will. Unless this biased "standard" is changed, you can count on it.

STUDENTS' RIGHTS

What's the answer? First, students need to know their rights and the freedoms we have in spite of all those that have already been stripped away. As of October 2004, these freedoms *still exist* in America—despite the harassment and threats you may receive for exercising them. You do not lose your First Amendment rights when you walk through the door of a public school. According to Federal court rulings, here are ten things you still have the freedom to do:

"THE STUDENT'S FREEDOM TO BELIEVE"

1. Freedom to bring your Bible to school
2. Freedom to meet with other students for prayer, Bible study, and worship

3. Freedom to share your faith on campus
4. Freedom to engage in voluntary school prayer
5. Freedom to hand out religious tracts on campus
6. Freedom to present school projects from a religious perspective
7. Freedom to wear religious T-shirts, symbols, and buttons at school
8. Freedom to study and practice religious holidays on campus
9. Freedom to have religious clubs on campus on an equal basis with other extra-curricular clubs
10. Freedom to live out your religious faith

Should any of these freedoms be put in jeopardy, you can go to www.f2a.org and find any number of people who will represent you for *free*. Groups like The AFA Center for Law and Policy, Liberty Counsel, the Alliance Defense Fund, the Pacific Justice Institute, and Thomas More Legal Center. They're all there in one place. Convenient, huh?

PUTTING SCHOOLS ON LEGAL NOTICE

Faith2Action partner Citizens for Community Values (CCV) has one of the best proactive solutions for protecting the 90 percent of American kids who attend public schools. We know homosexuality is three times more dangerous than smoking, and yet they are promoting it in the schools. What happens when one of these public school guinea pigs "tries it" as he's been prompted to do? What happens if he contracts HIV/AIDS, Hepatitis A, B, or C, gonorrhea, syphilis, Gay Bowel Syndrome, anal cancer, and/or anal and genital warts?

How about we take a page from the ACLU playbook? If Johnnie comes into harm's way because of what your school has taught him, *you can sue*. In fact, I'm convinced that *a lot* of little Johnnies have been harmed because they listened to what they were force-fed. And in case you didn't know, that's against the law. Yep. In every state there are laws that protect minors from being exposed to information that's harmful to them. But rather than wait for more children to be victimized and suffer the consequences of homosexual behavior, I say we act *now!*

CCV put every school board member/president/superintendent in Ohio *on legal notice* that should a child come into harm's way as a result of the homosexual agenda being taught at school, *they* will be held legally accountable.

How about that? Accountability for their actions. There's a concept. This needs to happen in every single state. If you're interested in protecting your kids, CCV will do the same for your state. Contact Faith2Action or go to www.f2a.org, and link to them directly. All it takes are the financial resources to customize the letters by state by coordinating with state laws that deal with protecting minors. Along with a legal opinion customized by state, every school board member in the remaining forty-nine states needs to receive the independent research revealing the dangerous consequences of homosexual acts. That way school board members and school superintendents will be armed with everything they need to *prevent* the homosexual agenda from being further promoted.

Joel Belz, publisher of *World* magazine, has a dream. He points to a generation ago, when 90 percent of America got its news from the big three: ABC, NBC, and CBS. No longer the case. However, while many Christians attend Christian and private schools and are homeschooled, 90 percent of America's children are still in public schools. If one monopoly can be broken, surely another can, as well.[32] This matters because, as Lincoln said, "The philosophy of the school room in one generation will be the philosophy of government in the next."

Chapter 10

ESSENTIAL HISTORY

T hough liberal judges and the ACLU haven't *yet* taken a bottle of Wite-Out to our historical documents, you know they'd like to. Bummer for them, the documents are heavily guarded and under glass. But they're doing all they can to keep them from being seen and implemented:

- A California teacher has been forbidden to show his students the Declaration of Independence because it refers to God.[1]
- Federal judge Jennifer Coffman actually declared the *Constitution* unconstitutional! She ordered that an "offensive" school exhibit that included our national motto (In God We Trust), the Declaration of Independence, the Mayflower Compact, proclamations by Presidents Lincoln and Reagan, and the Preamble of the Constitution of Kentucky be removed.[2]

Just what our Founding Fathers would have wanted, to be sure. You see, in this battle for our nation and our freedom, there are two sides. And just so you're clear, we're on the side of everything upon which our nation was founded: life, liberty, freedom of speech, and freedom of religion, just to name a few. We're the ones who believe that the Constitution's meaning and purpose don't change with the whims of judges. (Kind of like the Bible. We believe it says something explicit despite our desires to the contrary. A critical distinction for our future.)

So what does this all-important document really say? Can Johnny say God's name in school, or can't he?

WHAT THE CONSTITUTION REALLY SAYS

The First Amendment says *Congress* can't impose on our right of free exercise of religion: *"Congress* shall make no law respecting an establishment of religion or prohibiting the free exercise thereof." It doesn't say that Johnny can't pray in school or put a manger scene in the public square. It says what *Congress* can't do!

As George Washington so eloquently stated, "If I could entertain the slightest apprehension that the Constitution framed in the Convention, where I had the honor to preside, might possibly endanger the religious rights of any ecclesiastical Society, certainly I would never have placed my signature to it."[3]

Washington happened to be fairly knowledgeable about the Constitution because he presided over the Constitutional Convention, thereby overseeing the entire process from beginning to end. If he thought it was a threat to any rights at all—any religious freedoms—he wouldn't have signed the thing!

James Madison was the chief architect of the Constitution. Here's what he said to the Virginia Convention on July 12, 1788: "There is not a shadow of a right in the federal government to intermeddle with religion."[4] Incidentally, Madison also declared, "Religion [is] the basis and foundation of Government."[5]

WOW, THE ACLU BETTER HOPE THAT NEVER GETS OUT!

Okay. So there's no separation of church and state in the Constitution that limits the freedom of Americans to exercise their beliefs. The First Amendment says that Congress can't infringe on our religious freedoms. So

THE CRIMINALIZATION OF CHRISTIANITY

where does this "constitutional separation" come from? Maybe from Fisher Ames, the guy who was responsible for and introduced the original wording of the First Amendment in the House of Representatives. It must have been him, right? Otherwise our nation might have ended up with something as horrible as Bibles in public schools.

History reveals, however, that Fisher Ames actually spent a good portion of his life fighting to make the Bible a prominent book in public schools. He feared that the Bible was losing its importance in the schools. In 1801 he gave some clear insight into his position: "Should not the Bible regain the place it once held as a school book? Its morals are pure, its examples captivating and noble."[6]

One hundred years later, in their 1892 decision *Holy Trinity v. United States*, the Supreme Court cited eighty-seven precedents from the Founding Fathers, acts of the Founding Fathers, and acts of Congress and state governments proving that this nation was founded upon Christian principles. They could have cited a whole bunch more, but I guess they thought eighty-seven precedents were enough.

The Court's unanimous opinion stated, "These, and many other matters which might be noticed, add a volume of unofficial declarations to the mass of organic utterances that this is a Christian nation."[7]

That could really hurt an ACLU fund-raising letter.

So we've heard from the Constitution itself, the president of the Constitutional Convention, the chief architect of the Constitution, the congressman who wrote the specific language of the First Amendment, and the Supreme Court a hundred years later. Nowhere have we seen anything about protecting government from the church. Just the opposite.

What about Thomas Jefferson? He was in France at the time the Constitution was ratified and had nothing to do with it. But if you snoop around in his private letters, maybe you can find something he said that might be construed as a means to keep those Christians quiet.

The Danbury Baptists had heard some troubling rumors that a "national denomination" might be selected. They wanted to make sure the government wasn't intending to get involved in the establishment of a national denomination. In his private response to the Danbury Baptists, Jefferson wrote:

> I contemplate in solemn reverence the act of the whole American people which declared that their legislature should make no law respecting the establishment of religion or prohibiting free exercise thereof, thus building a wall of separation between the church and state.[8]

It is clear by the context that Jefferson's "wall of separation" was to protect the church from the state. This is the same guy who in the Kentucky Resolutions of 1798 said, "No power over the freedom of religion [is] delegated to the United States by the Constitution."[9]

Did you catch that? The United States has *no power* over the freedom of religion. No power. Maybe the proaborts and the ACLU would better understand their "separation" hero Thomas Jefferson if they read more than one private letter taken out of context.

I don't know how it could be any clearer. You have the freedom to exercise your religious beliefs and speak out as you see fit, and there's nothing the government can do about it—at least not according to the original intent of the Founding Fathers, the Constitution, the First Amendment, and the Supreme Court for the first 170 years after the birth of this nation. How about a direct message from the father of our nation, George Washington? In the Farewell Address he said, "Do not anyone claim to be a true American if they ever attempt to remove religion from politics." Wow, not only can you exercise your religious freedom, but you can even do it in politics. What do you know?

One of the first acts of the first Congress was to establish chaplains for the U.S. House and Senate. It was clear that there was no "impregnable wall," as has been proclaimed. It stands to reason that the Founding Fathers knew better what they intended when they ratified the Constitution than those in the twenty-first century who seek to undo it. If they meant for Christians not to influence public policy, they themselves would have had to step down from office!

Supreme Court Justice Antonin Scalia shed some light on why the current courts seem to have such a problem with this issue:

> Church and state would not be such a difficult subject if religion were, as the Court apparently thinks it to be, some purely personal avocation that can be indulged entirely in secret, like pornography, in the privacy of one's room. For most believers it is not that and has never been.[10]

GAG RULE FOR CHURCHES

If there is no separation of church and state that prohibits churches from exercising all their freedoms and influence in the public square, where did the gag rule for churches come in?

In 1954, Senator Lyndon B. Johnson (D-TX), was angry at some churches who opposed him. He thought he would teach them a lesson by legislating a gag rule for them and every other church in America. He offered an amendment that permanently extended the reach of the Internal Revenue Service into our nation's churches, parachurches, and nonprofit organizations. The amendment was accepted unanimously without debate.

"Since that time," said Congressman Walter B. Jones (R-NC), "the IRS has turned the 501(c)(3) code-section on its head in an attempt to punish pastors" for "communicating the principles of their faith during an election period." So Congressman Jones, along with colleagues House Majority Whip Tom DeLay (R-TX) and John Hostetler (R-IN), introduced the Houses of Worship Political Speech Protection Act, which would free churches to exercise their First Amendment freedoms just like everyone else.[11] If you care about restoring freedom to our churches, this bill *must be passed.*

Supporters of the act also note that while many churches—including those that support proabortion candidates—are active politically, there is a real double standard regarding pro-family churches. After attending Mass (and taking communion) at St. James Catholic Church in North Miami,

John Kerry attended a Baptist church where Pastor Gaston E. Smith went on the campaign trail for John Kerry: "For every Goliath, God has a David," he said. "For every Calvary's cross, God has a Christ Jesus. To bring our country out of despair, discouragement, despondency and disgust, God has a John Kerry."[12]

Kerry's agenda, it seems, is perfectly fine to promote in church. But ask people in church to vote in accordance with the Bible? That'll get you reported to the IRS. Like Pastor Ronnie Floyd, of First Baptist Church in Springdale, Arkansas, who came under fire because of "church snitches" who monitored his July 4 sermon. Floyd told Faith2Action listeners what we all need to hear: "It's time for evangelical America to wake up, because we are in a war!" As he told Fox News on July 31, he was not going to back down from telling his congregation to "vote God, His Ways, His will, His Word."[13] Saying "controversial" things like that will get you reported to the government.

Barry Lynn of the Americans United for Separation of Church and State is sending people to churches to videotape sermons for any "irregularities" and report them to the IRS. Lynn is joined by the so-called Mainstream Coalition, which has about a hundred volunteers monitoring churches to see whether pastors are abiding by federal laws governing political activity by nonprofit institutions.[14]

And not surprisingly, these people have also come after Reverend Jerry Falwell, attempting to silence him even from speaking as a private citizen. It's all part of a "scare-the-churches campaign," said Falwell, who is no stranger to attack.[15] Those tactics don't work against men of courage, but they do tend to scare everyone else. That's why the Houses of Worship Political Speech Protection Act is so necessary to protect the First Amendment rights of churches.

Rest assured, they will try anything they can to keep you on the sidelines. If the "constitutional separation of church and state" doesn't do the trick, they will try something else—like threats and intimidation. Even "monitors" sitting in your church, taping sermons to report to the government. *Are you ready to put your faith to action yet?*

STARK HISTORICAL SIMILARITIES

As we look back at our history, there are lessons that are far more recent. What happens when we don't follow those principles of freedom of speech and religion upon which our nation was founded?

We all know the most horrific modern example of *what* can happen— the Holocaust—but it wasn't until I visited the Holocaust museum in Washington, DC, that I gained a greater understanding of *how* it can happen.

I felt a chill as I witnessed a video presentation of the laws that were passed in pre–World War II Germany. One after another, law after law appeared on the screen along with the dates they were passed. Afterward, I bought Michael Berenbaum's *The World Must Know*, which describes the first of these laws:

> On April 7, 1933, it dismissed all non-Aryans from civil service, including notaries and teachers in state schools. It was the first of 400 separate pieces of legislation enacted between 1933 and 1939 that defined, isolated, excluded, segregated, and impoverished German Jews.[16]

So German Jews couldn't become teachers in state schools? Christians in Canada were told the same thing. The British Columbia College of Teachers denied Trinity Western University accreditation because of what they called "discriminatory" practices based on the pledge students make that they will not take part in activities the Bible condemns, including homosexual behavior. If you follow what the Bible says, they contended, you were not fit to teach school. The Supreme Court of Canada later overturned the decision, allowing Christian graduates to become public school teachers after all.[17] *For now.*

There are other parallels. Hitler turned Christmas and Easter into pagan holidays. Christmas became a pagan festival, and at least for the SS troops, its date was changed to December 21, the date of the winter solstice. Carols and nativity plays were banned from schools in 1938, and the name of Christmas was changed to Yuletide. Crucifixes were eliminated from classrooms, and

Easter was turned into a holiday that heralded the arrival of spring. Carols and nativity plays were banned from schools.[18] Does any of this sound familiar? Let me know when you get back from "spring break."

Signs saying "*Juden Unerwunscht,*" (Jews Unwelcome) were posted in public facilities, shops, theaters, restaurants, hotels, and pharmacies. Jews were forbidden to sit on public park benches and relegated to benches labeled "For Jews Only."[19] But *we* would never do anything like that today. How about an ad that ran in the *Village Voice* specifically stating "No Christians"?[20]

The seemingly "harmless" beginnings of the Holocaust started with negative representations of Jewish people in such things as political cartoons depicting them as rats (making it easier to "exterminate" them). Christians today are the subject of such negativity. A political cartoon (which you can see in my first book, *True to Life*) pictures Christians as rats pulling the Republican elephant into the "faith mission" with the quote, "You're being saved, like it or not." If only those pesky Christian rats would leave the Republican Party alone. Serves them right—just what do they think they're *doing* trying to influence public policy like that?

We've seen what happens when you refer to people as a disease. Nazi Propaganda Minister Joseph Goebbels said: "Some day Europe will perish of the Jewish disease."[21] In 1996, evolutionist Richard Dawkins was named Humanist of the Year by the American Humanist Association (past winners include Faye Wattleton and Ted Turner). In his acceptance speech, he compared the threat of AIDS and "mad cow disease" to the threat posed by faith. So faith is now a disease? According to Dawkins, faith is "one of the world's great evils, comparable to the smallpox virus but harder to eradicate."[22]

Eradicate. That's an interesting word. Kind of like *exterminate* and *eliminate.* Excuse me, but I thought humanists preached tolerance. Yet Dawkins still hasn't been admonished by his fellow humanists. Their "solution" seems *final.*

Historically, after ridicule, demonization, censorship, and discrimination comes persecution. In Germany, the call came for a *final solution.* There are lots of ways to implement a final solution. Gas chambers are one. Lions are another. Reggie Rivers of the *Rocky Mountain Times* wrote:

I can periodically understand the frustration and general fatigue that compelled the Romans to throw select Christians to the lions. It's not just that the lions were hungry; it was that the Romans were tired of listening to the self-righteous babbling of Christians who claimed to be experts on everything and had egos the size of…well, God.[23]

Send Christians to the lions. There's a suggestion.

In 1937, all Jewish property was registered. In 1938, all Jewish businesses that still existed were "Aryanized."[24] In 2003, the state of California passed Assembly Bill 17 (Chapter 752, Statutes of 2003), which requires that all employers who do business with the state provide domestic partnership benefits (like those afforded to spouses) for contracts of at least $100,000.[25] This effectively cut out Christian businesses that cannot morally comply with subsidizing relationships (homosexual or unmarried heterosexual) the Bible refers to as sin.

As I mentioned earlier, Christians in California can now also be put out of business with a single lawsuit based on the "Hey, Mister, Nice Dress Law," which forces business owners to shell out $150,000 for the "crime" of firing a man who comes to work wearing a dress.

In the thirties, crosses in German classrooms were replaced with pictures of Hitler. In August 1995, Germany's Constitutional Court ruled that crosses must be removed from public classrooms in overwhelmingly Catholic Bavaria, despite a state law vast public support for having crucifixes in classrooms.[26] See any crosses in public schools in America today? *Didn't think so.*

Dr. Joseph Goebbels "controlled the flow of public information through the press, radio, and film," and "those who listened to foreign broadcasts…were then subject to arrest."[27] Just like in Canada, where government officials have banned Fox News while approving the anti-American, anti-Semitic Al-Jazeera.[28] What's more, says Canadian writer Marni Soupcoff, if you're found viewing Fox News, you are…subject to arrest:

> Last year, the Canadian Supreme Court ruled that unscrambling foreign satellite signals (read transmissions of…"The O'Reilly

Factor" on Fox News) is against the law. And I don't mean against the law in the way that littering is against the law, with violations punished by sternly disapproving looks from elderly fellow citizens. The Royal Canadian Mounted Police (RCMP) are actually actively engaged in raiding satellite television shops, seizing DirecTV satellite equipment, and hanging onto it for months before finally levying charges of "conspiracy to sell and distribute American satellite systems."[29]

And just as the Nazis had "block wardens who monitored their neighbors," waiters who reported on their patrons, workers who made note of employer violations, government officials who monitored church activity, and children who reported on their parents, the trend continues.[30]

Remember the junior "thought police" in West Virginia and elsewhere who have been trained to do the very same thing—listen in and report any speech "violations" to law enforcement officials? What are they looking for? Anything that violates the homosexual agenda, including "homophobic slurs."[31] Did you ever think you'd live in a country where people attend church to take notes and report the sermon contents to government officials? Hitler's Germany even had an agreement with the church that it was not to "meddle in politics."[32] Ring any bells?

The laws in Germany between 1933 and 1939 "defined, isolated, excluded, segregated, and impoverished" German Jews. If you'll take a peek back at the previous chapters, you'll see even more similarities with American laws today. I don't know about you, but I would rather use my freedoms to speak out about where this trend is going than wait for our rights to be taken away.

We must never forget the warning from Pastor Martin Neimoller, a survivor of a Nazi concentration camp:

In Germany they came first for the Communists, and I didn't speak up because I wasn't a Communist. Then they came for the Jews, and I didn't speak up because I wasn't a Jew. Then they came for the trade unionists, and I didn't speak up because I wasn't a trade unionist.

Then they came for the Catholics, and I didn't speak up because I was a Protestant. Then they came for Me, and by that time no one was left to speak up.[33]

The good news is that evil can be and *has* been overcome. Ronald Reagan said:

I have seen the rise and fall of Nazi tyranny, the subsequent Cold War, and the nuclear nightmare that for fifty years haunted the dreams of children everywhere. During that time my generation defeated totalitarianism. As a result, your world is poised for better tomorrows. What will you do on your journey?[34]

A REMINDER

There are some self-evident truths we have lost sight of. Maybe this reminder from the Declaration of Independence would be good:

We hold these truths to be self-evident, that all men are created equal, that they are endowed by their Creator with certain unalienable rights, that among these are life, liberty and the pursuit of happiness. That to secure these rights, governments are instituted....

Our Founding Fathers said it was self-evident. Obvious, common sense, a no-brainer. But just so no one would miss it, they decided to write it down. I for one am glad they did. Because as truth has been replaced by tolerance, we have lost sight of what was once self-evident: "We are endowed by our *Creator*"—*not* by the state, *not* by the courts, but by our God. He's the one who gave us our inalienable rights—our liberty, our freedom of religion, and our freedom of speech.

Despite all that has happened to the contrary, *inalienable* still means absolute, undeniable, the kind of rights that can't be taken away. If the state had given us those rights, then the state could also take them away. But our rights come from God, so it doesn't matter *where* you live on this globe, those rights belong to you. "All men are created equal," after all. Freedom belongs to mankind, not just Americans.

I heard this idea somewhere else not too long ago. In his 2004 State of the Union address, President George W. Bush said, "Americans are a free people, who know that freedom is the right of every person and the future of every nation. The liberty we prize is not America's gift to the world, it is God's gift to humanity."[35]

When students in China got hold of that idea, it sparked something deep inside them, something etched on every human heart: a longing to be free. And for that freedom, they stood against all odds. For two months they stood in Tiananmen Square protesting the evil that would ultimately silence their cry for liberty.[36] And when the Chinese army, riding in tanks and armed with automatic weapons, rolled into Tiananmen Square and took aim at hundreds of freedom lovers, those students were holding our Declaration of Independence in their hands.[37]

That's that same Declaration of Independence that American teachers are told they can't show their students. I wonder if those students are forbidden from looking at their lunch money—it mentions God, too. By the way, if anyone *else* is offended by it, feel free to send that "objectionable" currency my way.

And next time you're standing at the beginning of a baseball game, think about this—the last verse of our National Anthem (the one you never hear sung):

O thus be it ever when free men shall stand
Between their loved home and the war's desolation!
Blest with victory and peace, *may the heav'n-rescued land*
Praise the Power that hath made and preserved us a nation!
Then conquer we must, when our cause it is just,
And this be our motto: *"In God is our trust!"*
And the star-spangled banner in triumph shall wave
O'er the land of the free and the home of the brave!

THE CRIMINALIZATION OF CHRISTIANITY

They still haven't stripped away all those nasty reminders of how and why our country was founded. It seems our Founding Fathers also knew how we might forget. That's why they also wrote things in stone. We would do well to remember them—we've seen what happens when they're lost.

Chapter 11

LESSONS FROM REAGAN

Let us renew our faith and our hope.
We have every right to dream heroic dreams.

RONALD REAGAN, FIRST INAUGURAL ADDRESS

D o you know where you were Friday, November 2, 1984? I was listening to President Ronald Reagan speak in Cleveland, Ohio. I had just cut a class, despite being sternly warned of the stiff repercussions, including having my grade for the class dropped by one letter.

Yet on that November day, while my fellow students went to class, my mom and I stood out in the cold holding signs. Even then the opposition tried to prevent us from exercising our First Amendment rights. Some busybody told us to take our signs down. When we refused, she suggested that they were in some way "illegal." We firmly stated our right to free speech, which didn't change with the volume of her voice. A man behind us overheard the exchange

171

and handed us his card. He was a lawyer ready to defend us. Rather prophetic, don't you think? On a full-page spread about the rally, two signs stood out in the crowd of faces: "Pro-Life Pro-Reagan" (mine) and "God Country Reagan" (my mom's).[1]

Ronald Reagan told us it was morning in America. He said the best was yet to come. And after four years of progress, he declared, "You ain't seen nothing yet." He was right. We saw the end of Soviet communism. We saw the Berlin Wall come down. We saw freedom triumph over oppression. Just like he said it would.

On that day I learned many things, including how to stand up to those who want to silence me and how one person can make a difference. I never for a moment regretted cutting class to hear Ronald Reagan speak. I wonder if any of my classmates who were afraid to miss class can now recall even a single word they heard on November 2, 1984.

TWENTY YEARS LATER

Fast-forward twenty years to May 17, 2004—a date that will live in infamy. That was the day the Massachusetts Superior Court, by a one-judge margin, redefined what marriage had been in every culture, every religion, for more than five thousand years of recorded history.

On that day we knew what was coming—what had already taken place— the effort to export these fraudulent "marriages" to every state in the country. I watched as agenda-driven public officials tried to impose it in San Francisco, Oregon, New Mexico, and New York. *Just to name a few.* And then courts like the one in Washington State ruled their state Defense of Marriage Law "unconstitutional."

May 17, 2004, was the day I started writing this book and the same day I...*quit writing.* Seriously, how much more could we possibly take? *I was tired. Overwhelmed. Battle-weary.* But then something happened to my attitude. I remembered the life of a great man—Ronald Wilson Reagan.

When Reagan died on June 5, like the rest of the country, I remembered him. As I soaked up every scene from his life, I remembered the greatest president of modern times and what he stood for. The valiant defender of life and freedom who in his first inaugural address urged us "to dream heroic dreams."

Heroic dreams? I asked myself. It had been a long time since I'd had those—we were getting clobbered down here. We were doing all we could just to *survive.* There was no time for heroic dreams. If we could just hang onto our freedoms a little longer, maybe our children could still grow up to know them.

But Ronald Reagan didn't set out to just *survive* the Cold War. He set out to *win* it. I believe the same thing applies to the cultural war. You can't win a war if all you know is defense. It seems as though we've been bailing water for so long that we've forgotten why we set sail in the first place. When you're in "survival mode," you don't have time to dream heroic dreams. Reagan embodied hope when the world looked grim. He was an optimist when there wasn't a lot to be optimistic about. *I was starting to remember.*

In his remarks at a White House reception for women appointees of the administration on February 10, 1982, Reagan put it this way:

> It's hard when you're up to your armpits in alligators to remember you came here to drain the swamp.[2]

"Alligator defense" has distracted us from our mission. We came to drain the swamp. We have been reacting, responding, and defending for so long that we've forgotten our mission. We've been changing the boundary markers on a shrinking piece of real estate for so long that we've forgotten that our goal was to "take the land."

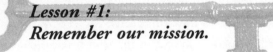

Lesson #1:
Remember our mission.

When the alligators were everywhere, Reagan remembered what he came to do. He stood for freedom and the strong defense that ensured it. But you may be among the skeptics who think the collapse of the Soviet Union was just a "coincidence" and had nothing to do with the policies of Ronald Reagan. Strobe Talbott is one of those. On the talk show *Inside Washington* he said:

The Soviet Union collapsed: the Cold War ended almost overwhelmingly because of internal contradictions or pressures within the Soviet Union and the Soviet system itself. And even if Jimmy Carter had been elected and been followed by Walter Mondale, something like what we have now seen probably would have happened.[3]

Really? That's not what former Soviet officials think. Oleg Kalugin, a former KGB general put it this way: "American Policy in the 1980s was a catalyst for the collapse of the Soviet Union." Yevgenny Novikov, senior staff member of the Soviet Communist Party Central Committee, said the Reagan polices "were a major factor in the demise of the Soviet system." Former Soviet Foreign Minister Aleksandr Bessmertnykh told Princeton conference attendees that programs like the Strategic Defense Initiative accelerated the decline of the Soviet Union.[4]

THAT WAS THEN...

Reagan knew the difference between good and evil: Communism is evil and freedom is good. Not hard. The difference was that he wasn't afraid to say it. I know what you're thinking. Calling evil *evil* was a lot easier back in Reagan's day. *Really?*

Let's go back well before the eighties and get a glimpse of what it was like. Reagan got an early taste of communism when, according to Soviet intelligence files, unions and organizations made attempts to take over Hollywood with the financial support of the Communist Party. Kirk Douglas recalled the event: "Thousands of people fought in the middle of the street with knives, clubs, battery cables, brass knuckles, and chains."[5] Ronald Reagan defiantly passed through the lines of communist picketers instead of sneaking through the storm drain, as security advised him.

Lesson #2: Hold on to the clear distinctions between good and evil.

Told to lie down on the floor of the shuttle so he wouldn't get hit with a flying Coke bottle or rock, Reagan refused. "A bus would pass through the human throng of violent picketers, with a solitary figure seated upright inside." Nor did he back down when the threatening calls started. One person told him he would never make films again. Another said if he continued to oppose the communist-backed strike, "a squad" would disfigure his face with acid.[6]

Reagan hired guards for his children and, looking over his shoulder, continued the stand. But even many of his "friends" turned on him. He later recalled an encounter with a previously friendly colleague: "My smile was already forming and I had just started to get them when one of the two thrust his face close to mine, his eyes burning with hatred. 'Fascist!' he hissed, literally spitting the words at me."[7]

Hmmm. Sounds kind of like the way things are now, doesn't it?

Jack Warner pointed to Reagan as a "tower of strength, not only for the actors but for the whole industry." Columnist Hedda Hopper stated that Ronald Reagan, through calmness and confidence, had "commanded the respect of his most bitter opponents."[8]

Communist backers in Hollywood saw Reagan's influence as a key reason for their defeat. Actor Sterling Hayden, a member of the Communist Party at the time, later testified before Congress about the strike and how the communists tried to paralyze the entertainment industry and take over the unions. Explaining why their efforts failed, Hayden said they had run into Reagan, "who was a one-man battalion."[9]

This is the kind of courage we saw in the White House. A man who stood against threats, violence, and all odds was a man who, unlike most national leaders, could stand up against criticism.

"EVIL EMPIRE"

On March 8, 1983, Reagan gave his famous "evil empire" speech. The original draft said, "I believe that communism is another sad, bizarre chapter in human history whose last pages even now are being written."[10] When his speechwriter, Tony Dolan, sent him the draft, Reagan took out his pen and made it even stronger. It went from, "surely historians will see they are the focus of evil in the modern world," to "they are the focus of evil in the modern world."[11] The words *evil empire* were removed *three times*—and Reagan reinserted them three times.[12]

Lesson #3: Stand boldly for good and against evil.

As expected, the media fallout was brutal. It reminds me of the time I was upset about a profile the *New York Times* ran about me. A friend gave me some very good advice: "Want to know the difference between Richard Nixon and Ronald Reagan, Janet? Richard Nixon *cared* what the *New York Times* wrote about him."

The *New York Times* called Reagan's "evil empire" speech "simplistic" and "sectarian," while *Time* magazine proclaimed that it couldn't possibly be taken seriously because of the "pure ideology."[13] Others on Capitol Hill ranted about how relations with Moscow would be set back. In the midst of all the finger pointing and criticism following the speech, yet *another* "seasoned diplomat" accused Reagan of undoing "twenty years of diplomatic relations."[14]

Watch this. Most everyone else would have caved and buckled under the criticism. I *love* what Reagan did next. "What did twenty years get you?" he responded. "A stronger Soviet Union and a weaker America."[15]

Reagan. He knew what he believed and he knew why. And all the criticism in the world wouldn't change that. Or his course of action.

While the liberal press was condemning Reagan, something else was going on that nobody could have imagined. Behind the Iron Curtain, people

THE CRIMINALIZATION OF CHRISTIANITY

were having a different reaction. In dark, damp prison cells, Russian political prisoners began to tap on walls and quietly repeat through toilets Reagan's words of inspiration. Word was spreading. So was hope. Natan Sharansky, who was one of them, "remembers feeling energized and emboldened."[16] Freedom's message was being heard, giving hope to those who knew its value more than most.

Reagan knew there was a titanic battle going on between good and evil. And he knew which side he was on. A month before the Geneva Summit, Reagan was in the presidential helicopter with New Hampshire Governor John Sununu. As they flew over Manchester, he said, "What I'd really like to do with Mikhail Gorbachev is to pick any house down there and introduce him to the 'working people' of America. I'd like to ask him to compare our way of life with that of the Soviet Union."[17]

KNOW WHEN NOT TO MINCE WORDS

Unashamedly, unapologetic, undaunted by the odds, the criticism, and the battle ahead, Reagan stated his case, fought, and eventually won the battle for freedom. He spoke directly and not with "politically correct" euphemisms. At the Geneva Summit, after some ice-breaking jokes, Ronald Reagan spoke directly to Gorbachev: "Let me tell you, Mr. General Secretary, why we fear you and why we *despise* your system."[18]

That was the system that fell. And that was the guy who attended Reagan's funeral. Maybe there is something to speaking directly and acting decisively.

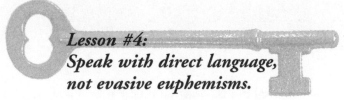

Lesson #4:
Speak with direct language,
not evasive euphemisms.

I hate it when I hear our people using the opposition's rhetoric. Euphemisms like "pro-choice" to describe child dismemberment and "tolerance" and "diversity" to describe the destruction of marriage and "hate crimes" to describe unequal justice. It must stop. Reagan spoke directly. When a reporter asked him what he thought of the Berlin Wall, his answer was, "It's as ugly as the idea behind it."[19] And he didn't care who heard it.

I'm feeling inspired. That's what I think of that fictitious "wall of separation" that's been used to incarcerate Christians. The only wall that exists in our Constitution is one that keeps *the state* out of the church. And following Reagan's lead, I say to the courts, the schools, and the legislatures: "Tear down this wall!"

Reagan was right. It's time to put freedom on the offensive again.

FREEDOM ON THE OFFENSIVE

If there is one lesson Christians can learn from Reagan, it's that freedom must be pursued. England's former Prime Minister Margaret Thatcher toasted President Reagan, praising him *"for putting freedom on the offensive where it belongs."*[20]

You see, Reagan didn't just talk about it. He did something about it. He commissioned his cabinet to spread the ideas of freedom to Eastern Europe and to dissident groups behind the Iron Curtain. "Project Democracy" was not to simply protect freedom, but to advance it. Reagan's friend Charles Wick, who had direct access to the president, managed the *Voice of America*, which beamed radio broadcasts into the Soviet bloc. Getting the truth to those behind the Curtain was crucial. It's just as essential to get the truth out to our troops in the cultural war. That's what Christian and conservative radio does.

Lesson #5:
Stay on the offensive.

But troops also need funds. The National Endowment for Democracy (NED) was created in the early eighties to provide money for oversees organizations working to develop democracies in countries around the world. In Poland, there were already government and private efforts to support solidarity, including trade unions, Catholic charities, and Polish ethnic organizations, which, along with the CIA, were sending money and supplies. NED provided funds for food, clothing, and medicine for Polish political prisoners and their families. It also funded books and materials that could be smuggled into Poland and help reduce the government control over information.

Do you see the Reagan model? If we want to win the battle for the future of our country, we need to do more than proclaim the truth; we must put it on the offensive. We must advance with our own *Voice of America* and National Endowment for Democracy, rushing supplies and funds to those fighting the battle in remote areas and behind enemy lines.

As we saw with regard to communism, when the government controls information, none of us are free. If they can control freedom of speech, we will lose our freedom of religion. This book will not be legal in Sweden. It will not be permitted in parts, if not all, of Canada. And if the current trend continues and what I'm saying is true, it could even be challenged in our own courts. But if America is informed, freedom has a chance. If we can send supplies and fund the pockets of resistance, the fight for freedom will prevail. Just like it did under Reagan.

KNOW WHEN TO LAUGH

Ronald Reagan was not overcome by evil, even when it seemed insurmountable. God gifted him with a wit and wisdom that left his opponents tongue-tied. When he was attacked, he used his famous humor. I can still see the gleam in his eye when he looked at the press "loaded for bear" and, as one reporter said, "flicked them off his sleeve," as in this exchange between Sam Donaldson and Reagan at a press conference in 1982:

> "Mr. President, in talking about the continuing recession tonight, you have blamed the mistakes of the past and you've blamed Congress. Does any of the blame belong to you?"

> "Yes, because for many years I was a Democrat."[21]

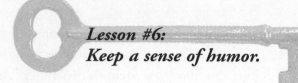

Lesson #6:
Keep a sense of humor.

He's the guy who after he was shot told his wife, Nancy, "I forgot to duck." The one who told the surgeons, "I hope you're all Republicans." And when hooked up to all the equipment following surgery scribbled to Nancy, "All things considered, I'd rather be in Philadelphia." Other notes said: "If I had this much attention in Hollywood, I would have stayed there" and "Send me to LA, where I can see the air I'm breathing" and "Winston Churchill said nothing so exhilarating as to be shot at without result."[22]

STAY THE COURSE

Reagan lived his statement of principle:

> A leader, once convinced a particular course of action is the right one, must have the determination to stick with it and be undaunted when the going gets rough.[23]

I have seen the downfall of many governors, congressional, and state leaders who run on principle, only to cave into the perceived "sound reason" to keep their power. Ask former president George H. W. Bush how he feels about being talked into the "necessity" of a "tax increase" after running against one. If you don't want to listen to what he has to say, you can "read his lips."

Lesson #7: Stand on
principle, not opinion.

It is an epidemic problem in the Republican Party. Some Republicans are so afraid of losing "power" that they back down from every principle that got them into office—just in case it might offend the opposition, who were never with them to begin with. I have campaigned for, worked for, raised money for, and had these people to my home. They include U.S. Senators who ended up voting for outrageous affronts to our freedoms like hate crimes (or thought crimes legislation) and *against* state marriage referendums. It's enough to make you want to forget the whole process. If there hadn't been men of principle like Ronald Reagan, I might have done just that.

Surrounded by naysayers, most people cave. They don't know what they believe or why. They don't have the resolve to stand against those who make popular and seemingly logical arguments, who say there is no other way but the "obvious" solution agreed upon by "everyone." Reagan was one of the few who weren't turned by the counsel of men or afraid to stand alone. And he was one of the few who could actually allow people who strongly disagreed with his philosophy into his inner circle of counselors and not cave into their "demands."

WHAT TO DO WITH FEAR

Reagan overcame the major objection of the time, best demonstrated by an anti-nuclear banner displayed in Germany that stated simply: "I am afraid."[24] Dick Cheney said it this way: "Terrorist attacks are not caused by the use of strength. They are invited by the perception of weakness."[25] He is right. The text of one of the anti-Kerry bumper stickers that found its way to my e-mail box read: "Kerry '04: Because the Sears Tower is an Eyesore Anyway." Weakness invites attack.

Lesson #8:
Appeasement doesn't work.

Speaking to the homosexual lobby at the 2004 Democratic National Convention, Teresa Heinz Kerry said, "You're pushing the envelope, and we, as a country, have to respond with policies and cultural acceptance."[26]

No we don't.

If Reagan taught us anything, it was that the policy of appeasement is not the answer. Winston Churchill would tell you the same thing. Not appeasement, not containment, but peace through strength.

While we're on the subject of fear, it's important to note that Reagan didn't change his statements or actions based on what the other side, the press, or the naysayers said. My friend Gary Glenn, who named his daughter Reagan after the president, told me the same thing when I called him for advice. "Gary, if I do this, then the other side will do *that* (so to speak). What do you advise?" He sounded Reaganesque when he told me what I already knew was true: "Never fail to do the right thing for fear that the opposition will attack you in response. The other side can and will attack you anyway, at a time of their own choosing rather than yours, regardless of whether you act."

Lesson #9:
Expect attack, and do the right thing anyway.

Another lesson Republicans would do well to heed.

But, as much as I admire Reagan, he was not perfect—he made a tragic mistake that still haunts us long after his death. *Roe v. Wade* would likely have been overturned if it hadn't been for the votes of Reagan appointees Sandra Day O'Connor and Anthony Kennedy. Reagan was also the guy who appointed Justice Scalia—a phenomenal move. And he moved Justice Rehnquist (appointed in 1972) to Chief Justice—an excellent decision. But a couple of great appointments do not make up for even a single bad one. Especially not when the decisions are 5–4 and the stakes are millions of lives.

When I think of this otherwise great man and all he stood for, I know this is not part of the legacy he would have wanted to leave. After all, it was Reagan himself who said:

We cannot diminish the value of one category of human life—the unborn—without diminishing the value of all human life.... There is no cause more important.[27]

He was right.

In *Reagan's War,* Peter Schweizer documents Ronald Reagan's congressional testimony *against* blacklisting communists. Why did Reagan do this? Because he believed there was a better way to fight wrong ideas. As Schweizer explains: "In a straight ideological battle between freedom and communism, [Reagan] was confident freedom would always come out on top."[28] It took him leading the charge for forty years of his life, but he was right.

History has shown it. Even *Time* magazine, which formerly criticized Reagan ended up crediting him with success. Joe Klein, in his article "The Secrets of Reagan's Success" wrote this: "Reagan will mostly be remembered for his unyielding opposition to the Soviet Union, for his willingness to call a regime that murdered at least 40 million of its citizens 'evil.'"[29]

Really? "Murdering at least forty million of its citizens" is "evil"? Let's think about that for a minute. Forty million, forty-*five* million…what other country has killed that many of its own citizens? Oh yeah, *we did.* The "secret of Reagan's success" was that he relentlessly proclaimed the evil of communism and worked to bring that evil to an end. What would Ronald Reagan say about the evil of abortion?

We don't need to speculate. He said, "We must with calmness and resolve help the vast majority of our fellow Americans understand that the more than one and one-half million abortions performed in America in 1980 amount to a great moral evil, an assault on the sacredness of human life."[30]

Reagan stood firm against the evil of communism and won—against all the odds, the political pundits, the media, the money, and much of the world. But we are endowed by *our Creator* with the inalienable right to liberty. Oh yeah, "life," too. That's why we stand against abortion. That's why we will never stop standing. Reagan said it best: "Human-life legislation ending this tragedy will someday pass the Congress—and you and I must never rest until it does."[31] Because when the truth prevails, history will show it.

Lesson #10: Trust truth and freedom to prevail.

For that reason I opposed the so-called Campaign Finance Reform gag rules. And I disagree with President Bush's stand against the 527s—those independent contributions that funded ads from groups like moveon.org and the Swift Boat Vets for Truth. Sure, the Left funded Bush-bashing entities with millions. *So what?* That's their right. The same right the Kerry-bashing Swift Boat Vets should have. The same right *we* should have.

Silencing people's right to speak isn't the answer; presenting better ideas and winning the public debate is. When they start clamoring to take away the right of ordinary groups to speak, fight it. If you value free speech, fight it with everything you have. *But they have more money than we do,* you say. Maybe it's time we learned how to raise it. (By the way, if anyone out there knows how, please fill me in on it, *will you?*)

You see, the answer to our dilemma isn't to silence all voices with whom we disagree; it's to let all voices have an opportunity to be heard—and to let the *best ideas win*. Reagan knew freedom was a better idea than communism. He was right. He had the courage to speak the truth in the crowded public square, and that truth prevailed.

THE BEDROCK OF GENUINE FAITH

There was another side to Reagan that not everyone knew. He had a very deep Christian faith. When I had George Otis Sr. on my Faith2Action radio show following Reagan's death, I learned something about Reagan. Back when he was governor and most believed he was too old to run for president, George Otis spoke prophetically to him. He told him that if he would follow God and all His ways, He would reside at 1600 Pennsylvania Avenue.[32] Otis told me that Pat Boone asked the president years later if he remembered what Otis had told him. His answer was, "Oh yes!" Reagan knew from where his power came. And he knew that God gives us power in order for us to *use it.* The Republicans in Congress would do well do remember this.

Reagan knew he had a divine purpose, especially after he survived an assassination attempt. At the National Prayer Breakfast on February 4, 1982, he said, "I've always believed that we are, each of us, put here for a reason, that there is a plan, somehow a divine plan for all of us."[33]

Lesson #11: Look to God for strength and guidance.

When Reagan was governor of California, Pastor James Robinson once asked him:

"Governor, is Jesus real to you?" With the bobbing of the head and the opening word that became so familiar, Reagan said, "Well…my father was an alcoholic. My mother was the greatest influence in my life. And Jesus is more real to me than my mother."[34]

When Robinson left that day, he believed he had "just spoken to the future president of the United States, a man who would preserve freedom." And when he spoke with Governor George W. Bush, he left with the same feeling. Bush said:

My life is changed, I had a drinking problem. I won't say I was an alcoholic, but it affected my relationships, even with my kids. It could have destroyed me. But I've given my life to Christ.

I feel like God wants me to run for president. I can't explain it, but…something is going to happen, and, at that time, my country is going to need me. I know it won't be easy, on me or my family, but God wants me to do it.

In fact, I really don't want to run. My father was president. My whole family has been affected by it. I know the price. I know what it will mean. I would be perfectly happy to have people point at me someday when I'm buying my fishing lures at Wal-Mart and say,

"That was our governor." That's all I want. And if I run for president, that kind of life will be over. My life will never be the same. But I feel God wants me to do this, and I must do it. [35]

Time magazine called President George W. Bush "Reagan's son." I'm not sure they meant it as a compliment, but it is. And I agree. As Reagan spoke of the shining city on a hill, of letting that light shine before men, he knew the source from where light was drawn and from where our freedom comes. While his track record is far from perfect, I believe President George W. Bush does as well.

"You are the light of the world. *A city on a hill cannot be hidden.* Neither do people light a lamp and put it under a bowl. Instead they put it on its stand, and *it gives light to everyone* in the house. In the same way, let your light shine before men, that they may see your good deeds and praise your Father in heaven." (Matthew 5:14–16)

Chapter 12

LESSONS FROM GOD

Our struggle is not against flesh and blood, but against the rulers,
against the authorities, against the powers of this dark world and
against the spiritual forces of evil in the heavenly realms.

EPHESIANS 6:12

When we talk about the battle, I think it's important to take a step back and look at the big picture—the *really* big picture. Another battle is going on, one beneath the surface between forces more powerful than every obstacle we face…more powerful than everything we see and hear and feel. The fact of the matter is that we are in a spiritual war. Don't believe me? Doesn't matter. As you may have heard me mention, some things are true whether you believe them or not.

I once met some interesting people around three in the morning while spending the night at Kinko's working on a project. They explained to me that they were satanists working on graphics for their heavy-metal CD. They listed some of their songs as if to inquire if I had ever heard them. I said, "I can go out to my car and check, but I'm pretty sure I don't have any of your CDs."

The conversation went something like this:

"So you guys are really satanists?" I asked.

"Yeah."

"Not just a gimmick…"

"Nope."

"So…you worship *Satan*."

"Yep."

"I have a question for you: How did you find out that Satan even *exists?* From the *Bible*—right?"

"Among other places."

"The thing I don't understand is that if you look in the Bible to find out about your hero Satan, you'll find out that he's not just out to 'kill, steal, and destroy *your enemies*'; he's out to 'kill, steal, and destroy *you.*'"

No response.

"And I don't know how to break this to you, but if you look in the back of the book, those that follow Satan…don't turn out so good."

You see, unlike my Kinko's friends' "god," the God I serve is *for* me. He came to give me life and life abundantly. Every good and perfect gift comes from Him. And if He didn't spare His own Son for me, do I really think He's going to hold back anything else?

He who did spare his own Son, but gave him up for us all—how will he not also, along with him, graciously give us all things? (Romans 8:32)

God speaks to us through His Word just as clearly as He would through a cloud or a burning bush. Specific and direct. I know it because I've seen it. A little more than a year ago, I wanted to quit. That's right. Give up fighting this cultural war and close down Faith2Action. I had started it a year earlier and had seen a lot accomplished. As far as I knew, a unified effort like this had never been made before. But I had gone from having a staff of managers, researchers, writers, personal assistants—from having everything, including my speaking engagements and travel, booked *for* me—to *just* me.

I had reached the breaking point. I'd had all I could take. The way I saw it, with a few phone calls I could make *a lot of money* by quitting this fight and selling widgets instead of staying in this battle making nothing. I told God that if I didn't have a direct word from Him, I was throwing in the towel. That's the *precise moment* I read this:

> I suggest that you finish what you started a year ago, for you were the first to propose this idea, and you were the first to begin doing something about it. Now you should carry this project through to completion just as enthusiastically as you began it. (2 Corinthians 8:10–11, NLT)

Lesson #1: God communicates clearly through His Word.

Okay. *I'm back.* What else do you do when you get the equivalent of a Mailgram from God? I guess He didn't want me selling widgets for the good of mankind. Whatever widgets are. That verse kept me going for a long time. I could give you dozens of examples *just like that*—specific, detailed, direct, and unmistakable. Growing up, I never knew that God talks to us so directly. If I had known the specific encouragement, enlightenment, and empowerment available to me, I would have read my Bible a lot more.

THE SPIRITUAL PLAYERS

As I mentioned earlier, I believe there is a God. He's not found in a crystal or in a tree trunk. He's not a nebulous "Force," no matter how many *Star Wars* movies you've seen. He is who He says He is—a good Father. Not a distant grandfather winking at sin. He's involved in our lives and wants what's best for us. He's also all-powerful, almighty, and all-knowing. Pretty good traits to be plugged into. But there's a battle going on between good and evil, between God and Satan, between our rights and those who would take them from us. And if you're placing bets: God trumps Satan. Any way you look at it. It's not an equal yin and yang kind of thing. God created Satan, and the *Creator* is far more powerful than His *creation*.

**Lesson #2:
God (the Creator) trumps
Satan (the creature).**

That's tough to remember when we can't see what's really going on. The prophet Elisha didn't have that problem. His servant was in a panic because they were surrounded by the enemy. Pretty good reason to panic. But Elisha wasn't afraid because God had given him a glimpse of what was happening in the spiritual realm. "Don't be afraid," he told his servant. "Those who are with us are more than those who are with them." Elisha prayed and said, "O LORD, open his eyes so he may see" (2 Kings 6:16–17). The Lord opened the servant's eyes, and he saw the mountain full of warring angels he hadn't known were there. Who is doing battle on our behalf that we don't know about? Pray that He gives you a glimpse.

I have met with many national leaders over the years and had the opportunity to talk candidly with most of them. *Nearly every one* of them fighting this battle for our liberties—fighting the steamroller of the homosexual threat—has at times felt completely alone. When you're on the tip of the arrow, there don't seem to be a lot of people on either side of you. They're there; you just can't see them.

Elijah felt as if he was alone, too, but he didn't know there were seven thousand others hiding out in caves. That's my point. Not only are there more of us *spiritually*, there are more of us *physically* than we know about. That's why we need to come out of the Bat Cave and join together in fighting the forces of evil. I'm back to writing like a cartoon, but you get the idea.

I've been told that there is only one phrase that appears in every book of the Bible: "Be not afraid." Courage. It is the essential ingredient for victory—for life. No matter what comes your way, remember this:

> Therefore, LORD, we know you will protect the oppressed, preserving them forever from this lying generation, even though the wicked strut about, and evil is praised throughout the land. (Psalm 12:7–8, NLT)

EQUIPPED FOR BATTLE

Getting back to the strategic map, when Satan left heaven, he took a third of the angels with him. That means there are *two-thirds left*. Two-thirds with God, one-third with Satan. God trumps Satan. And two-thirds beats one-third. God wins. The question I keep asking is if that's the case, why aren't we doing better in this fight?

One reason may be that we're not using all the tools available to us.

We're getting blindsided because we don't have on that armor God tells us about:

> Finally, be strong in the Lord and in his mighty power. Put on the full armor of God so that you can take your stand against the devil's schemes. For our struggle is not against flesh and blood, but against the rulers, against the authorities, against the powers of this dark world and against the spiritual forces of evil in the heavenly realms. Therefore put on the full armor of God, so that when the day of evil comes, you may be able to stand your ground, and after you have done everything, to stand. (Ephesians 6:10–13)

Lesson #3:
Put on spiritual armor
for spiritual battle.

We have to put on armor because we're in a war and we need protection. In Ephesians 6:14–18, Paul, most likely inspired by the Roman prison guards around him, said we need to:

- buckle the belt of truth around our waist
- put on the breastplate of righteousness
- fit our feet with the readiness of the gospel of peace
- take the shield of faith, with which we will be able to extinguish all the flaming arrows of the evil one
- take the helmet of salvation
- the sword of the Spirit, which is the word of God

I've given you only a brief introduction to God's armor, but you can start by putting on the belt of truth by referring to a list of key Scripture passages I've provided on my web site at www.f2a.org.

COMPROMISE

Another reason we're not doing better may be because we're living in compromise. It's highly probable that if Daniel had compromised by eating the king's food, he would have compromised about other things, too, like bowing to his image. "Oh, I'll still pray to God, but I'll just bow to this thing to spare my life, because, after all, I can do a lot of ministry for God if I survive." That wasn't Daniel or his uncompromising buddies Shadrach, Meshach, and Abednego. When you obey God in the small things, it becomes a lot easier to obey Him in the big things. That's when God shows up. He can shut the mouths of lions and protect you from the flames.

Lesson #4:
Never compromise with evil.

THE CRIMINALIZATION OF CHRISTIANITY

Perhaps another reason we're not doing better in this battle is because we're at arm's length from God. Living in lukewarm mediocrity, bored in church, disappointed with God. It's been so long since we've seen a prayer answered that we've stopped praying—although we retain the option to do so should a catastrophic crisis arise. The Bible says to ask and it shall be given to us—right? Then how come we keep asking but get nothing?

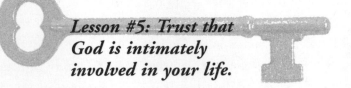

Lesson #5: Trust that God is intimately involved in your life.

I think the answer is found in John 15. If our prayers aren't being answered, it just might be something *we're* not doing. Jesus said "if *you remain in me* and *my words remain in you*, ask whatever you wish, and it will be given you" (v. 7). We haven't been plugged into the source and have been asking for the wrong stuff.

If we were in Christ and His words were in us—if we were really living and breathing those words—our lives and our nation would be transformed. If we really relied on every word He spoke, if we held tightly to His promises and listened for His direction, if we looked for His purpose everywhere we went, in everything that happened to us and stepped out in faith, we'd start seeing God-sized feats and "impossible" victories. Remember, God is the same God revealed in the Bible—capable of pulling off the same kinds of "impossible" victories!

I have a question for you: If they made a movie about your life, would anyone want to watch it? You see, God is the producer of the movie of your life. He's also the director. What you may not know is that He also wrote the script. Psalm 139:16 says that all the days of your life were already written in God's book before one of them came to be. God has an action adventure that, according to Ephesians 3:20, is "immeasurably more" than all you could "ask or imagine." If God can come up with something immeasurably better than anything I could ever dream up, then I want God's script for my life.

You may have heard that every movie has already been made…only the characters change. Stale, trite, boring. But when you surrender to God and let Him direct the movie of your life, it's new, exciting, and action-packed. With God there aren't any accidents, no coincidences. He is deliberate and purposeful, and when you surrender to Him, He weaves the plot together into a masterpiece that even Steven Spielberg couldn't come up with.

He's involved. Intimately. Even in writing this book. After speaking once on the phone to Linda Swearingen, a woman I had never met, she informed me that she felt God leading her to "pray me through" this book. So she called several of her friends, including Jeannie Fuller, Pastor Greg Fry, Pat Cerjan, and Amelda Thomas-Jones, and one of mine, Fred Hammack. Amelda then introduced us to the concept of a "Clarion Call" and proceeded to show us what it meant: intense, focused intercessory prayer every day for one hour…for nearly four months—until this book was finished.

During one of the calls, out of the blue, Amelda "just happened" to mention that a year and a half earlier she had stayed at a place called Conklin's Guest House, a bed-and-breakfast in remote Sisters, Oregon. She remembered talking to Marie, the owner at the time, who "happened" to mention that an author from Multnomah had just stayed there.

And for some reason Amelda told all of us on the call about it. "God sparked something in me to pray for that author. I didn't know her *either,*" she said. "It was the only other time I prayed for an author I had never met. I'm not even sure why I'm telling you all this, but all I knew was that I was praying for a "female author of Multnomah" who had recently stayed there. I felt God telling me to pray specifically for the "middle and end" of the book.

As of this writing, I have never met Amelda. She didn't even know the name of my publisher. And she had no way of knowing that just over a year and a half earlier I had gone skiing near Sisters, Oregon. And stayed at a bed-and-breakfast called…*Conklin's Guest House*. Amelda was praying for *me*.

She was praying specifically for the middle and the end of the book. Not so coincidentally, I had already finished the beginning.

Now do you see what I'm talking about with this "movie stuff"? God is purposeful and deliberate. And if you're close enough to hear Him, He's going to give you a glimpse of what He's doing. If there's anything of value in this book, it is because of the power of God working through that small group of prayer warriors who walk closely with Him.

If the LORD is pleased with us, he will lead us into that land, a land flowing with milk and honey, and will give it to us. (Numbers 14:8)

HE MAKES ALL THE DIFFERENCE

In Acts 1:8, Jesus said, "You will receive power when the Holy Spirit comes on you; and you will be my witnesses in Jerusalem, and in all Judea and Samaria, and to the ends of the earth." So the disciples were waiting for that kind of power. They were saved. They believed that Jesus had died; they had witnessed His resurrection and ascension to heaven. They just didn't have the power yet.

What did they do? Well, they had to fill the vacancy left by Judas. They had an open spot on the first church council, so they interviewed the candidates to fill it. They narrowed it down to two and drew lots to decide. Matthias was chosen...and you never hear from him in the Bible again. Pastor Bob Coy, of Calvary Chapel, Ft. Lauderdale, had a perspective on this I hadn't heard before. These guys didn't have any power. They did church business like so many churches do—they fill the open vacancies, and nothing comes of it.

Lesson #6:
Draw on the power of
God's indwelling Spirit.

You see, until they had the power of the Holy Spirit guiding and empowering them, they didn't do much of anything. In fact, after they saw Jesus resurrected, they didn't immediately start witnessing and healing and transforming the world. They went fishing.

Peter said he was going fishing, and the others went with him. But "they caught nothing"—until Jesus showed up (John 21:3, 6). We've been filling vacancies; we've been going fishing and coming up empty. It's time we hear the "rushing mighty wind" and are filled with the power of the Holy Spirit. Until we have tapped into the Source, we're not going to see change.

HIGH-OCTANE PRAYER

When the apostles couldn't cast out a demon, they asked Jesus why. And He told them it was "because of your *unbelief*" (Matthew 17:20). Faith is the starting place. But if you have mountains to move, as we do, you're going to need more. Jesus continued, "I say to you, if you have *faith as a mustard seed,* you will say to this mountain, 'Move from here to there,' and it will move; and nothing will be impossible for you. However, this kind does not go out except by prayer *and fasting*" (v. 21, NKJV).

Did you catch that? If you want the mountain to move, you need faith that God is capable of such a feat, and you need to trust Him enough to do some seemingly illogical things—like going without food. Doesn't make much sense, does it? That's what I thought. But His thoughts are higher than ours.

Lesson #7: Express fervency in prayer by fasting.

A little while ago I had a conversation with my friend Jeff Froling, who told me he was praying for an answer about what job to take, but hadn't gotten one. I asked him if he'd thought about fasting. "I haven't fasted, but I *have* been eating poorly." *Uh, not the same thing.*

I remember meeting with Dr. Bill Bright of Campus Crusade for Christ one day in Orlando. I had skipped lunch and was feeling faint. I wasn't sure I was going to make it through the meeting. That was when Dr. Bright told me he was on day thirty-six of his forty-day fast. Do you want to be used by God as mightily as He used Dr. Bill Bright? Do what Bill did. Take God seriously. Pray like you mean it—fast—and watch what God does with those high-octane prayers. Dr. Bright is enjoying a feast right now in heaven, I'm sure.

And are you really serious about taking your country back?

The first time I really took this seriously was during the 2000 elections. On the Sunday morning before Election Day, my pastor announced from the pulpit that Christian leaders had called for a day of fasting for the elections and for our country. I had skipped breakfast, so I was a third of the way there. But I came home to a refrigerator full of food—a rare thing for me. I had just gone shopping and had all my favorite things to choose from. I remember sitting in my backyard that day, praying: *Look, God, if that fasting thing has to do with making time to pray, I have an idea, I can pray while I eat! I am fully capable of praying with my mouth full. I mean, I would hate for that food to go to waste. What do You say?*

I didn't get an answer.

So I decided to obey God, and I made it through the day. And then two days. Then I decided to fast until *I found out the results of the election.*

As you may recall, the results of the election *didn't come right away.* And neither did food. I fasted for seventeen days—until my family persuaded me to eat some Thanksgiving dinner. While I had hardly been able to skip lunch without fainting, when I was focused on God and crying out to Him to have mercy on us as a nation, I could fast for seventeen days. With God, *all things* are possible. Those prayers were answered by the way.

THE VICTORIOUS MINORITY

There's so much at stake. When are we going to start taking God seriously? When are we going to start obeying Him even when it doesn't make sense to us?

When Ronald Wilson Reagan was inaugurated, he raised his right hand and put his other hand on his mother's Bible, which was open to 2 Chronicles 7:14 (KJV): "If my people, which are called by my name, shall humble themselves, and pray, and seek my face, and turn from their wicked ways; then will I hear from heaven, and will forgive their sin, and will heal their land."[1]

Ronald Reagan knew what I had yet to really learn:

If My people, who are called by My name will:

- humble themselves
- pray
- seek My face
- turn from their wicked ways

Then I will:

- hear from heaven
- forgive their sins
- heal their land

Some of us have heard that verse a hundred times, but check out who God is talking about: *His* people. You see, for God to move, we don't have to have a majority. Surprised? His ways are not our ways. Do you want to know why we won that election? Because God's people in America prayed like they have never prayed before in recent history.

Lesson #8: A humble, prayerful, repentant minority will win.

During that election, I lived in Broward County, Florida—the land of the "hanging chad." I spent my vacation counting ballots, and let me tell you what I saw. People praying. Everywhere. In the recount waiting room, outside the Palm Beach Operations Center, kneeling in the street outside the Broward County Courthouse. Praying like they meant it and not caring about who saw them or what they thought. People were crying out to God for His mercy. Waking up at 4:00 A.M. to pray. Praying for children not yet born to be protected so they could sing His praises. I have never seen anything like it in my life.

A spiritual battle was being waged, and I was right in the middle of it.

I remember that, with everything on the line, I didn't want to waste a minute doing anything else when I could be doing something to change the outcome—praying. Yes, the votes were cast, but the outcome was anything but certain. Judges had a say in the matter, and I know God can turn the hearts of Judges just like He can with Kings (Proverbs 21:1). That's what He said, and I believe Him. But when I saw the Florida Supreme Court rule on our side, I saw it up close.

With everything on the line, we need to act like it. Have faith. God is who He says He is. He works the way He's told us. Pray. It changes the outcome. Fast. Show Him you really mean it. When those prayers are high octane, you take them a lot more seriously, and so does God. That's how He says mountains move. That includes changing the results of an election. That includes changing the course of our nation right now.

A NATION CAN CHANGE

Nineveh was a city that badly needed to adjust its course. Its inhabitants were evil. Wicked. *Really, really bad.* You may recall that Jonah wasn't big on going there. When God told him to go warn the Ninevites to repent before He destroyed them, Jonah went the other way. But God wanted them to hear His message, so He sent a big fish to swallow Jonah and then spit him out so he could do what he was told to do. What message was so important that God would go to such great lengths to deliver it?

Lesson #9: God desires national, not just personal, repentance.

The message was that in just over a month, they were *toast:* "'Forty more days and Nineveh *will be overturned*'" (Jonah 3:4). God said it. And He didn't say *maybe*. These people had just over a month, and that was it. How else do you read "*will be* overturned?"

But listen to what happened next:

The Ninevites believed God. They declared a fast, and all of them, from the greatest to the least, put on sackcloth. When the news reached the king of Nineveh, he rose from his throne, took off his royal robes, covered himself with sackcloth and sat down in the dust. Then he issued a proclamation in Nineveh: "By the decree of the king and his nobles: Do not let any man or beast, herd or flock, taste anything; do not let them eat or drink. But let man and beast be covered with sackcloth. Let everyone call urgently on God. Let them give up their evil ways and their violence. Who knows? God may yet relent and with compassion turn from his fierce anger so that we will not perish." When God saw what they did and how they turned from their evil ways, *he had compassion and did not bring upon them the destruction he had threatened.* (Jonah 3:5–10)

God saw what they did. They prayed, fasted, humbled themselves with sackcloth and ashes. And they "turned from their evil ways." See a pattern? Those prayers reached a compassionate God who changed His mind and "did not bring upon them the destruction He had threatened." That's the same God we have today.

WHEN YOU JUST AREN'T UP TO IT

Feel inadequate? Good. That's just the kind of people God uses. Father Bill Witt from Youngstown, Ohio, once told me, "The only ability you need to serve God is availability." It's true. I know it firsthand. You see, when I found out that children were being dismembered in this country, I was a shy high school sophomore afraid to give a speech in class. What in the world could I possibly do about it? I wrote some school reports, but I never even *thought* about starting a pro-life group. I'm embarrassed to say that I was even afraid to voice my opinion in a college class when abortion came up. I did voice it to the girl sitting next to me, however. She just happened to be a girl who was starting a pro-life group on campus. Did I want to help? That's all it took. Someone to lead.

Lesson #10:
You are inadequate;
God is adequate.

I was asked to speak on the subject. That wasn't my "strength," I told them, but I knew other people who could do it. Then I weighed the logic of my argument. Which was more important: the fact that four thousand babies are killed every day, or the fact that I was afraid to tell anyone about it? My fear of public speaking lost that contest, and I dragged my mom with me to pro-life speaker's training. She did great, but I'm surprised they passed me. Years later, I was asked to give the keynote speech at the Pro-Life Memorial for 2500 Clevelanders at the Music Hall (I think they were looking for someone who would speak for free). Backstage I ran into someone from my speaker's training class of several years prior who said, "I'm really surprised *you* ended up being our spokesperson." Kind of says it all. The only ability you need to be used by God is *availability.*

Recording artist Charlie Peacock said it this way:

It's just like God to make a hero from a sinner,
It's just like God to choose the loser not the winner,
It's just like God to tell a story through the weak,
To let the Gospel speak through the life of a man.[2]

Then there was Gideon. The thing about God is that He sees us as we *can* be in His adequacy, not as we are in our inadequacy. Gideon was a scaredy cat, too. That's when the angel of the Lord addressed him as a "mighty man of valor!" (Judges 6:12, NKJV). I'm sure he looked behind him to see who the angel was talking to. "How can *I* save Israel?" Gideon was quick to point out that his clan was the weakest and that he was the "least" in his father's household. Didn't matter. That's just the kind of people God likes to use. "Surely I will be with you, and you shall defeat the Midianites as one man" (v. 16).

It's not about what we can do anyway. It's about what God can do through us if we'll just let Him. It's just like God to choose the loser, not the winner. That way everyone will know that what happens isn't from any brilliance of our own, but from Him and Him alone.

The long and the short of the story is that God pared down Gideon's army of thirty-two thousand soldiers to only three hundred. Then Gideon knew they were ready to win because they were relying solely on God and listening to His every direction. God was the only chance they had. He's the only chance we have, too.

> Some trust in chariots and some in horses,
> but we trust in the name of the LORD our God. (Psalm 20:7)

Fear is the opposite of trust. And God wants to make sure our trust is in Him.

OVERWHELMED?

I was driving to work one day and got three phone calls in a row—each with bad news. The third was from a friend who wanted to know if I had seen Rosie O'Donnell on television lobbying to overturn Florida's adoption law, which protects vulnerable children from being placed in homosexual homes. Why do I oppose that? For a hundred reasons, including the fact that it guarantees that children will never have both a mother *and* a father—what ten thousand studies show is best for them. This caller, like others, wanted to know what *I* was going to do about it. At that moment, the only thought that came to mind was throwing the stupid phone out the window.

I felt overwhelmed. And if you've been in the battle for the soul of our country, I know you can relate. What can we do? Numbers 14 provides some answers. In that story there are ten people who felt just like I did—spies who were given the task to scope out the Promised Land and provide Moses with a strategic military analysis. You know the drill. "There we saw the giants…and we were like grasshoppers in our own sight, and so we were in their sight" (Numbers 13:33, NKJV). So let's go back to slavery in Egypt—at least there we're "safe." Reminds me of those who would exchange freedom for "safety" now.

Before I give you the minority report, let's look at God's response to the majority report. Did He say: "I understand. Those bad ol' giants are really big and scary, aren't they?" No. Listen to what God really said:

> "How long will these people treat me with contempt? How long will they refuse to believe in me, in spite of all the miraculous signs I have performed among them?" (14:11)

Wow. Did you catch that? Being overwhelmed by the giants is the same thing as *treating God with contempt*. I don't want to do that anymore!

The minority report presented by Joshua and Caleb was what God was looking for:

> If the LORD is pleased with us, he will lead us into that land, a land flowing with milk and honey, and will give it to us. Only do not rebel against the LORD. And do not be afraid of the people of the land, because we will swallow them up. Their protection is gone, but the LORD is with us. Do not be afraid of them. (14:8–9)

I found another verse while reading Isaiah. Check this out:

> It is He who sits above the circle of the earth, and its inhabitants are like *grasshoppers*. (40:22, NKJV)

Lesson #11: God is bigger than every giant.

Notice that God knew it was a "circle of the earth" before anyone else did. And He does make every single giant we face look like a grasshopper. So when you feel overwhelmed, remember to "look up."

WHO IS THIS UNCIRCUMCISED PHILISTINE?

I had been traveling and was scheduled to be on *Hannity and Colmes* a while back. I had just been told that I would be debating Patricia Ireland. *Great,* I thought. *That's all I need. I'm exhausted, and I'm just not up for a debate tonight.* I was overwhelmed, so to speak. That was when my former communications director Chris Gorbey walked into my office quoting one of my speeches in which I talked about what David said as he faced Goliath. "Who is this uncircumcised Philistine, that he should defy the armies of the living God?" (1 Samuel 17:26, NKJV). Immediately, my faith was restored, and I said, "*Yeah!* My God makes her look like a grasshopper!" *Nothing personal.*

What we have to remember is that our land was founded in covenant with God. Go back and take a peek at chapter 10 to see what our Founding Fathers really believed. And while some who *occupy* our land are out of covenant with God, they are not its rightful owners. We can look to them as David looked at Goliath and say, "Who is this uncircumcised Philistine, that [they] should defy the armies of the living God?" Remember that. And one more thing: *Goliath lost.*

Lesson #12:
Stay focused on God,
not on circumstances.

To get out of the boat in the deep water requires faith you'll never get by wading along the shore. When you're in over your head, you have to trust that God is who He says He is and will back up every single claim He makes. I love Peter. He's the guy who got out of the boat when he saw Jesus walking on water. Walking on water is pretty cool. It's also something you *can't* do—unless you're completely focused on God, that is.

When Peter started looking at the waves and focusing on the wind, he started to sink. If you want to stop treading water and start *walking* on water, change your focus. Want to do "impossible" things? Want to "dream heroic dreams"? If we want to live this radical New Testament kind of life, we must take our eyes off the wind and waves, off the giants. And we must look up to the God who makes them look like grasshoppers.

TWO WAYS TO START YOUR DAY

"Get a grip on reality." That's a statement usually uttered by "realists" to "idealists" who believe in accomplishing something. The realist says, "It can't be done." The idealist knows that sometimes it can. We often forget one thing: Newspaper headlines are *not* reality. Ask the people of Missouri, who saved marriage in their state by a 71 percent of the vote, *despite* what the papers said.

Reality is every word spoken by our mighty God. *Votes schmotes.* We have a God with a plan. He can get around votes, judges, elections. That's what He does. He only requires that we trust Him. That's it. So put the newspaper down and pick up the only thing that matters: every word God has spoken.

We are in a spiritual battle, but the good news is that we have a God who is *for* us, who trumps Satan, who conquers every giant, and who beats all the odds. So "suit up" with His armor, arm yourself with His Word, pave the way with prayer, and move the mountains with fasting. If we will focus on Him, He will empower us to accomplish God-sized feats and win "impossible" victories.

Chapter 13

THE PLAN

Several years ago when I was at a national conference with some friends, we were deciding which workshop to attend. I was intrigued by one workshop's title: "How to Transform Your State for Life." I talked my friend Jeff Kolozy into going with me. We had served on the board of Greater Cleveland Right to Life together and had been in the pro-life movement for years.

I sat down, pen in hand, ready to gather new strategic information to save lives and change the course of human events. The speaker droned on in a way that, I'm sad to admit, I have imitated on more than a few occasions. Her solution to transforming your state was to "write letters to the editor—and call and lobby your legislators—that makes a difference—you'd be surprised."

Jeff, seated a few rows ahead of me, turned around and glared at me. His face said it all: "You talked me out of the workshop I wanted, for *this?*" I, however, sat on the edge of my chair, acting enthralled with the speaker, pretending to take copious notes, as if writing letters to the editor was some remarkable new bit of strategic intelligence.

In case you missed that workshop on the basics, here are some notes on how to get started:

- Register to vote.
- Register your church members to vote.
- Find out where the candidates stand (through candidate surveys and voter guides from many sources, including www.f2a.org).
- Start a social issues group in your congregation to keep others informed.
- Vote.
- Get your church members, rotary clubs, and neighborhood groups to vote (that's what those directories are for!).
- Get involved in the pro-life movement and become a liaison to your church.
- Recruit church liaisons in other churches (begin with your friends).
- Actively seek candidates to run.
- Support them.
- Run yourself!

Oh yeah, don't forget to "write letters to the editor—and call and lobby your legislators—that makes a difference—*you'd be surprised.*" It also helps to call secular radio stations and enter the discussions on such things as why marriage matters. Talking points are available through the partnering groups on www.f2a.org.

At the same time, I don't believe that winning is necessarily about working harder. It has everything to do with working smarter and working together. And instead of getting beaten down on the defense, it's about taking the offense. And being on the offense is a whole lot more fun.

I know what it's like to fight giants without resources. Without an adequate army. Without enough time to pull it all together. But all those obstacles can be tackled on the offense with a seldom-used but very powerful weapon: creativity.

TATTOOS TO THE RESCUE

On my last day as legislative director of Ohio Right to Life, I received a going-away present of sorts. We were working to pass a bill in the Ohio House that would remove abortion coverage from state insurance policies. Had heard the slogan so long that we finally decided it was time to take "the government out" of the abortion business.

At that time I knew the players and the press so well that I was able to predict the next day's headlines: "State Employees Denied Abortion Coverage" or "Ohio Workers Denied Reproductive Health Care." But I set out to change that.

It all started with a bit of research down in the bill room. As it turns out, just a few months earlier, nearly every legislator in the Ohio General Assembly had voted to require a parent's permission (or consent) before a minor could get a *tattoo* or body piercing. These legislators, including the prime sponsor of the Tattoo Parental Consent bill, wanted parents to have to give permission before their daughter could get a tattoo—but not before she could have an *abortion!*

Now, legislators think no one will remember how they voted four months earlier or hold them accountable.

They were wrong.

I went to my favorite novelty store and purchased some temporary tattoos—one for each legislator and member of the esteemed press. I printed up a flyer that read: "Parental Consent for Tattoos and NOT ABORTION?" Then I listed the name of every representative who voted for parental consent for tattoos. I stapled the tattoos on the corner of each of the flyers and gave them to Representative Ron Hood, who sat on the floor of the House waiting for the right moment to unveil them.

It was high drama. The bill everyone knew about was being debated, but I had counted and we had the votes. That was when Representative Jim Jordan moved to amend the bill. The proaborts looked around in dismay, clearly taken by surprise. This wasn't in their plans. Then they found out that his amendment would require parental consent before "an unemancipated minor could obtain an abortion." This was just not done! A major bill of this kind had never been passed without going through weeks and weeks of laborious committee hearings and debate.

We waited for the floor debate to get going before launching our little tattoo surprise. "This is outrageous! How *dare* you say that parents can interfere with their daughter's right to choose what to do with her own body?" "They have the right to choose without parental interference!"

That's when Representative Hood looked up at me in the balcony and mouthed, *"Now?"*

I nodded and mouthed back, *"Now."* The flyers were passed out throughout the entire House, and the atmosphere was immediately transformed. As legislators were handed their colorful flyers, with lively temporary tattoos attached, they immediately started laughing. Some turned around to others who hadn't gotten theirs yet, while others began comparing tattoos. "I'll trade you my Ohio State tattoo for your tiger!" Some began to put on their tattoos—but all scanned the list to see if their name was on the list of those who had voted for parental consent for tattoos. Nearly everyone was on that list.

One proabortion Republican woman was overheard saying, "Shoot! *Now* we have to vote for it!" (The word wasn't *shoot*, but you get the idea.)

The pro-life reps were in their glory. They were no longer being asked to make a "difficult vote" that wouldn't play well in the press. They were on the winning side of the debate, public opinion, and common sense. Even the media couldn't ignore this little stunt. The message was clear: "Look at the hypocrisy. You mean to tell me that you think a tattoo is more significant, more important for parents to be informed about, than a surgery that could leave a girl sterile or take her life and the life of her unborn child?"

Yes, my last day at Ohio Right to Life was an enjoyable one. And instead of the headlines talking about poor state employees losing their right to abort their children, they all talked about—you guessed it—tattoos and hypocrisy.

Creativity before the vote goes a lot farther than all the whining in the world afterward. The problem is that each organization in each of the cities in each of the fifty states comes up with creative things independently of the others. Each working on slogans, sound bites, and strategy…alone. Pouring out our hearts. I've had a glimpse of it while traveling all over the country. Each one has a slightly different take. Most good. Some great. Each exhausting themselves in isolation from the rest. Don't have it? I guarantee there is an ally on our side who does—and probably has the flyers and bumper stickers already printed. That's why we need to work together. Want to expose the hypocrisy of the Left? Do it in a fun, exciting, and *creative* way.

A WINNING PLAN

After looking at the strategic map, I couldn't come up with a single scenario in which we could *win* the culture war if we continued to fight it in the exact same way we had been. The following is the "Faith2Action plan" I put together for pro-family leaders because I believed that if we are to win, we must change how we do battle.

It's clear that we in the pro-family movement have not made the kinds of gains in public policy that our numbers, our passion, and the truth of our positions warrant. This is not to say that there haven't been valiant efforts and hard-fought victories. For the most part, however, they've been on the defensive: protecting the definition of marriage and the family, fighting abortion funding and regulations, but achieving very limited results.

Hard work. Heroic efforts. But if success is our goal, we must do better.

While groups meet frequently to "report" on what they're doing, there has been very little planned collaborative effort. A major hurdle is that each group has its *own lists*—its own members and donors it wants to protect (which is perfectly understandable considering that its very existence depends upon them). There is also the matter of limited budgets, overcommitted staff, tough economic times, and public relations acknowledgment in a joint venture where contributions are unequal.

The good news is that every obstacle that has kept the pro-family movement from working together can be overcome. We must be engaged in the *most significant* battles—where what we do makes an essential difference in the outcome of the war. While there are scores of important issues from which to choose, the most significant affect the greatest number of human lives and pose the greatest threat to our freedoms.

They are the issues we discussed in chapter 2:

- Abortion
- Embryonic stem-cell research/cloning
- Marriage
- Homosexuality
- Pornography
- Assisted suicide
- Evolution
- Abstinence
- Evangelism

WE'VE DONE IT BEFORE

In 1998, eighteen national organizations joined together in the "Truth in Love" campaign to express hope for change for those struggling with homosexuality. This unified effort, which ran full-page ads and television commercials across the country, was the first of its kind and enjoyed unprecedented success. Every network and every show from *Today* to *20/20,* even *Hard Copy* and *Extra,* clamored to cover it. Every newsmagazine covered it multiple times, and it even made the cover of *Newsweek.*

In 1999, after the shootings at Columbine, the "Yes, I Believe in God" campaign equipped more than ten thousand high school leaders across the country with "Yes, I Believe in God" kits to help them boldly proclaim their faith in Jesus Christ. This joint effort combined the resources of the Alliance Defense Fund, the American Center for Law and Justice (ACLJ), and Liberty Counsel to show students their First Amendment rights and how to get free legal representation should those rights be violated.

Then in 2001 and 2002, the "Shake the Nation Back to Life" campaign combined the efforts of more than twenty groups to work for the nomination of pro-life judges. That campaign produced and aired award-winning commercials nationally, collected forty-five thousand baby rattles with pro-life messages to "shake things up" in the Senate, and appeared on the front page of the *New York Times* (above the fold), as well as on CNN, Fox News, and elsewhere.

When groups work together, they break out of their mailing lists and into the culture.

"I AM AN AMERICAN"

While sitting in Pizzeria Unos in Washington, DC, I thought of a way to draw the groups together on January 22, 2003, the thirtieth anniversary of, *Roe v. Wade,* the Supreme Court ruling that sentenced more than forty-five million children to death by abortion.

My friend Dierdre was with me, watching me write crazy ideas on a napkin. Then it hit. At that time most people still remembered the post-9/11 "I Am an American" campaign, in which those words were spoken over and over by every type of American under the sun. But there were some Americans we had forgotten—the ones alive but not yet born. Combining that phrase with a 3-D ultrasound image of a child in the womb would say it all.

I made a call to David O'Stein, Executive Director of National Right to Life. He loved it and helped fine-tune the wording of the full-page ad before it went out—*along with bumper stickers*—to every right-to-life chapter in nearly every city in every state in the country.

A call to my friend Don Van Curler also helped pave the way, and the "I Am an American" ad campaign was announced on January 15 at the National Press Club. It had the support of groups such as Concerned Women for America, Family Research Council, Prison Fellowship, Eagle Forum, American Values, the Christian Coalition, and Traditional Values Coalition. Thirty-five national pro-life groups had signed on!

With the help of Greg Darby of the Christian Interactive Network, we filmed 4-D (3-D with movement) ultrasounds and made a television

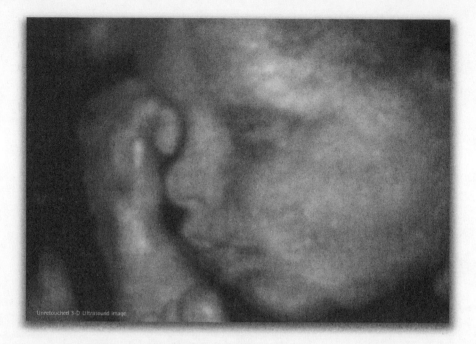

Unretouched 3-D Ultrasound image

I Am An American.

I am endowed by my Creator with the inalienable right to life.

Just like you, and every other American.

You know who I am.

Now that you can see my face,

will *you* use your voice?

Please tell America,

I am an American, too.

30 years of denying this self-evident truth is long enough.

America, it's time to protect your children again.

Alliance for Life	CatholicVote.org	Deacons in Service for Life	Lutherans For Life	ProLife Info.org
American Collegians for Life	Christian Coalition of America	Eagle Forum	National Center for Freedom and Renewal	Roe No More
American Family Association	Christian Interactive Network	Family Research Council	National Right to Life	Sound Wave Images
American Values	Christian Medical Association	Focus on the Family	Operation Outcry	Teachers Saving Children"
American Victims of Abortion	Common Good	Heartbeat International	Priests for Life	Traditional Values Coalition
Care-Net	Concerned Women for America	Liberty Counsel	Prison Fellowship	The Van Curler Foundation
Catholic Online	Council for National Policy, Inc.	Life Issues Institute	Pro Life Communications	Your Catholic Voice

commercial. Phil Cooke Pictures did the production, and with the help of my friend Marty Kincaid, it aired on the Family Network and Inspiration Network, as well as more than a dozen other venues, reaching more than thirty million homes.

Now, nearly two years later, it's still being used. A few weeks ago while I was in Traverse City, Michigan, to speak at a pro-life banquet, I drove by an "I Am an American" billboard. It even became an ad in Canada, with the words "I am a Canadian."

God can do a lot with a paper napkin. *I know.*

WE CAN DO IT AGAIN

To win, we must break through the confusion with a message of truth that the American people can recognize, understand, and embrace. We must regain control of the public debate and the battlefronts in:

- the schools
- the legislatures
- the courts
- the media
- Hollywood
- businesses
- science
- music

We cannot achieve victory by doing things the way we are now. *To win, three things must change .*

1. We must work *together.*

Jesus…said to them: "Any kingdom divided against itself will be ruined, and a house divided against itself will fall." (Luke 11:17)

Imagine trying to fight the war in Iraq (or any war) if each branch of the military fought independently of the others—if the Army didn't coordinate with the efforts of the Navy, Marines, Air Force, and Special Forces and the allied coalition forces never communicated. The results would be very different.

For each major issue, there are more than one hundred local, state, and national groups—each with a different name, a different "niche," and a different approach, each with its own constituency unaware of the big picture of what the allied groups are doing. For example, the Abstinence Clearinghouse has discovered more than four thousand independent abstinence programs and curricula. Because independent organizations are not coordinated, they are spending time, energy, and precious resources reinventing what has already been done. It's no wonder groups feel so overwhelmed! To win, we must *share* our resources. Working together, not reinventing the wheel.

Many of these overextended, underfunded, battle-weary troops are also trying to fight *every* battle on all sides. But as large or as good as each group may be, it simply cannot be all things to all people and lead the charge in every battle.

Our isolated "island" approach has also given us an inferiority complex. The members of each group feels the weight of the entire battle because they don't see the allied troops who, like them, also feel they are fighting alone. As Christ said and Lincoln reiterated: United we stand; divided we fall.

This new approach combines the strengths of each allied organization and provides a platform for it to speak with a unified voice. It's a revolutionary idea of combining our strengths to win without losing each organization's essential autonomy and individuality. It is about plugging people in where God is already at work and sending reinforcements to the troops where they are needed most.

Now, imagine the different branches involved in the cultural war actually working in unison—focused not on their uniforms, but instead on where the battle is the hottest, where our freedoms are most at risk. Not just reporting to each other, but strategizing together to set the agenda, control the debate, and take back ground.

Through the grace of God, the trust and good will of our nation's pro-family leaders, and the culmination of collective efforts over the past several years, for the first time in history our nation's leading pro-family groups have come together in one place: Faith2Action. That's because Faith2Action is a service to them, highlighting what they do and sending people to them. Offering them ideas and pointing to projects they may want to support, like the 2004 voter guides. Because of a unified effort, F2A voter guides went to over two million people. We had to go through five sets of lawyers, but it was worth it.

I'd like to see this effort expand to every significant Bible-based issue, for every national, state, and local affiliate, as well as international efforts, on the most critical fronts.

2. We must move from defense to *offense*.

Have I not commanded you? Be strong and courageous. (Joshua 1:9)

In virtually every arena, we in the pro-family movement are scrambling to respond, to defend, to put out the brushfires the opposition is setting. In each battle, we pour all our time, energy, and money into trying to keep what we already had. But in a defensive posture, even when we "win," we lose. You see, if they set a dozen brushfires, and we put out nine, we still have a net *loss* of three.

Put another way, while they push boulders down the hill, we scramble to try and push them back to the top—something that requires a great deal more effort and results in far, far fewer victories. In an effort to appear "reasonable" and "non-confrontational," we compromise with a relentless agenda that demands twenty acres—and celebrate when we lose only ten. We've been hanging on to a shrinking piece of real estate, and we simply cannot win like that.

To win, we must become proactive.

3. We must *control the debate*.

We demolish arguments and every pretension that sets itself up against the knowledge of God. (2 Corinthians 10:5)

There are two worldviews at odds with each other. One stands for God and the principles in His Word, and the other seeks to destroy them ("The thief comes only to steal and kill and destroy" [John 10:10]).

We have debated the issues on our opponents' terms for too long, responding, defending, reacting. On virtually every issue, they have succeeded by portraying their position as one of "neutrality" ("choice," "tolerance," "diversity") and our position as one of "hostility" ("narrow-minded," "arrogant," "judgmental"). With this posture, even those who agree with us side with the opposition because they don't want to "impose their morality" on others and be viewed as the media portrays us. As long as they continue to portray their side as "neutral," they win.

What is not communicated properly is that if we lose, *their* (im)morality is imposed on all of us. We are debating whether we should be "allowed" to pray in public, say the Pledge, post the Commandments, wear a cross or a particular T-shirt. Instead of defending our basic rights in response to their attacks, we need to be initiating and debating what will gain us ground we didn't previously have.

As with debates on partial-birth abortion and a woman's right to know, since we introduced the legislation, we named it. Groups opposed to protecting children and informed consent had to speak about it in our language. They lost the debate before it ever started. And for the first time, the American people got a glimpse of how brutal abortion really is and how extreme those who work against us really are. Every independent poll since the congressional debate on partial-birth abortion has gained between eight and ten points for the pro-life movement.

To win, we must draw the lines, set the stage, and choose the terms of discussion.

THE BELIEVABLE DREAM

Lincoln said it this way: "Freedom is the natural condition of the human race, in which the Almighty intended men to live. Those who fight the purpose of the Almighty will not succeed. They always have been, they always will be, beaten."

I have a dream. I can see this network in all fifty states. Why should you miss out on what's happening where you live just because you don't happen to be on the mailing list of the group taking the lead where the battle is the hottest? Why shouldn't you know about the Hate Crimes Bill being voted on in your state legislature? Or about the Leadership Institute training seminar on how to run for office that's being conducted down the street from you? Ever get frustrated when you can't find out where the local candidates stand on an issue? You can't keep up with all the school board votes, I know that. But *somebody* is. It's a shame they don't know how to find you to tell you who's on our side. If we linked to all those people finding all that information, you could get to it from one place.

Here are some of the things that can be done to take us to the next level. We just need people willing to invest in a new way of doing battle—a proactive, strategic, creative, and unified way.

State and local groups. Connecting the network of state and local affiliates of the national groups through state and local web pages will provide a secure area in which to strategize and a means to inform the grassroots in an immediate, informative, and effective way through live "Intelligence Briefings," which include streaming video and audio from our nation's leaders.

Ongoing voter registration. F2A provides a way for users to register to vote and find out where candidates stand on the issues that matter most. Users can plug in to the groups that are already surveying candidates and keeping track of their voting records and positions, such as the Christian Coalition, and National Right to Life. F2A developed voter guides for the 2004 presidential race and key senate races for all the partnering groups to use. More than two million were sent out as a result. E-mail armies are perfect for this, and our groups have them. Individuals can take it from there and provide their friends, neighborhood, church, and precinct with that critical information.

Prayer page. If we really believe that prayer paves the way for what's ahead, we need to make this the best we can in order to allow different groups to post prayer requests and link groups who are already praying together. Prayer chat rooms could connect every division of our army, from university groups all the way to international organizations. Daily/weekly/monthly conference "Clarion Calls" could be reserved and used by any group that wants to call the conference number, accommodating as many people as want to pray.

Evangelism sites/methods/tools. These allow groups helping the poor and feeding the hungry to partner with groups already effectively spreading the gospel.

Schools. Connecting Intervarsity Christian Fellowship, Campus Crusade for Christ, Youth for Christ, as well as homeschool networks and high school groups like First Priority and Teens for Life would allow them to share information, materials, and strategy without them starting from scratch.

Streamline training. Training can be posted both nationally and broken down by state to channel recruits to training offered by allied seminars, conferences, workshops, and meetings as well as provide it online.

Entertainment. Leaders like Ted Baehr and Larry Poland are well known, but there are groups set up to influence Hollywood that most of us aren't even aware of. Unfortunately, they aren't aware of each other, either. F2A can provide the same model for entertainment-related organizations—from those evangelizing to those training, writing, and producing Christian and pro-family films.

International. Many groups look to the U.S. for leadership. Among them are the representatives from France who fly to the March for Life in Washington, DC, every year. As one representative told me, "We don't have anything like this where we live. Abortion is accepted, and there aren't any protests there like there are here. I come here to be encouraged." F2A could provide international chats, password protected posting, and resources to download and help collaborative efforts to translate materials. This could also be a forum for reporting Christian persecution overseas.

Secure posting. This is a place where national, state, and local allied groups can post and download the best developments and discoveries, from campaigns to charter amendment language that has been found constitutional. Groups can put their own organization's name on this information and run with it. They can also post nonconfidential information directly on their web sites without having to come up with it on their own. This has already worked for thirteen states with marriage laws on the ballot. They each shared strategy, literature, video, artwork, and ideas via F2A, and it paid off. All won with an average of 70 percent of the vote!

Grassroots action. Recruit an army of volunteers from across America who can be called upon as needed. By linking to the e-mail armies of the allied partners, we can utilize the most cost-effective and efficient way to reach large numbers of people quickly.

Political action committee. F2A is working toward creating a PAC in order to help influence candidates, focusing on primary elections in order to have the most impact. The network is in place; now all that's needed is the funding.

REPORT FOR DUTY!

While we focus on the most significant battles affecting human life, human freedoms, and the human mind, we must also focus on *where* those battles are being waged. And we must fight the battle *our way.*

If you're sick of talking and tired of losing battles we should win, partner with the Faith2Action team and be a part of revolutionizing the cultural war! Because faith without action isn't a "nice outlook"; it isn't called a "good start." Faith without action is…"dead" (James 2:17). Through the Faith2Action network, we can accomplish what each group could not do alone—achieve victory on the issues that matter most.

This is just one plan. And Faith2Action is but one networking group. Others are moving forward that give me great hope. This is an essential component for victory.

Chapter 14

IT'S LATER
THAN YOU THINK

If the watchman sees the sword coming and does not
blow the trumpet to warn the people and the sword comes
and takes the life of one of them, that man will be taken away because
of his sin, but I will hold the watchman accountable for his blood.

EZEKIEL 33:6

Jeffrey Satinover, who holds degrees from Princeton and doctorates from Yale, MIT, and Harvard, was on my radio program one day, and I asked him about where we are in history. He explained that according to the *Babylonian Talmud,* the book of rabbinical interpretation of the Scriptures written a thousand years before Christ, there has been only *one time in history* that reflects where we are right now.

According to these writings, at only one other time in history were men given to men in marriage and women given to women. Want to venture a guess as to when? No, it wasn't at the time of Sodom and Gomorrah, although that was my guess. Homosexuality was rampant there, but according to the Talmud not homosexual "marriage." What about ancient Greece? *No.* Rome? *No.* Babylon? *No again.* The one time in history when homosexual "marriage" was practiced, Satinover reports, was…during the days of Noah. And according to Satinover, that's what the *Babylonian Talmud* says was the final straw that led to the flood.[1]

A VERSE COMES TO MIND

When I heard Satinover say that, my mind immediately went to a verse, one I've heard many times but never with such relevance. It's found in Matthew:

> "As it was in the days of Noah, so *it will be* at the coming of the Son of Man." (24:37)

There's something you should know about me. I don't naturally gravitate to end-times theology. I haven't even finished all the *Left Behind* novels. So when I first heard that verse, I thought sure, it was *really, really bad* during the days of Noah. And while it's really bad now, it has been really, really bad at other points in history, too. But if what Satinover says is true, it is *uniquely* like the "days of Noah" right now—and only right now.

But it can't be yet, you say? You have a lot going on in your life? You're getting married? Here's how the New Living Translation describes that very sentiment in Luke:

> "When the Son of Man returns, the world will be like the people were in Noah's day. In those days before the flood, the people enjoyed banquets and parties and weddings right up to the time Noah entered his boat and the flood came to destroy them all." (17:26–27)

Happily going about as if everything were fine. That's what *they* did, too.

REASON TO LISTEN

Do you know that about one-fourth of the Bible is prophecy? A quarter of the Bible is a lot—it's a big book. And do you know God's standard? Perfection. That means that if even one of those prophesies is wrong, you can discount all of them. Kind of like a prophet who makes a false prediction—that made him a *false* prophet and a candidate for stoning.

Do you know that four thousand prophecies in that Bible have already come true down to the last detail? If four thousand out of five thousand prophecies have already occurred exactly as the Bible predicted they would, you *might* want to pay attention to the rest.[2] The one thousand yet to be ful-filled are the ones regarding the last days before the return of Christ, and they're being checked off the list right now.[3]

The Bible made more than three hundred prophecies about the coming Messiah. Here are just a few:

- From the tribe of Judah (Genesis 49:10; Luke 3:33)
- Born in Bethlehem (Micah 5:2; Luke 2:4)
- Proceeded by a forerunner (Malachi 3:1; Luke 7:24, 27)
- To minister in Galilee (Isaiah 9:1–2; Matthew 4:13–16)
- Rejected by the Jews (Isaiah 53:3; John 1:11)
- Triumphal entry on a donkey (Zechariah 9:9; Mark 11:7)
- Betrayed for thirty pieces of silver (Zechariah 11:12; Matthew 26:14)
- Accused by false witnesses (Psalm 35:11; Mark 14:57)
- Spat on and struck (Isaiah 50:6; Matthew 26:67)
- Pierced through hands and feet (Zechariah 12:10; Luke 23:35)
- Soldiers gambled for His clothes (Psalm 22:17–18; Matthew 27:35)
- None of His bones were broken (Psalm 34:20; John 19:32–33, 36)

- Pierced through His side (Zechariah 12:10; John 19:34)
- Buried with the rich (Isaiah 53:9; Matthew 27:57–60)
- Resurrected (Psalm 16:10 and Psalm 49:15; Mark 16:6)

One man fulfilled every single one of these prophecies—and 285 more. His name is Jesus Christ. Coincidence, you say? Just what are the odds of such a coincidence? Try this: Cover the entire state of Texas with silver dollars two feet deep, put a red *X* on just one of them, and then blindfold someone and give him one chance to pick it. That's what scientists have said are the odds that Christ would have fulfilled just *eight* of those prophecies. And Christ fulfilled more than three hundred.[4]

I don't know about you, but if all those other prophecies came true, I'm going to expect more of the same when it comes to the remaining ones.

A GLIMPSE AHEAD

Here's what I remember from Sunday school: In the end times there's a one-world government and a good-looking charismatic leader that people really fall for. He seems like a great guy, but he happens to be the Antichrist. He talks about peace and requires that everyone take his mark in order to buy and sell. The upside of taking the mark is that you get to buy and sell; the downside is that you go to hell forever.

Not really a difficult choice, but a lot of people are going to make the wrong one. In case you're unsure, hell is worse than anything else—*anything* else. Oh yeah, and it's forever…and ever. Don't pick it, no matter what's behind the other curtains. Starvation, beheading, being shot, tortured—all are better options than hell forever. All of them *combined* are better options than hell forever. Just want to be clear.

People in previous generations have rejected the book of Revelation because many of the prophecies were considered absolute impossibilities. For example, Revelation 11 predicts that two witnesses who prophesy in Jerusalem will be killed and that "for three and a half days men from every people, tribe, language and nation will gaze on their bodies and refuse them burial" (v. 9). How could all the people in the world see an event like this? *Couldn't happen.* For centuries, people discounted the whole book of Revelation, and sometimes the entire Bible, because if this "impossibility." But today, television and the Internet have made it possible for people from every nation and language to see such an event.

Keeping in mind that there are a thousand prophecies regarding what's to come, here's a peek at just a few about that really likeable Antichrist.

- The Antichrist is a man (Daniel 7:21–25).
- He will arise from a union of ten kings (prime ministers/ presidents) (Daniel 7:24).
- He will uproot three of those kings (Daniel 7:8).
- The ten-nation union will merge into a dominant world government (Daniel 7:23).
- He will destroy many by peace (Daniel 8:25).
- His appearance will be "greater than his fellows" (Daniel 7:20).
- He will sit in the rebuilt Jewish Temple, claiming to be God (2 Thessalonians 2:3–4).
- He will be promoted by a miracle-working partner (Revelation 13:12).
- He will speak "great things" (Daniel 7:8).
- He will persecute God's people (Revelation 13:7; Daniel 7:21).
- He will dominate the world, but will face resistance (Daniel 11:21–45).
- He will not regard "the desire of women" (Daniel 11:37).
- The number of his name will be 666 (Revelation 13:18).

I'm not going to speculate about whether the Antichrist comes from the European Union or about when the rapture will occur—or even if there will be a rapture (Christians taken to heaven before the bulk of the worldwide persecution kicks in). But in a book about the criminalization of Christianity, I think I would be remiss if I didn't at least pass along some signs and possible ways this might be carried out.

Take a closer look at that last prophesy for a minute:

"This calls for wisdom. If anyone has insight, let him calculate the number of the beast, for it is man's number. His number is 666." (Revelation 13:18)

What does that mean? Are people really going to have "666" written on their foreheads? I'm sorry, but I just don't see that happening. Not in my lifetime anyway. But what if it's not a Manson-like mark? What if this thing is "logical" and "rational"? Viewed as "essential"? People have speculated that it could be anything from Social Security numbers to bar codes, but just what does the Bible say?

A third angel followed them and said in a loud voice: "*If anyone worships the beast and his image and receives his mark on the forehead or on the hand,* he, too, will drink of the wine of God's fury, which has been poured full strength into the cup of his wrath. He will be tormented with burning sulfur in the presence of the holy angels and of the Lamb. And the smoke of their torment rises for ever and ever. There is no rest day or night for those who worship the beast and his image, or for anyone who receives the mark of his name. (Revelation 14:9–11)

"Tormented with burning sulfur [or with fire and brimstone, as another translation puts it]...forever and ever"? One thing's for sure, *whatever* that mark is, *you don't want to take it.*

THE BEGINNING OF THE END?

According to the original Greek, the "mark" comes from the word *Chi-xi-stigma,* or *stizo,* which means "to stick" or "to prick."[5] Here's how Strong's concordance defines it:

5516. **chi xi stigma** *khee xee stig'-ma;* the 22nd, 14th and an obs. let-ter (4742 as a cross) of the Greek alphabet (intermediate between the 5th and 6th) used as numbers; denoting respectively 600, 60 and 6; 666 as a numeral:–six hundred threescore and six[6]

4742, **stigma**, *stig'-mah;* from a primary **stizo** (to "stick," i.e. *prick*); a *mark* incised or punched (for recognition of ownership), i.e. (fig) scar of service:—mark {1x}[7]

It's sticking or pricking an identification mark into someone for recognition of ownership or service. That doesn't sound to me like a Social Security number or a barcode. I'm not saying I know what it is, but I do know one thing that's exactly like that—a microchip.

I remember listening a few years ago to a news anchorman reporting on a computer chip about the size of a grain of rice that was inserted into a dog for identification—by pricking his skin. What he said never left me: "Here ya go, little fella. It won't be long before we get these, too." Since that broadcast, the microchips have been implanted in more than *a million* pets.[8]

I'm not suggesting that Rover is going to hell forever because he's been pricked with a mark "for recognition of ownership." But you have to admit that the concept could fit if it were applied to humans to identify them and allow them to buy and sell.

It turns out that this thing is really starting to catch on. The microchip has many names, including the "Radio Frequency Identification," or RFID. Here's how it's being used already:

- **Airports:** "[Hong Kong Airport] announced that to 'improve cus-tomer satisfaction,' a baggage tracking infrastructure using Radio Frequency Identification (RFID) will be installed."[9]
- **Marines:** "'In-transit visibility' [IVT] is defined as the ability to track the status of supplies needed for the mission. By combining information transmitted from satellites and radio identification

devices, the Marine Corps is recreating the way it handles logistics." This system allows Marines to log onto a web site, type in a supply container's tracking number, and pinpoint its approximate location.[10]

- **Babies:** It is now being used in the neonatal ward in the bracelet around the wrist of newborns to prevent mix-ups and kidnappings. "If someone leaves the room with the baby who is not authorized to do so, alarms go off."[11]
- **License plates:** "The German Green Party intends to designate the centre of Munich as a tolled zone to significantly reduce the amount of traffic on its streets, and has suggested using RFID tags for car registration. Every vehicle would have to carry a RFID transponder card emitting a unique registration code. The number plates of unregistered cars entering the city would be photographed, so they could be charged later."[12]
- **"Loyalty cards":** "The applications use an RFID-enabled loyalty card that can identify a customer as he or she walks through a store. The chip in the loyalty card transmits to a nearby reader when the customer is within 8 feet of the reader, triggering an avatar to appear on a nearby computer screen. The RFID reader identifies the information in the loyalty card and feeds the data to the avatar, which welcomes the customer to the store in an animated fashion."[13]

Loyalty, huh? The word the *Left Behind* end-times novels use for the mark of the beast is the same one retailers in Germany tried to use to track their customers. In March of 2004, activists in Germany protested "loyalty cards" that used radio frequency IDs to track customers. Their efforts forced one of Europe's largest retailers to back down from a trial run of the tags. A German privacy organization, FoeBud, led the charge against Metro Extra Future Stores, who agreed to stop putting RFID tags in their shopper "loyalty cards" and promised to replace RFID cards already issued to consumers.[14]

A victory for freedom in Germany. For now. The arguments of the privacy groups are good: Do you really want to be in a prison without walls, where the government can keep track of every single thing you do and everywhere you go? At every single minute? Kind of like a prisoner's ankle bracelet, only not as bulky. Do you want someone to be able to deduct money from your bank account without your knowing whether it's through a chip in your license plate charging a toll, or a store charging a purchase, or a government agency exacting a penalty or limiting your access?

As I make the case for the criminalization of Christianity, there are many who balk at this idea. I don't blame you. I was one of them. But if what we believe becomes illegal, just how are they going to put all those Christians in jail? How in the world are they going to control everybody? Can't people just vote for change? Yeah, that's why I'm writing this book. But if we don't, the same Bible they're trying to make illegal has given us a thousand clues as to how Christianity will *ultimately* be criminalized. This is all coming because God said it was going to come.

BANNED FROM THE GROCERY STORE?

The Bible says this mark isn't just for "recognition or ownership"; you're going to need it to *buy and sell:*

> He causes all, both small and great, rich and poor, free and slave, to receive a mark on their right hand or on their foreheads, and that no one may *buy or sell* except one who has the mark or the name of the beast, or the number of his name. (Revelation 13:16–17, NKJV)

Okay, you can't buy your way out of this. Rich and poor take the mark. Influence doesn't get you out. Small and great take the mark. If you want to buy or sell, you take the mark of the beast. Of course if you do, you burn in hell forever. As long as we have our options straight.

RFID technology is even being used now in order to buy and sell. Club hoppers in Spain are now getting a microchip implanted under their skin to get VIP access and to keep from having to carry a wallet or purse. If you want a drink, you can wave your RFID implant within a few feet of a scanner, and you're done.

How very convenient it all is. Except that now instead of stealing your wallet, thieves can just chop off your hand. Before assailants start pulling out other people's hands to pay for stuff, perhaps somebody needs to find a way to disable the thing if the person isn't alive. That's what I'd do if I were the one developing the mark of the beast. (I can't believe I just wrote that.) By the way, if you're running commercials to pitch the mark of the beast, the first thing you have to do is rename it. *Duh.*

Here's how I envision the Mark of the Beast commercial:

MARK OF THE BEAST COMMERCIAL

Voiceover: You're not still carrying around that *heavy* purse, are you?

[VIDEO: Grandma hunched over heavy pocketbook while would-be thieves give each other the nod for the post-purchase mugging.]

Voiceover: Don't you know that makes you an easy target for crime?

[VIDEO: Grandma hoists her heavy purse onto the fast food counter while very attractive teens walk in, roll their eyes at grandma, wave their hands, and begin to eat while she's still looking for her change.]

Voiceover: Don't listen to the kooks who think there's something wrong with being smart, safe, and secure.

[VIDEO: Airport security line of all the attractive "chipped" people smiling as they go through the express security lane, while all the nerds, geeks, old, and ugly finger-pointing people stand in long, winding lines while the security people shake their heads at the antiquated, outdated extremists.]

Voiceover: Secure-a-chip. It's smart, safe, and secure…and so small you'll forget you have it!

[VIDEO: Man looks for his wallet until he realizes that he has the chip and waves it by the scanner, as his attractive wife looks at him smiling, shaking her head playfully. They both laugh and the Secure-a-chip image appears on the screen.]

Voiceover: [Read very low and very fast.] Those with high blood pressure, pacemakers, pregnant women, or those planning to become pregnant should consult with their doctor before implantation. Possible side effects of the Secure-a-chip include infection, allergic reaction, boils, and burning in hell forever.

I should really get more sleep than I do.

Back to what I was saying about possibly disabling this thing so a thief won't be inclined to cut off a body part to go shopping. About ten years ago I heard some scientists talk about a million-dollar study that had been conducted to determine where in the body you could find the most temperature fluctuation. The thought at the time was that this location could provide a means of "charging" a battery for an implant under the skin. After all that money and all that studying they found out what most mothers already know. When your child has a fever, what do you do? You automatically place the back of your hand on the child's forehead. That's what the study reportedly found. The hand and the forehead provide the most temperature fluctuation in the body. Could that be connected with a way to recharge or disable this device should it be removed from the body? It's possible.

PROLIFERATION OF THE CHIP

Okay, okay, some freaky people in Spain are using this technology to pay for drinks. They'll probably do it in California, too, but that doesn't mean anyone is going to take this thing seriously. Or that it will be required. *Really?*

The Attorney General of Mexico and at least 160 people, including the top federal prosecutors and investigators in his office, have been implanted with RFID tags to obtain access to restricted areas inside the AG's headquarters. The Associated Press reported that "more are scheduled to get 'tagged' in coming months, and key members of the Mexican military, the police and the office of President Vicente Fox might follow suit." They reported that the chips were *required* to enter a new federal "anti-crime information center."[15]

I guess you could still quit if you didn't want to accept the implant. So it's not really *required;* it's just take the chip or lose access to those high-security areas. Or maybe if they're lucky, high-ranking public officials can get a demotion—they haven't required the access chip for those people just yet.

In addition to the chips being used by the Mexican government, more than one thousand people have implanted them for medical reasons—in Mexico alone. That same article reported, "The Food and Drug Administration had yet to approve microchips as medical devices in the United States."[16] As of the July 14 article, the microchip wasn't FDA approved for use in humans in America. *Whew!*

Newsflash: *It is now.*

On my birthday, October 13, 2004, the FDA approved RFID tags for medical purposes. I would've rather had cake.

Now, I'm not saying that people who get RFID chips right now are taking the mark of the beast. I just see the technological foundation being laid for something that I find scary. I can tell you that *I'm* not going to let anyone put anything in my hand (or forehead), *period.* No matter how logical, reasonable, or practical it may seem. If it's inserted into the hand (or forehead) to identify, buy, or sell, no matter what you say, *I'm out.* I don't care if it means I can't buy anymore. I don't care if it means I can't fly anymore. I don't care if it means I die. You can make your case, but I already made that decision— *when I was about ten.* Before any of this technology even existed. Four more words come to mind: Fear God, not man.

This just in: On February 10, 2005, the U.S. House of Representatives voted 261 to 171 for the "Real ID Act," which will mandate that driver's licenses (and other ID card) include undefined "machine-readable technology, with minimum data elements," such as an RFID tag. As an antiterrorist measure, the White House and about 95 percent of Republicans supported it, while three-fourths of the House Democrats opposed it. Rejecting this new ID card would mean you could be denied access to "airplanes, trains…and other areas controlled by the federal government."[17] I have to tell you, it is not often that I'm on the side of the ACLU, but I oppose this measure that moves us toward a national ID card—a step closer to the Mark—an ID that, if inserted, conveniently won't get lost.

BECAUSE I CARE

You may not believe a single word of any of this. That's why I'm writing it *before* this thing is viewed as so "practical" and so "logical" that you find yourself being swayed. This was prophesied nearly two thousand years ago when the prospect of some mark on your hand or forehead to identify, buy, and sell was ludicrous and "impossible." Do not be deceived. The same God who predicted it was very clear about what happens if you take the mark, *whatever* it is: eternity in hell.

Don't believe in hell? Doesn't matter. Some things are true whether you believe them or not. I happen to care more about where you spend your eternity than I do about whether or not you like me. And while I expect a lot of hate speech as a result of this book, I *never* want to hear these words:

WHERE "TOLERANCE" LEADS

When we disagreed while watching the news,
You chose to ignore my misguided views.
I trusted you and thought you were my friend,
But you stood by and watched me come to this end.

When I fell for the lie "my body, my choice,"
Fear of offending me silenced your voice,
"Don't let me die!" the child in me implored,
But you drove to the clinic and dropped me off at the door.

You didn't tell me Jesus took all of my blame,
Because you didn't want to be called a mean name,

It was all about you, not shining the light,
You didn't speak up to show me what was right.

That my sins were paid for by a God who loved me,
You could have explained it so I could see.
Yes, you were "tolerant," when love would have cost more,
When there was time to choose heaven's door.

But for the first time, I can now tell,
With a warm, pleasant smile, you let me go to hell
You called it "tolerance," but it was not love,
You let your friend go to hell, *who* were you thinking of?

—Janet L. Folger

Are you sure you're going to heaven? Refusing the mark of the beast won't ensure your entrance into heaven. Being pro-life or even voting Republican won't get you in. Belief in God is not enough (even the devil believes in God). To be sure you're going to heaven, the Bible says you must:

- **Recognize that you're a sinner.** "There is no one righteous, not even one" (Romans 3:10). We can't make excuses or blame others or our circumstances for our actions, "for all have sinned and fall short of the glory of God" (v. 23).

- **Recognize that Jesus died on the cross for your sins.** "God demonstrates his own love for us in this: While we were still sinners, Christ died for us" (Romans 5:8). "The wages of sin is death, but the gift of God is eternal life in Christ Jesus our Lord" (6:23). *He paid your admission price…with His life.*

- **Repent of your sins.** Repent means to change direction. "Repent, then, and turn to God, so that your sins may be wiped out, that times of refreshing may come from the Lord" (Acts 3:19). *God commands us to repent and turn away from things that displease Him.*

- **Receive Jesus as your Savior—and Lord** (the one who calls the shots). Don't try to clean up your life first. Come to Jesus just as you are and allow Him to change your life. "To all who received him, to those who believed in his name, he gave the right to become children of God" (John 1:12). Jesus said, "All that the Father gives me will come to me, and whoever comes to me I will never drive away" (6:37).

- **Pray.** "Dear Lord Jesus, I know that I am a sinner and am in need of forgiveness. I know that You died on the cross to give me that forgiveness. I accept the ultimate gift You gave to pay the penalty for my sins. I invite You to be my Savior and the Lord of my life. I trust You and want to follow Your way all the days of my life. In Jesus name, Amen."

- **Know for sure that you have eternal life.** "For it is by grace you have been saved, through faith—and this not from yourselves, it is the gift of God—not by works, so that no one can boast" (Ephesians 2:8–9). "He who has the Son has life; he who does not have the Son of God does not have life.… I write these things to you who believe in the name of the Son of God so that you may know that you have eternal life" (1 John 5:12–13).

When you really mean those things you prayed, your life will change. Jesus said if you love Him, you'll keep His commandments. We love God when we actually do what He says. That's where putting your faith to action comes in. *"Faith by itself, if it is not accompanied by action, is dead"* (James 2:17).

There may not be much more time to proclaim the gospel. Rest assured, if they can silence the truth, they *will* silence the gospel. The criminalization of Christianity is coming. Not because my book says so, but because God's does.

DANGEROUS TIMES ARE COMING

Mark this: There will be terrible times in the last days. People will be lovers of themselves, lovers of money, boastful, proud, abusive, disobedient to their parents, ungrateful, unholy, without love, unforgiving, slanderous, without self-control, brutal, not lovers of the good, treacherous, rash, conceited, lovers of pleasure rather than lovers of God—having a form of godliness but denying its power. Have nothing to do with them. (2 Timothy 3:1–5)

Sort of like reading the paper, isn't it?

In fact, everyone who wants to live a godly life in Christ Jesus will be persecuted, while evil men and impostors will go from bad to worse, deceiving and being deceived. But as for you, continue in what you have learned and have become convinced of, because you know those from whom you learned it, and how from infancy you have known the holy Scriptures, which are able to make you wise for salvation through faith in Christ Jesus. (vv. 12–15)

Yes, persecution is coming. If you live in Sudan, North Korea, China, or *any* Muslim country, it's *already here.*

Sudan: "African slaves, especially Christians, are viewed as lower than animals.… The story of 'Joseph,' a Christian, is told in a recent newsletter of the Persecution Project Foundation, an organization that monitors Christian persecution in Africa. While Joseph was at church, some of the camels he was in charge of escaped, and his master flew into a rage. 'Ibrahim,' Phillips writes, 'swore he would kill Joseph and do to him what had been done to Jesus…he would crucify him.' After brutally beating Joseph on the head and all over his body, the master laid him out on a wooden plank. He then nailed Joseph to the plank by driving nine-inch nails through his hands, knees and feet. He then poured acid on Joseph's legs to inflict even greater pain, and finally left him for dead.... To say that Christians are second-class citizens in much of the Islamic world [not just the Sudan] is a cruel understatement."[18]

North Korea: "Since 1953, about three hundred thousand Christians have 'disappeared.' Anyone found with a Bible may be shot. One woman reported seeing Christians killed when molten steel was poured on them. She also stated that Christian prisoners were often not given clothes and were treated like animals."[19]

Saudi Arabia: "O'Conner, thirty-six, has been tortured and threatened with death if he does not renounce his faith and convert to Islam.... The Indian Christian told friends who visited him in prison he then was dragged to a religious police office where his legs were chained and he was hung upside down. For the next seven hours, his captors alternately kicked and beat him in the chest and ribs, O'Conner claimed.... [H]e was 'whipped on his back and soles of his feet by electrical wires,' causing intense pain."[20]

Iraq: "In the latest and most dramatic evidence an all-out jihad has been declared against Iraq's minority Christian population, car bombs exploded outside at least five Christian churches today."[21]

India: "Pastor Kumar was told he would be killed in front of his wife and two-year-old son if he conducted church services. The more than forty new believers in this south Indian village—whom Kumar led to Christ over the past two years—were also threatened with death if they set foot inside the church."[22]

Kazakhstan: "On two separate occasions a pastor and church members have been physically attacked by a group of people punching them, throwing them from a moving lorry, stealing and destroying religious literature, as well as stealing money and a mobile phone."[23]

Palestine: "After slaughtering a Muslim-turned-Christian, Islamic extremists have reportedly returned the man's body to his Palestinian family in four pieces."[24]

China: A Chinese Christian man named Zhang Yi-nan was severely beaten after arriving at a "re-education through labor" camp.[25]

WAKE UP!

Persecution of Christians is happening around the globe in communist and Muslim countries, where it's *the rule* rather than the exception. We need to use our voices to speak for them.

Xiao Bi-guang, a Chinese Christian who was arrested with Zhang Yi-nan, was charged with "subverting" the Chinese government and "socialist system," but he was released from prison after publicity from his case elicited the prayers and protests of Christians worldwide. Xiao said he was released because he got his story out on the Internet. The more people know about what's going on, the more we can do to stop it.[26]

Just because we know persecution is coming doesn't mean we can't fight it. It doesn't mean we have to put out a welcome mat and usher it through our doors. It doesn't mean we have to lie down in front of the tanks that seek to silence the voice for freedom and the voice of truth.

Make no mistake, if they can silence the truth, they will silence the gospel and criminalize Christianity. And the longer you stay on the sidelines, the sooner it will happen.

Chapter 15

REASON FOR HOPE

The only way they can win is if we give up.

MAGGIE GALLAGHER

Once upon a time there was a great big elephant called Tiny. That wasn't his real name, but that was what everyone called him. His real name was Mighty, but he hadn't heard his real name for so long that he had forgotten who he was. Mighty was born at the circus and never knew what it was like to run free in the jungle as his parents had done. He ate only what was fed to him and never got to choose anything else.

Since birth, he had been told what to do and where to go by all those around him. He was even put on a big heavy chain to keep him from escaping. But Mighty wanted to be free. He had heard from his parents about what it was like in the jungle—to roam and play wherever you wanted to go. Mighty tried and tried to break free from the heavy chain, but he always failed.

There was a mean circus man everyone called Judge. And when Judge would see Mighty try to break free, he would hit him with a big stick and say, "Tiny, you'll *never* be free." He said it over and over and louder and louder so that every time Mighty thought about roaming free in the jungle as his parents had, he would hear Judge's words again and again in his mind: "Tiny, you'll *never* be free." Mighty didn't like the way that stick felt either. So finally he quit trying. He quit dreaming. And he even forgot his real name.

Then young Mighty grew up. That heavy chain couldn't hold him anymore, but Judge had done such a good job of beating him down that Mighty didn't know it. In fact, that chain was replaced with a thin little rope tied to Mighty's leg and a small stake in the ground.

Mighty could snap that rope in an instant. But he had been told so often that he couldn't that he didn't even try. And so there he stayed, tied to a teensy-weensy rope that only let him take two steps forward and two steps back. Mighty swayed back and forth and back and forth, going nowhere. Day in and day out, told what to think and what to eat, back and forth, going nowhere.

One day some troublesome teens came to the circus and saw Mighty tied up behind the big tent. One bully was named PC and the other one was called TV. They started pelting Mighty with trash and rocks, shouting, "What are you going to do about it, 'Tiny'?"

Mighty looked down and saw the little rope and hung his head low, trying to turn away from the stinging rubbish being thrown at him. He rocked back and forth and back and forth, going nowhere.

Then a little girl came and chased the bullies away. She was little, but she had a big loud voice and wasn't afraid to use it. She walked up to Mighty and held out a hand full of peanuts. "Hello, Mr. Elephant," she said. "My name is Truth, but they call me Trudy—*even though I hate it.*" Mighty moved closer to the little girl and ate the peanuts from her hand.

"You're so big. Your name can't be Tiny like the sign says. What's your *real* name?"

Real name, Real name. Mighty thought hard. "Everyone calls me 'Tiny.'"

"Everyone calls me Trudy, but that doesn't mean it's my name. I'll bet your name is Big, or Powerful, or Mighty, or something like that!"

Mighty couldn't believe his ears. He remembered! "Yes! That *is* my name! My name is Mighty!"

Truth reached into her pocket and brought out another handful of peanuts. "Well, if your name is Mighty, then you'd better start acting like it."

"What do you mean?" Mighty asked. "I can't do anything. I'm tied to this rope."

"You call *that* a rope? You could break that thing in your sleep."

"No, Judge said I can't, and PC and TV told me I'm bad and stupid and weak."

"Those bullies? You're going to listen to those bullies? What's your name again?" asked Truth.

"My name is Tin— uh, Mighty."

"And what do you want to do, Mighty?" Truth asked.

Mighty remembered the jungle he had heard about when he was young. "I used to dream heroic dreams of roaming free in the jungle…but that was a long time ago."

"You can do whatever you want," said Truth. "What do you most want?"

Mighty looked down. "Of course, it's not so bad here. They feed me what they want and I eat it, and I get to walk two steps forward and two steps back."

"Two steps? Say what you want, but I wouldn't call that *free*. Two steps forward and two steps back is the same as going nowhere!"

Mighty looked at how far he was allowed to step and had to agree. "You're right. I really don't like going nowhere."

"What *do* you want?" Truth asked a final time.

"I want to be free," Mighty said.

"Then snap the rope," the little girl replied.

"But Judge said I couldn't."

"Snap the rope."

"But PC and TV—"

"Snap the rope," she said emphatically. "There is a big old woods on the other side of the street. It's not quite a jungle, but you could go anywhere you wanted. Even over to my house to visit. I live in the white house at the corner, and the woods are my backyard. If you want to be free, you need to forget about the lies and remember the truth. You must remember who you are. You are an elephant. You are big and strong. And before I go, I have two questions."

"Yes?" Mighty asked.

"Do you want to be free?"

"Yes," replied the hesitant elephant.

"My final question…" asked Truth, "What is your name?"

"My name is…Ti…Mighty."

"*What* is your name?"

"Mighty," he said more elephantically.

"What is your name?" she asked a third time.

"MIGHTY!" And with that Mighty snapped the rope. He kissed Truth on the cheek with his trunk and ran free to the woods, where he lived happily ever after.

In case you didn't make the connection, the elephant is *us*. Christians. The ones history will show to be the good guys. The ones who say dismembering children is wrong. The ones who stand for marriage between a man and a woman. The ones who believe what the Declaration of Independence and the Constitution have to say, including the part about our inalienable rights endowed by our Creator. But we've been beaten down so long that we don't even remember our name. We are *Christians*. Sons and daughters of the Most High God. The "Mighty" God who empowers and enables us to move *mountains* and snap ropes. And He came to set the captives free.

So forget what the judges say—we have the power to limit them and impeach them. Forget what's PC and what the TV tells us. I'd rather listen to Truth.

We've been playing by the opposition's made-up rules. Treated worse than an elephant in a circus act, Christians have been ridiculed, blamed, assaulted, censored, fined, fired, and thrown in jail.

The bullies of the courts, the media, the educators, and Hollywood have been beating us with big sticks only because we've stood by and allowed it. Bullies have always fought against what is right. We need to quit going nowhere and snap the rope. Quit reacting and responding and start using the freedoms with which we're endowed.

Snap the rope.

A WOMAN NAMED PHYLLIS

There once was a woman named Phyllis. And she didn't have a chance. She was facing a freight train powered by every earthly power broker. *Every* power broker. Congress had just passed legislation for a constitutional amendment—one Phyllis didn't want. But it seemed that everybody *else* did. The vote in the U.S. House of Representatives was 354 to 23. The Senate vote was 84 to 8. Now the thirty-eight states were rushing to see who could ratify it the fastest. In the first month, fourteen states passed it, and by the end of the first year, the total was up to thirty.[1] With eight states to go, this amendment was unstoppable. The media spearheaded the crusade, and no voice of opposition was heard. The conservatives caved because of fear. Wow, *there's* a surprise.

Phyllis didn't think she had a chance either. After all, she's a smart lady. But she knew that opposing the freight-train amendment was "the right thing to do." She had a phone, and she had a newsletter, and she was going to use them for everything they were worth. So she made a four-page, two-column case in her newsletter and sent it to three thousand people.

Then she got a call from a woman in Oklahoma who took that newsletter to the Oklahoma State Legislature and stopped the amendment dead in its tracks. It was then that Phyllis realized that she had something.[2] That was the beginning of the end of a dangerous amendment and an "impossible" victory.

That amendment was the ERA. That woman was Phyllis Schlafly.

OUR TOOLS

If you check out the end of the book—not mine, but God's—those on His side win. And if we will humble ourselves, pray, seek His face, and turn from our wicked ways, He will hear from heaven, forgive our sins and heal our land. We are to "occupy" until He comes (Luke 19:13, KJV)—not run or retreat. It's time we do that again. Our nation *is* "under God," as we continue to say in the Pledge (despite attempts to stop us). Our motto remains "In God we trust."

If you don't like the idea of being silenced or the prospect of your beliefs being criminalized, you must act. *We* must act. In a unified way as the body of Christ. And He's given us some very powerful weapons.

Truth. I have often spoken on the abortion issue and laid out the odds. Say we have a scale. On one side are the courts, Congress, the White House, the media, Hollywood, the schools, the power brokers, and a ton of money; on the other is…the truth. Guess which side I'd pick? I would pick the truth. It doesn't matter what the issue is; I would pick the truth. Because not only does truth exist, but as you may have heard, the truth will prevail.

Persistence. How do we get to the Promised Land? The answer: *Keep walking.* The abortion movement said we'd be gone by now. They said after three long decades we would have packed our bags and called it quits. They were wrong. We're not going away until children are protected again. And that may happen a lot sooner than they thought. How do I know that? Because regardless of the odds, regardless of the issue, persistence wins.

Love. A woman approached me after a talk I gave in Minnesota and introduced herself as a "former abortionist." She said she had many friends in the abortion business that "desperately want out, but they feel like they have nowhere to go." She was a member of a group that called themselves the Centurions. "You know," she explained, "like the Romans who killed Christ." I asked her to deliver a message to those she knew who were still performing abortions, something I hope every abortionist in the country hears: "If you will walk away from killing children, we will *welcome you with open arms.* You *do* have a place to come."

That's what the Cross is all about. Whatever you've done, God can forgive you, just like He's forgiven me. His love will transform your life no matter what your sin. How do I know? Because He said so and because love conquers all.

      THE CRIMINALIZATION OF CHRISTIANITY

Faith. Jesus said that if we had faith the size of a mustard seed, we could move mountains (Matthew 17:20). You may have noticed we have some mountains to move. You may not have much faith. The good news is that you don't need much. Imagine what God could do with the mountain ranges in front of us if we trusted Him with every fiber of our being? We have faith, and faith moves mountains.

God. Again, it's not that God's on our side as much as it is that we're on His—on the side of His principles, His commandments, His way. That's where you want to be if you want to win. That's why Christians spend all that time reading the Bible. The strategy, the encouragement, and the means to fulfill the destiny you were created for are in that book. The words of naysayers don't matter. The odds don't matter. The headlines don't matter. The circumstances don't matter. Your feelings don't matter. What God says matters, and it will happen. With God, *all things* are possible.

We will see the goodness of the Lord in the land of the living. When God's people start acting on what they say they believe, we will see victory and take the land. We have the truth and the truth will prevail. We have persistence, and persistence wins. We have love, and love conquers all. We have faith, and faith moves mountains. And we have God—with whom all things are possible.

I have great hope we will win this battle for our future. Because despite the attacks on us, we have more reasons to be hopeful than ever before.

TWENTY YEARS

I finished writing this book twenty years—to the day—after I cut class to go hear President Ronald Reagan speak. It is now November 2, 2004, the day America will elect our next president of America. The next Supreme Court and the future of our nation is at stake. And as the results pour in, it is clear that we are a nation divided. As Rabbi Lapin said, "We are two nations occupying the same piece of real estate and engaged in a giant cultural tug-of-war."[3] But as I watch the results, I will remember that the God we serve is bigger than the billionaires, more powerful than the pundits, and mightier than the media and movie makers. That is why, as I write this, I have the optimism of Ronald Wilson Reagan, who told us that "the best is yet to come." And judging from the results I see, he was right.

VICTORY ON THE HORIZON

1. Values voters have turned the tide.

Not only did marriage win across the board (in eleven out of eleven measures) on November 2, 2004, but moral values elected the president. "Moral values" was cited by voters in exit polls as the number one issue that "mattered most in deciding how [they] voted for president," and of the 22 percent who listed it, 80 percent voted for Bush.[4] President George W. Bush captured the "attend church weekly" and "nearly weekly/monthly" group, while John Kerry captured the "seldom/never attend church" group.[5] There's a voting block to brag about. People of faith became people of action and voted the values that matter most. They also sent a strong signal through changes in Congress, including Republican gains and the stunning defeat of Senate Minority Leader Tom Daschle (D-SD).

2. Traditional marriage is *the* most winning electoral issue in the nation.

The antifamily elements clearly overplayed their hand. In every state that voted to amend its constitution to protect marriage between one man and one woman, marriage won by a landslide. That's seventeen out of seventeen for those of you keeping score at home. If you're a politician wondering about which side to take, have a look at those margins:

- Alaska—passed 68 to 32 percent
- Arkansas—passed 75 to 25 percent
- Georgia—passed 77 to 23 percent
- Hawaii—passed 69 to 29 percent
- Kentucky—passed 75 to 25 percent

THE CRIMINALIZATION OF CHRISTIANITY

- Louisiana—passed 78 to 22%
- Michigan—passed 59 to 41%
- Mississippi—passed 86 to 14%
- Missouri—passed 71 to 29%
- Montana—passed 66 to 34%
- Nebraska—passed 70 to 30%
- Nevada—passed 70 to 30% (2000); 67 to 33% (2002)
- North Dakota—passed 73 to 27%
- Ohio—passed 62 to 38%
- Oklahoma—passed 76 to 24%
- Oregon—passed 57 to 43%
- Utah—passed 66 to 34%[6]

3. The media monopoly has been broken.

The days of the news monopoly by the big three networks is over. It's a different world now. Ninety percent of America has switched to other news sources. Web loggers (or bloggers), alternative radio like Rush Limbaugh and Sean Hannity, Christian radio, and Internet news sites like www.worldnetdaily.com have now become conservatives' preferred avenues for information. Another welcome player is Fox News, which, though not perfect, is making a sincere effort to remain balanced in its coverage—and is number one in cable news as a result.

Those alternative news sources led to the exposure of "Rathergate"—the preelection attack on President Bush's National Guard service with the now-famous forgery that led to Dan Rather stepping down as CBS anchor. Rumor has it that in the interest of fairness, CBS may soon be dropping the C from their name.

4. I still see men and women of courage.

Like Pastor Joe Wright. When he was asked to open the session of the Kansas Senate in prayer, this is what the senators heard:

"Heavenly Father, we come before You today to ask Your forgiveness and to seek Your direction and guidance.

We know Your Word says, 'Woe to those who call evil good,' but that is exactly what we have done. We have lost our spiritual equilibrium and reversed our values.

We confess that we have ridiculed the absolute truth of Your Word and call it pluralism.

We have exploited the poor and called it the lottery.

We have rewarded laziness and called it welfare.

We have killed our unborn and called it choice.

We have shot abortionists and called it justifiable.

We have neglected to discipline our children and called it building self-esteem.

We have abused power and called it politics.

We have coveted our neighbor's possessions and called it ambition.

We have polluted the air with profanity and pornography and called it freedom of expression.

We have ridiculed the time-honored values of our forefathers and called it enlightenment.

Search us, O God, and know our hearts today; cleanse us from every sin and set us free. Guide and bless these men and women who have been sent to direct us to the center of Your will and to openly ask these things in the name of Your Son, the living Savior, Jesus Christ. Amen!"[7]

Legislators walked out during the prayer in protest. Within six weeks, the Central Christian Church where Reverend Wright is a pastor received more than five thousand phone calls—only forty-seven of them negative. Requests for copies of his prayer have come from as far away as India, Africa, and Korea. Commentator Paul Harvey aired it on his program and reportedly received "a larger response" than "any other he has ever aired."[8]

OUR CHOICE

Bob Knight's speech asserting that the homosexual lobby seeks the criminalization of Christianity is one I didn't believe and, frankly, didn't want to hear. But some things are true whether *I* believe them or not—and true whether or not I listen. We now know the very real threat to our values and our freedoms. And now that we know, we have a choice. We can either speak the truth with the freedoms we have left or use our "right to remain silent" until those words are being read to us before we join Sweden's pastor Ake Green in a prison for the politically incorrect.

Christian, it is time to snap the rope. To win, we must work *together.* We must move from defense to *offense.* And we must *control the debate.*

We must live our faith in every segment of our culture—not on the retreat, but taking truth and freedom forward. We must work together where the battle is the hottest, set the agenda, and take back ground. We must also use the freedoms our Founding Fathers worked so hard for, including our most basic: We must vote.

What gives me hope is that the battles we've been losing have been lost by default. In the 2000 election, out of sixty million evangelical Christians, only fifteen million voted. We've been playing the game with only one-fourth of our players. Imagine what would happen if we came back onto the field with all *eleven* of them! We could start playing as a team…on the offense, carrying the ball across the goal, and winning!

By the way, this has already begun to happen. According to the National Election Pool exit poll, in 2004 Bush's vote among evangelicals was up by 10 percent from 2000. In fact, the evangelical vote constituted 36 percent (over a third) of Bush's voters. By comparison, African-Americans, the "most loyal of Democratic constituencies" constituted only about 21 percent (or one-fifth) of Kerry's voters.[9]

Christianity was never intended to be a spectator sport! It is meant to be played out in every area of our life. Faith without action isn't a "nice outlook"; it isn't called a "good start." Faith without action is…"dead" (James 2:17).

We would do well to heed William Wallace's words in the movie *Braveheart*:

William Wallace: I am William Wallace. And, I see a whole army of my countrymen, here in defiance of tyranny. You've come to fight as freemen, and freemen you are. What will you do without freedom? Will you fight?

Man: No…we will run…and we will live.

William Wallace: Aye. Fight and you may die. Run and you'll live—at least a while. And, dying in your beds, many years from now, would you be willing to trade all the days from this day to that for one chance, just one chance, to come back here and tell our enemies, that they may take our lives, but they'll never take our freedom![10]

Like Wallace, Patrick Henry epitomized the American spirit with his famous words: "Give me liberty or give me death."

If I asked Americans if they would die for their freedoms, most of them would say yes. At least the people I know. But perhaps a more important question might be: Are you willing to *live* for your freedom? That means to use it to its fullest. Right now we have the freedom to proclaim the name of Jesus Christ. But are we really using it? I know *I* haven't used that freedom fully.

But the fact that it may soon be taken away makes me want to proclaim the name of Jesus and God's truths even more. I have come to learn that speaking the truths of God's Word in the public square is critical, not just for the future of our nation, but for the future of our freedom. Because if they can silence the truth, they will silence the gospel.

NOTES

Chapter 1

1. "University Cuts off Christian Fraternity," *WorldNetDaily*, 15 August 2004. http://www.worldnetdaily.com/news/article.asp?ARTICLE_ID=39975.
2. Michael Harmon, "Persecution of Christians Is Growing—in Sweden and Canada," *Press Herald*, 30 July 2004.
3. "Swedish Pastor Sentenced to One Month's Jail for Offending Homosexuals," *Ecumenical News International*, 30 June 2004.
4. Bob Knight, radio interview, *Faith2Action with Janet Folger*, 20 January 2004.
5. "Pastor's Imprisonment for Sermon Protested," *WorldNetDaily*, 30 July 2004. http://www.worldnetdaily.com/news/article.asp?ARTICLE_ID=39687.
6. Alan Sears and Craig Osten, *The Homosexual Agenda: Exposing the Principal Threat to Religious Freedom Today* (Nashville, TN: Broadman & Holman, 2003), 183.
7. John Leo, "Stomping on Free Speech," *townhall.com*, 12 April 2004. http://www.townhall.com/columnists/johnleo/jl20040412.shtml.
8. Sears and Osten, *The Homosexual Agenda*, 182.
9. Art Moore, "Bible Verses Regarded as Hate Literature," *WorldNetDaily*, 18 February 2003. http://www.worldnetdaily.com/news/article.asp?ARTICLE_ID=31080.
10. Mathew D. Staver, *Same-Sex Marriage: Putting Every Household at Risk* (Nashville, TN: Broadman & Holman, 2004), 63.
11. Center for Disease Control, *HIV/AIDS Surveillance Report*, 9, no. 2 (May 1998). "Divisions of HIV/AIDs Prevention, Centers for Disease

Control" Survey Report, National Center for HIV, STD and TB Prevention, Vol. 14, Table 1. http://www.cdc.gov/hiv/stats/hasr1402/table1.htm.

12. Sears and Osten, *The Homosexual Agenda*, 183.

13. "Court Upholds Firing of Worker Who Opposed 'Gay' Poster, Finds Employer Did Not Discriminate against Worker Based on His Religion," *The Employment Law Authority*, Ogletree Deakins February/March 2004, 8. http://ogletreedeakins.inherent.com/images/ns_attachment/attachment62.pdf.

14. "Christian Stripped of Workplace Signs," *WorldNetDaily*, 24 August 2004. http://www.worldnetdaily.com/news/article.asp?ARTICLE_ID=40112.

15. Author telephone interview with Enoch Lawrence, 10:30 EST, 27 September 2004.

16. Ibid.

17. Julie Foster, "Christians Sue Lab for Discrimination: Accuse Sandia of Giving Special Rights to 'Gays,' Denying Believers Equal Treatment," *WorldNetDaily*, 2000. http://www.worldnetdaily.com/news/article.asp?ARTICLE_ID=17871.

18. Lorne Gunter, "Bill Means End of Free Speech," *Edmonton Journal*, 28 March 2004.

19. Ibid.

20. Folger, *:30 Seconds to Common Sense*, 194.

21. Sears and Osten, *The Homosexual Agenda*, 185.

22. Ibid., 183.

23. Robert A. Jason, "My Radio Interview with Janet Folger," e-mail, 29 June 2004.

24. Divisional Court, *"Brillinger and the Canadian Lesbian and Gay Archives v. Imaging Excellence Inc. et al.,"* Board of Inquiry Decisions, Ontario Human Rights Commission, 29 September 1999 and 24 February 2000; Art Moore, "Freedom of Conscience Debated in Ontario," *WorldNetDaily*, 17 December 2001. http://www.worldnetdaily.com/news/article.asp?ARTICLE_ID=25673.

25. Moore, "Freedom of Conscience Debated in Ontario."

26. "The New Totalitarianism: On Its Way to the USA," *Issues & Views*, 17 June 2002.

27. Liam Reid, "Legal Warning to Church on Gay Stance," *The Irish Times*, 2 August 2003. http://www.ireland.com/newspaper/front/2003/0802/720611077HM1POPE.html.

28. Allyson Smith, "Vatican Statement Against Homosexual Unions Encourages Pro-Family Advocates," Concerned Women for America: Culture and Family Institute, 6 August 2004. http://www.cultureandfamily.org/articledisplay.asp?id=4410& department=CFI&categoryid=cfreport.

29. Doug Windsor, "Vatican Calls Gay Marriage 'Gravely Immoral,'" *365Gay.com*, 31 July 2003. http://www.365gay.com/NewsContent/073103popeMarriage.htm.

30. Smith, "Vatican Statement Against Homosexual Unions Encourages Pro-Family Advocates."

31. Jon ben Asher, "Distribute Vatican Anti-Gay Marriage Document and Face Jail Irish Priests Warned," *365Gay.com*, 2 August 2004. http://www.365gay.com/NewsContent/080203irishPriests.htm.

32. Staver, *Same-Sex Marriage,* 64.

33. Karen Holgate, radio interview, *Faith2Action with Janet Folger,* 24 August/30 June 2004.

34. California Assembly Bill 1785 Chartered Bill Text, introduced by Assembly member Villaraigosa, 26 January 2000, Section 4 (b) 3. http://www.californiafamily.org/Site/isBrief_Detail.asp?PID=73.

35. Holgate radio interview, 24 August 2004.

36. Mathew Staver, "Colorado Court Vacates (For Now) Trial Court Order That Prohibits a Mother From Exposing Her Child to 'Homophobic' Religious Upbringing Or Training," Liberty Counsel Press Release, 1 July 2004. http://www.lc.org/libertyalert/2004/la070104b.htm.

37. "Hate-Crimes Law Worries Pastors," *WorldNetDaily*, 30 June 2004. http://www.worldnetdaily.com/news/article.asp?ARTICLE_ID=39204.

38. Phyllis Edwards, "Meeting Disruption Case Goes to Trial," *NewsofDelawareCounty.com,* 29 September 2004. http://www.zwire.com/site/news.cfm?newsid=13030781&BRD=1725&PAG=461&dept_id=45529&rfi=8; James Taranto, "The Bible as 'Hate Speech,'" editorial, *Wall Street Journal,* 1 October 2004. http://www.opinionjournal.com/best/?id=110005704.

39. Pastor Harding, radio interview, *Faith2Action with Janet Folger,* 25 August 2004.

40. Art Moore, "Punishment Includes Islam Indoctrination," *WorldNetDaily*, 31 October 2002. http://www.worldnetdaily.com/news/article.asp?ARTICLE_ID=29483.

41. Ibid.

42. Ibid.

43. Holgate radio interview, 24 August 2004.

44. Benjamin Lopez, "California Governor Signs Drag Queen/Hate Crime Law," Traditional Values Coalition Press Release, 23 September 2004. http://www.traditionalvalues.org/modules.php?sid=1920.

45. Rabbi Daniel Lapin, *America's Real War: An Orthodox Rabbi Insists That Judeo-Christian Values Are Vital for Our Nation's Survival* (Sisters, OR: Multnomah, 1999), 46.

Chapter 2

1. Chuck Colson, "Why Christians Are Losing the Culture War," *Christian Research Journal* (Summer 1996), A9.

2. "Americans Are Most Likely to Base Truth on Feelings," *The Barna Group*, 12 February 2004. http://www.barna.org/FlexPage.aspx?Page=BarnaUpdate&BarnaUpdateID=106.

3. "Declaration of Principles on Tolerance," The Member States of the United Nations Educational, Scientific and Cultural Organization, meeting in Paris at the twenty-eighth session of the General Conference, from 25 October to 16 November 1995.

4. Reuters, "Has Church of Satan Gone to Hell?" *CNN Custom News—World*, 26 January 1999. http://customnews/cnews/pna.show_story?p_art_id=3373001&p_section_name=World; Jack Boulware, "Has the Church of Satan Gone to Hell?" *New York Times—Features*, 17 June 1988.

5. Janet L. Folger, *:30 Seconds to Common Sense* (Ft. Lauderdale, FL: Coral Ridge Ministries, 2001), 76.

6. Josh McDowell and Bob Hostetler, *The New Tolerance: How a Cultural Movement Threatens to Destroy You, Your Faith, and Your Children* (Wheaton, IL: Tyndale, 1998), 25.

7. "Excerpts from the Eulogies: Recollections of Hope, Humor and One Very Big Heart," *New York Times*, 12 June 2004.

8. Robert B. Reich, "The Last Word," *The American Prospect Online*, 17 June 2004. http://www.prospect.org/web/page.ww?section=root&name=ViewPrint&articleId=7858.

9. McDowell and Hostetler, *The New Tolerance*, 92.

10. Ibid., 95.

11. "Paralyzed Woman Walks Again After Stem Cell Therapy," *Agence France-Presse*, 28 November 2004.

12. Center for Disease Control, *HIV/AIDS Surveillance Report*, 9, no. 2 (May 1998); "HIV Infection and Risk Behaviours Among Young Gay and Bisexual Men in Vancouver," *Canadian Medical Association Journal*, 11 January 2000.

13. "Scientific Evidence on Condom Effectiveness for STD Prevention," National Institutes of Health, 2001.

14. "Facts & Answers about STDs," *American Social Health Association*, 2005. http://www.ashastd.org/stdfaqs/statistics.html.

15. Alan Guttmacher Institute, *Sex and America's Teenagers* (New York: Alan Guttmacher Institute, 1994), 19–20. http://www.mfc.org/legmanual/education%202.pdf.

Chapter 3

1. Bernard N. Nathanson, MD, *Aborting America: A Doctor's Personal Report on the Agonizing Issue of Abortion* (Toronto, Canada: Life Cycle Books, 1979), 51.

2. Ibid.

3. Ibid., 52.

4. Ibid., 52–53.

5. Ibid.

6. Janet L. Folger, *True to Life: The Incredible Story of a Young Woman Who Spoke up for the Unborn and Found Herself in the National Spotlight* (Sisters, OR: Multnomah, 2000), 81.

7. Michael Weisskopf, "Energized by Pulpit or Passion, the Public Is Calling," *Washington Post*, 1 February 1993, A1.

8. "Christians: Easy Targets for the Media," *Impact*, May 1993.

9. "Ted's Latest Insults," *Cincinnati Enquirer*, 2 March 1999, A16.

10. D. James Kennedy and Jerry Newcombe, *The Gates of Hell Shall Not Prevail* (Nashville, TN: Thomas Nelson, 1996), 114.

11. From an Ohio Human and Civil Rights Commission questionnaire, published by the Ohio Education Association, December 1994.

12. Charlene K. Haar, "National Education Association: Convention Delegates Debate Change," *Education Policy Institute*, September 1997. http://www.educationpolicy.org/files/Orgtrnds997.htm.

13. Doug Ireland, "Gay Ed for Kids," *The Nation* 268, no. 22 (14 June 1999): 8.

14. George Varga, "The Real Deal, Linda Ronstadt's Current Tour— 'A History Lesson of Music'—Reflects Her Dedication to Authenticity and Quality," *San Diego Union-Tribune*, 15 July 2004.

15. Andy Rooney, "As God Told Me...," *60 Minutes*, 22 February 2004. http://www.cbsnews.com/stories/2004/02/19/60minutes/rooney/main601254.shtml.

16. "Mel Gibson's 'Passion' Worldwide Film Receipts Top $609 Million," Kingdom Ventures Press Release, 19 July 2004.

17. John Wheeler, "Assault of Faith," *Christian American*, 15 September 1994, 4.

18. Ralph Reed, *Mainstream Values Are No Longer Politically Incorrect* (Dallas, TX: Word, 1994), 10.

19. "The 'Left' Melts Down," *American Renewal*, 16 December 1998.

20. Robert Knight, "If All Else Fails, Silence Them!" *WorldNetDaily*, 1 September 2004. http://www.wnd.com/news/article.asp?ARTICLE_ID=40244.

21. Family Research Council, *Culture Facts*, 11 November 1993.

22. Kennedy and Newcombe, *The Gates of Hell*, 88.

23. Ibid.

24. "Clear Channel Nixes Howard Stern, Faced with a $495,000 FCC Fine, the Radio Chain Drops Stern Show from Six Stations," *CNN*, 8 April, 2004.

25. Daniel Rubin, "Howard Stern Finds Freedom, $500 Million in Satellite Deal," *Seattle Times*, 7 October 2004.

26. "Sidelights—News Scraps," *American Enterprise*, November/December 1995. http://www.taemag.com/issues/articleid.16431/article_detail.asp.

Chapter 4

1. Ron Kessler, "Tired of the Bush-Bashing? By Election Day, There Will Be 50+ Anti-Bush Books in Stores from Liberals like Michael Moore, Maureen Dowd, Al Franken," New York, *Sentinel*, 9 August 2004; Cliff Kincaid, "Smearing President Bush," *Accuracy in Media*, 27 August 2004.

2. Oliver North, radio interview, *Faith2Action with Janet Folger*, 16 December 2004.

3. Andrea Peyser, "Ignorance on the March," *New York Post*, 30 August 2004.

4. Ibid.

5. "Gore: Bush Faith Akin to Fundamentalist Islam," *WorldNetDaily*, 8 September 2004. http://www.worldnetdaily.com/news/article.asp?ARTICLE_ID=40357.

6. Matt Drudge, "Drudge Report," *Drudge Report*, 22 August 2004. http://www.drudgereportarchives.com/data/2004/08/22/20040822_215403_flash5.htm.

7. Ibid.

8. "Lesbian Scene Nixed Because Bush President?" *WorldNetDaily*, 4 August 2004. http://www.worldnetdaily.com/news/article.asp?ARTICLE_ID=39783.

9. "Slim-Fast Trims Whoopi from Ads," *CNN.com*, 14 July 2004. http://www.cnn.com/2004/SHOWBIZ/07/14/slimfast.whoopi/.

10. "Hillary Clinton: 'This Is a Battle,'" *CNN.com*, 27 January 1998. http://www.cnn.com/US/9801/27/hillary.today/.

11. Michael Lind, "Understanding Oklahoma Scofflaw Conservatism: Beyond the Hyperbole, Ideas Have Consequences," *Washington Post*, 30 April 1995, C1.

12. John Leo, "Not the Way to Stop Abortions," *U.S. News & World Report*, 29 March 1993, 17.

13. David Crary, "We Are Women, Where's the Roar? Many Lesbians Aren't Getting the Health Care They Need," *Times-Picayune*, San Francisco, 26 June 2004.

14. "Schwarzenegger's 'Girlie Men' Line Under Fire," *CNN*, 20 July 2004.

15. M. V. Lee Badgett and Rhonda M. Williams, "The Economics of Sexual Orientation: Establishing a Research Agenda," *Feminist Studies* 18, no. 3 (Fall 1992): 649–57; Peter Sprigg and Timothy Dailey, *Getting It Straight: What the Research Shows about Homosexuality* (Family Research Council: Washington, DC, 2004), 58; Maricks M. Klawitter and Victor Flatt, "The Effects of State and Local Antidiscrimination Policies on Earnings for Gays and Lesbians," *Journal of Policy Analysis and Management* 17, no. 4 (1998): 662; Sprigg and Dailey, *Getting It Straight*, 57; "National Marketing Studies Confirm the Affluence of the Gay and Lesbian Market," RainbowReferrals.com, 23 April 2003, http://www.rainbowreferrals.com/sponsors/statistic.asp; Sprigg and Dailey, *Getting It Straight*, 65.

16. Bob Jones IV, "Shouting Down Christians?" *World* 13, no. 49 (19 December 1998). http://www.worldmag.com/displayarticle.cfm?id=2519.

17. Ibid.

18. John Leo, "Avoid 'Climate' Control," *Incorrect Thoughts: Notes on our Wayward Culture* (Somerset, NJ: Transaction Publishers, 2001), 153.

19. Ibid.

20. From a letter from City of San Francisco Board of Supervisors to Coral Ridge Ministries in response to the announcement of the Truth in Love Campaign, 19 October 1998.

21. Katie Couric, *Today Show,* 12 October 1998.

22. Stuart Shepard, "Ministry Calls on NBC to Apologize," *Family News in Focus,* 7 December 2004, http://www.family.org/cforum/fnif/news/a0034812.cfm; Michael Medved, "Media Finally Face the Truth on Shepard Case," *Jewish World Review*, 6 December 2004. http://www.jewishworldreview.com/ cols/medved120604.asp.

23. Allyson Smith, "Remembering Jesse Dirkhising: A Young Life Snuffed Out by Homosexual Lovers," Concerned Women for America, 18 September 2002. http://www.cultureandfamily.org/articledisplay.asp?id=2093&department=CFI&categoryid=cfreport.

24. Sprigg and Dailey, *Getting It Straight,* 126.

25. Allyson Smith, "'Gay' Reaction to Mrs. Stachowicz's Murder: Silence to Applause," Concerned Women for America, 4 December 2002. http://www.cultureandfamily.org/articledisplay.asp?id=2877&department=CFI&categoryid=cfreport.

26. Ibid.

27. Ibid.

Chapter 5

1. Quoted in Michael Wilrich, "Uncivil Disobedience," *Mother Jones* (December 1990), 16; Scott Lively, *Seven Steps to Recruit-Proof Your Child* (Keizer, OR: Founder's Publishing Corporation, 1998), 173.

2. John Leo, *Two Steps Ahead of the Thought Police* (New York: Simon & Schuster, 1994), 148.

3. Ibid., 148, 258–59.

4. Scott Lively and Kevin Abrams, *The Pink Swastika: Homosexuality in the Nazi Party* (Sacramento, CA: Veritas Aeterna Press, 2002), 290.

5. Ibid., 295.

6. Roy Maynard, "Zero Tolerance," *World,* 22 March 1997. http://www.reformednet.org/refnet/nwscover/970324/970324.htm.

7. Ibid.

8. Ibid.

9. Chuck and Donna McIlhenny and Frank York, *When the Wicked Seize a City: A Grim Look at the Future and a Warning to the Church* (Lafayette, LA: Huntington House, 1993).

10. Lively and Abrams, *The Pink Swastika*, 290–91.

11. Janet L. Folger, *:30 Seconds to Common Sense* (Ft. Lauderdale, FL: Coral Ridge Ministries, 2001), 183.

12. Quoted in Kirk Kidwell, "Homosexuals Flex Muscles in Washington"; Lively and Abrams, *The Pink Swastika*, 210.

13. Jeffrey Satinover, *Homosexuality and the Politics of Truth* (Grand Rapids, MI: Hamewith Books, 1998), 32.

14. Ibid.

15. Ibid., 33.

16. Ibid.

17. Ibid., 34.

18. Ibid., 35.

19. Ibid., 36.

20. "APA, Dr. Laura Respond," *Impact*, November 1999, 2.

21. Jon Dougherty, "Student Sues College for Psychiatric Abuse," *WorldNetDaily*, 5 January 2001. http://www.worldnetdaily.com/news/article.asp?ARTICLE_ID=21225.

22. "Scouting Legal Defense Fund," letter, American Civil Rights Union, Washington, DC, July, 2004.

23. Roger J. Magnuson, Are *Gay Rights Right? Making Sense of the Controversy*, Portland, Oregon, Multnomah, 1990, 70–71.

24. Ibid., 71.

25. David Wooding, "EU Bans Girl-Only Ads," Online Sun, 22 September 2004.

26. Pat Dostine, "Hate Messages Target Ferndale Residents," *Ferndale (MI) Mirror,* 14 November 2002.

27. Ibid.

28. Ibid.

29. Center for Reclaiming America, "FastFacts—Homosexuality" (Ft. Lauderdale, FL: 1999).

30. "'Miami Arrests, Massachusetts Debacle Show Homosexual Lobby's Win-at-Any-Cost Strategy,' Rios Says," Concerned Women for America, 20 August 2002, http://www.cwfa.org/articledisplay.asp?id=1194&department=MEDIA&categoryid=family; Tere Figueras, "Two More

Arrested in Probe of Gay Rights Repeal Drive," 16 August 2002. http://www.miami.com/mld/miamiherald/3881224.htm; Peter J. LaBarbera, "Prosecutor Defends Arrest of Pro-Family Leader in Miami," Concerned Women for America, 28 August 2002. http://www.cultureandfamily.org/articledisplay.asp?id=745&department=CFI&categoryid=cfreport.

31. J. Michael Bailey and Richard C. Pillard, "A Genetic Study of Male Sexual Orientation," *Archives of General Psychiatry*, 48 (December 1991): 1089, 1094.

32. Gary L. Bauer, "Quotas—For Homosexuals?" Campaign for Working Families—End of Day Report, 14 May 2004. http://www.theinterim.com/2004/june/10quotasfor.htm.

33. "Historic Gay Advocate Now Believes Change Is Possible," National Association for Research and Therapy of Homosexuals, 9 May 2001. http://www.narth.com/docs/spitzer3.html.

Chapter 6

1. Janet L. Folger, *True to Life: The Incredible Story of a Young Woman Who Spoke up for the Unborn and Found Herself in the National Spotlight* (Sisters, OR: Multnomah, 2000), 205.

2. Brad Bauman, letter to the editor, Florida International University *Beacon*, 9 February 1999. http://www.clorinfo.org/GAP/gap-quotes.html.

3. Diane Brooks, "Religious Talk Is a Bus-Stopper, Woman Says," *Seattle Times*, 7 April 1999.

4. "The Gospel according to Balmer," *World*, 2 July 1994.

5. "Atheists to Demonstrate at San José Nativity Display," *American Atheist*, 25 November 1998; *San José Mercury News*, 4 December 1994; Dave Kong, "San José Public Nativity Protest," *American Atheist*, 5 December 1994.

6. Ron Strom, "Google Bars 'Hate' Sites' Ads, but Runs Porn Ads," *WorldNetDaily*, 18 August 2004, http://www.worldnetdaily.com/news/article.asp?ARTICLE_ID=40012; Google search of "gay porn" ads listed on page 1, 13 September 2004.

7. Janet L. Folger, *:30 Seconds to Common Sense* (Ft. Lauderdale, FL: Coral Ridge Ministries, 2001), 89.

8. Jodi Veenker, "Christian Group Labeled 'Cultic,'" *Christianity Today*, September 1999, 26.

9. Ibid.

10. C. Boyden Gray, "Claude Allen and His Enemies: Understanding the Judge Fights," *National Review Online*, 7 July 2004.

11. Ibid.

12. "Judges May Have to Quit Groups that Discriminate against Gays," *Arizona Daily Sun*, 7 August 2004.

13. Kay Daly, interview, *Faith2Action with Janet Folger*, 23 August 2004.

14. Kay Daly, "Judge for Yourself: Are Senate Democrats Determined to Keep Believers off the Bench?" *Wall Street Journal*, 25 July 2003.

15. Audrey Mullen, "CFFJ Calls on Senate to Confirm Leon Holmes, Anti-Believer Litmus Test Must Be Stopped," Coalition for a Fair Judiciary Press Release, 6, July 2004.

16. Associated Press, "Holmes Confirmed by Senate," *Fox News*, 7 July 2004.

17. Folger, *True to Life,* 208.

18. "The One World Church," *Discerning the Times* 1, no. 6 (July 1999), http://www.discerningtoday.org/members/Digest/1999Digest/July/The%20One%20World%20Church.htm.

19. "History and Organizational Design," *United Religious Initiative*, United Nations, 2003. http://www.factindex.com/u/un/united_religions_initiative.html

20. Gary Kah, *The New World Religion* (Noblesville, IN: Hope International Publishing, 1999); "The New Religious Order," http://www.garykah.org/html/hftwec.html.

21. "Declaration of Principles on Tolerance," proclaimed and signed by the member states of UNESCO on 16 November 1995, http://www.unesco.org/tolerance/declaeng.htm; Berit Kjos, "Media Bias Matches UNESCO Intolerance," Kjos Ministries, 16 September 2004, http://www.crossroad.to/articles2/2002/tolerance.htm.

22. "Historic Judgement Finds Akayesu Guilty of Genocide," United Nations Press Release, 2 November 1998. http://www.un.org/ictr/english/pressrel/PR138.htm.

23. "Presidential Debate Transcript: What Is Kerry's Position on Preemptive War?" *CNN*, 1 October 2004. http://www.cnn.com/2004/ALLPOLITICS/10/01/debate.transcript.13/index.html.

24. "Classic Reagan Quotes," Annual Meeting of the 30 March 1961 Phoenix Chamber of Commerce, Geocities Web site, 26 August 2004. http://www.geocities.com/Pacific_Future/quotes_reag.html.

Chapter 7

1. Gary L. Bauer, "Quotas—For Homosexuals?" Campaign for Working Families—End of Day Report, 14 May 2004. http://www.theinterim.com/2004/june/10quotasfor.html.

2. David Barton, *Original Intent: The Courts, the Constitution, and Religion* (Aledo, TX: Wallbuilder Press, 1997), 14.

3. Marshall Allen, "Watch That Invocation: Prayer in Jesus' Name Forbidden in California Legislative Meetings," *Christianity Today*, 8 July 2003.

4. "ACLU of San Diego Challenges Sectarian Prayers at City Council Meetings on Behalf of Resident," American Civil Liberties Union, 5 May 2004. http://www.aclu.org/ReligiousLiberty/ReligiousLiberty.cfm?ID=15666&c=29.

5. Barton, *Original Intent*, 17.

6. Ibid., 15.

7. Bill O'Reilly, "Santa is Appalled," *WorldNetDaily*, 2001.

8. Ibid.

9. "On Festive Holiday, Do Only Bigots Dare Mention the C-Word?" *Columbus Dispatch*, 8 A, 24 December 1996.

10. Barton, *Original Intent*, 14.

11. Ibid.

12. "LA County to Remove Cross from County Seal after ACLU Challenge," *ABC7.com*, 2 June 2004, http://abclocal.go.com/kabc/news/060204ap_nw_county_seal.html; Bill O'Reilly,"Another Victory for the ACLU and Its War on Christianity," *FoxNews.com*, 28 June 2004. http://www.foxnews.com/story/0,2933,124012,00.html.

13. "Capitol Flag under Fire over Cross," *Palm Beach Post*, 23 July 2004.

14. Family Research Council, "Washington Update—American Renewal," 22 April 1994.

15. Janet L. Folger, *:30 Seconds to Common Sense* (Ft. Lauderdale, FL: Coral Ridge Ministries, 2001), 91.

16. "*Michael Chandler, et al., v. Fob James, et al.,*" United States District Court for the Middle District of Alabama, Northern Division, October 29, 1997, National Legal Foundation. http://www.nlf.net/dmtordr.html.

17. "National Endowment for the Arts," Concerned Women for America, 11 November 1997. http://www.cwfa.org/articledisplay.asp?id=1992&department=CWA&categoryid=pornography.

18. "Transcript of Excerpt of Proceedings Before the Honorable Samuel B. Kent, U.S. District Court for the Southern District of Texas," CA No. G-95-176, 5 May 1995, 3–4.

19. Robert B. Bluey, "Author of Homosexual Marriage Ruling Is Under Fire, Won't Budge," *CNSnews.com*, 28 April 2004. http://www.cnsnews.com/ViewCulture.asp?Page=%5CCulture%5Carchive%5C200404%5CCUL20040428a.html.

20. "Liberty Counsel Files Amicus Brief on Behalf of Mother Who Was Ordered by Court to Not Expose Her Child to 'Homophobic' Religious Upbringing or Training," Liberty Counsel Press Release, Orlando, Florida, 29 October 2003.

21. Ibid.

22. Phyllis Schlafly, *The Supremacists: The Tyranny of Judges and How to Stop It* (Dallas, TX: Spence Publishing Company, 2004), 117.

23. F. James Sensenbrenner Jr., "House Approves Legislation Protecting Marriage Policy for the States," U.S. House of Representatives Committee on the Judiciary Press Release, 22 July 2004. http://www.judiciary.house.gov/legacy/news072204.htm.

24. Ibid.

25. Jim Abrams, "House Votes to Protect 'Under God' in Pledge," *Houston Chronicle*, 23 September 2004.

26. "Roy Moore Plans Bill to Curb Federal Courts," *WorldNetDaily*, 17 November 2003. http://www.worldnetdaily.com/news/article.asp?ARTICLE_ID=35666.

27. "Roy Moore-Inspired Bill Limits Federal Courts," *WorldNetDaily*, 30 March, 2004. http://www.worldnetdaily.com/news/article.asp?ARTICLE_ID=37796.

28. Michael J. Meade, "Judges Have Too Much Power in Social Issues Scalia Says," *365gay.com*, 29 September 2004. http://www.365gay.com/newscon04/09/092904scalia.htm.

Chapter 8

1. "Pastor Sued for Alleged Hate Speech Urges the Church to Avoid Timidity," *Charisma Now*, World News, 5 October 2004. http://www.charismanow.com/a.php?ArticleID=9860.

2. Michael Marcavage, "Narrative of Incident at the Lansdowne Borough Council Meeting on July 21," Repent America Press Release, 21 July 2004. http://www.repentamerica.com/narrative7–21–04.html.

3. Ibid.
4. "Man Prosecuted for Reading Bible at Council Meeting," *WorldNetDaily*, 1 October 2004. http://www.worldnetdaily.com/news/article.asp?ARTICLE_ID=40710
5. Ibid.
6. Scott Brooks, "Mass. Man Is Facing Hate Crime Charges," *Union Leader*, 21 August 2004.
7. James Jacobs and Kimberly Potter, *Hate Crimes: Criminal Law and Identity Politics* (Oxford University Press, 1998), 5. http://users.ox.ac.uk/~mert1230/hatecrimes.pdf.
8. Marshall Kirk and Hunter Madsen, PhD, *After the Ball: How America Will Conquer Its Fear and Hatred of Gays in the 90s* (New York: Doubleday, 1989), 183.
9. Ibid.
10. Leah Farish, "Hate Crimes: Beyond Virtual Reality," Family Research Council, 15 October 2004. http://www.frc.org/get.cfm?i=IS03K01.
11. "Gunman Opens Fire at Texas Church; 8 People Dead," *CNN.com*, 15 September 1999. http://www.cnn.com/US/9909/15/church.shooting.04/index.html.
12. Farish, "Hate Crimes: Beyond Virtual Reality."
13. Ibid.
14. "Crying Wolf?" *World*, 1 August 1999, 8.
15. John Leo, "Faking the Hate," *U.S. News & World Report*, 5 June 2000, 22.
16. "Combating Hate Crimes" (Bill at issue: S622), Senate Judiciary Committee hearing, chaired by Sen. Orrin Hatch (R-UT), 11 May 1999.
17. Ibid.
18. Jody Brown, "California's Hate Crimes Expansion Potentially 'Dangerous' for Christians; Activists Say Pending Legislation Would Punish Those Who Speak Out against Homosexuality," *AgapePress*, 18 August 2004. http://headlines.agapepress.org/archive/8/182004a.asp.
19. Benjamin Lopez, "California Governor Signs Drag Queen/Hate Crime Law," *Traditional Values Coalition News*, 23 September 2004. http://www.traditionalvalues.org/modules.php?sid=1920.
20. "What's Happening in My State," Human Rights Campaign, 1 August 2004. http://www.hrc.org/Template.cfm?Section=Your_Community.
21. Brian Fahling, radio interview, *Faith2Action with Janet Folger*, 5 January 2005.
22. John Leo, "Stomping on Free Speech," *townhall.com*, 12 April 2004. http://www.townhall.com/columnists/johnleo/jl20040412.shtml.

THE CRIMINALIZATION OF CHRISTIANITY

23. Ibid.

24. "Hate Propaganda," Consolidated Statutes and Regulations, Department of Justice, Canada, 30 April 2003. http://laws.justice. gc.ca/en/c-46/41491.html.

25. California Assembly Bill 1785 Chartered Bill Text, introduced by Assembly member Villaraigosa, 26 January 2000, Section 4 (b) 3.

26. Karen Holgate, "Hate-Crime Legislation: Promoting the Gay Agenda in the Schools?" California Family Council, *CaliforniaFamily.org.* www.californiafamily.org/Site/isBrief_Detail.asp?PID=73.

27. California Assembly Bill 1785 Chartered Bill Text, Section 2 (a) 1.

28. Karen Holgate, radio interview, *Faith2Action with Janet Folger,* 24 August/30 June 2004.

29. "Iowa Transsexuals Able to Obtain New Birth Certificates," *Advocate,* 14 September 2004.

30. Dr. James Dobson, *Marriage under Fire: Why We Must Win This Battle* (Sisters, OR: Multnomah, 2004), 54.

31. Stanley Kurtz, "Death of Marriage in Scandinavia," *Boston Globe,* 10 March 2004, A23.

32. Michelangelo Signorile, "Bridal Wave," *OUT* magazine, December/January 1994, 161.

33. Tom Stoddard, quoted in Roberta Achtenberg, et al., "Approaching 2000: Meeting the Challenges to San Francisco's Families," *The Final Report of the Mayor's Task Force on Family Policy, City and County of San Francisco,* 13 June 1990, 1.

34. Michelangelo Signorile, "I Do, I Do, I Do, I Do, I Do," *OUT* magazine, May 1996, 30.

35. Paula Ettelbrick, "Since When Is Marriage a Path to Liberation?" in William Rubenstein, ed., *Lesbians, Gay Men and the Law* (New York: The New Press, 1993), 401–05.

36. Judith Levine, "Stop the Wedding! Why Gay Marriage Isn't Radical Enough," *The Village Voice,* July 23–29. 2003. http://www.villagevoice.com/news/0330,levine,45704,1.html.

37. Judith Levine, *Harmful to Minors: The Perils of Protecting Children from Sex* (Minneapolis: University of Minnesota Press, 2002), 88–89.

38. Pamela Manson, "Utah Suit Challenges Laws on Polygamy," *Salt Lake Tribune,* 4 August 2004.

39. Ibid.

40. The National Gay and Lesbian Task Force, "Arguing the Case for Domestic Partnership Benefits," *The NGLTF Domestic Partnership Organizing Manual*, 19 October 2004. http://www.ngltf.org/downloads/dp/dp3.pdf.

41. "National Homosexual Lobby Cut Same-Sex Benefit for Its Own Employees," *Washington Blade*, 7 March 2003, http://www.washblade.com/local/030307ngltf.php3?

42. Dobson, *Marriage under Fire*, 58.

Chapter 9

1. "'It's Elementary' under Attack," *youth.org*, 17 March 1998. http://www.youth.org/loco/PERSONProject/Alerts/Old/1998/attack.html.

2. Norma Bowles and Mark E. Rosenthal, eds, *Cootie Shots: Theatrical Inoculations against Bigotry for Children, Parents and Teachers* (New York: TCG Books, 2001).

3. "Play Wedding," Gay, Lesbian and Straight Education Network of Colorado—Cootie Shots Companion Guide—Lesson Plans. http://www.glsenco.org/.

4. "Fox Special Report with Brit Hume," *Fox News*, Transcript # 021803cb.254, 18 February 2002 (Online. Nexis.).

5. Bowles and Rosenthal, eds, *Cootie Shots*.

6. John Leo, *Two Steps ahead of the Thought Police* (New York: Simon & Schuster, 1994), 149.

7. Ibid.

8. Gay, Lesbian and Straight Education Network of Colorado, "Books for Elementary," http://www.glsenco.org/.

9. "British Columbia Schools and the Law," *Planet Out*, 23 June 2000. http://www.sodomylaws.org/world/canada/canews002.htm.

10. Ibid.

11. Linda Harvey, "West Virginia Attorney General Uses Students as Informants on 'Homophobic' Speech, Federal Agencies, States Abusing Power to Promote Homosexuality,"Concerned Women for America, 17 July 2002. http://www.cwfa.org/articles/696/CFI/cfreport/

12. Ibid.

13. Ibid.

14. Tony Perry, "Lawsuit Pits Gay Rights, Free Speech," *Los Angeles Times*, 16 September 2004.

15. "The Health Care Costs of Smoking," *New England Journal of Medicine* 338, no. 7 (12 February 1998); "HIV Infection and Risk Behaviours among Young Gay and Bisexual Men in Vancouver," *The Canadian Medical Association Journal*, 11 January 2000.

16. Jeffrey Satinover, *Homosexuality and the Politics of Truth* (Grand Rapids, MI: Hamewith Books, 1998), 51.

17. "President Signs $15 Billion Emergency AIDS Bill," *PBS*, 28 May 2003. http://www.pbs.org/newshour/extra/features/jan-june03/aids_5–28.pdf.

18. Janet L. Folger, *:30 Seconds to Common Sense* (Ft. Lauderdale, FL: Coral Ridge Ministries, 2001).

19. Ibid, 98.

20. "Most Parents Think Their Kids Never Had Sex While Data Shows 50% Sexually Active," *Medical News Today*, 17 August 2004.

21. "Teacher Has Kids Tasting Flavored Condoms," *WorldNetDaily*, 22 July 2004. http://www.worldnetdaily.com/news/article.asp?ARTICLE_ID=39588.

22. President George W. Bush, "State of the Union, 2004," January 20, 2004. http://www.whitehouse.gov/news/releases/2004/01/20040120-7.html.

23. Keith Peters, "New Booklet Exposes Ideology Behind Sex Ed," *Family News in Focus*, 10 August 2004.

24. Janet L. Folger, *True to Life: The Incredible Story of a Young Woman Who Spoke up for the Unborn and Found Herself in the National Spotlight* (Sisters, OR: Multnomah, 2000), 156; Tony Snow, "Subsidizing the Condom Cult," *Jewish World Review*, 18 October 1999. http://www.jewishworldreview.com/tony/snow1018199.asp.

25. "Abstinence-Only 'Sex' Education," *Planned Parenthood*, July 2004. http://www.plannedparenthood.org/pp2/portal/files/portal/medicalinfo/teensexualhealth/fact-abstinence-education.xml.

26. Associated Press, "Sharon Stone Says Keep Condoms Near," *Washington Post*, 2 December 1998. http://search.washingtonpost.com.

27. Oliver Moore, "Winnipeg Makes Crack Smoking Safer," *Globe and Mail*, 26 August 2004.

28. Ibid.

29. Folger, *:30 Seconds to Common Sense*, 141.

30. George Archibald, "'How to be Gay' Course Draws Fire at Michigan," *Washington Times*, 2003. http://washingtontimes.com/national/20030818-122317-3268r.htm.

31. Steve Jordahl, "Gay-Friendly News Urged," *Family News in Focus*, 15 October 2004.

32. Joel Belz, "Rather Likely: The Decline of the Major Media Should Give Us Hope That Other Monopolies Might Fall, Too," *World* 19, no. 39 (9 October 2004): 4.

Chapter 10

1. Dan Whitcomb, "Declaration of Independence Banned at Bay-Area School," *SignOnSanDiego.com*, Los Angeles, 24 November 2004. http://www.signonsandiego.com/news/state/20041124-1309-life-declaration.html.

2. Janet L. Folger, *:30 Seconds to Common Sense* (Ft. Lauderdale, FL: Coral Ridge Ministries, 2001), 97.

3. George Washington, 10 May 1789, quoted in William J. Federer, *America's God and Country Encyclopedia of Quotations* (Coppell, TX: Fame Publishing, 1994), 653.

4. John Eidsmoe, *Christianity and the Constitution: The Faith of Our Founding Fathers* (Grand Rapids, MI: Baker, 1987), 108.

5. James Madison, 20 June 1785, quoted in Federer, *America's God and Country*, 410.

6. Ibid., 26.

7. U.S. Supreme Court, *Church of the Holy Trinity v. United States,* argued and submitted 7 January 1892, decided February 1892. http://members.aol.com/TestOath/HolyTrinity.htm.

8. Thomas Jefferson, 1 January 1802, quoted in Federer, *America's God and Country*, 325.

9. Thomas Jefferson, 16 November 1798, quoted in Federer, *America's God and Country*, 323.

10. Justice Antonin Scalia, Dissent in *Lee v. Weisman*, 505 U.S. 577 (1992). http://supct.law.cornell.edu/supct/html/90-1014.20.html.

11. "Houses Of Worship Political Speech Protection Act Introduced in House," Center for Reclaiming America, June 2002. http://www.reclaimamerica.org/Pages/NEWS/newspage.asp?story=147.

12. Stephen Dinan, "Kerry, Jackson Tell Blacks to Ignore Gay 'Marriage' Issue," *Washington Times,* 11 October 2004.

13. Erin Curry, "Ronnie Floyd, on Fox News, Discusses Pulpits and Politics" *BP News,* 2 August 2004.

14. Joseph Farah, "Political Snitches Monitor Sermons, Groups Threaten

Churches with Loss of Tax-Exempt Status over Activism," *WorldNetDaily*, 23 July 2004.

15. Ibid.

16. Michael Berenbaum, *The World Must Know* (Boston: Little, Brown & Co., 1993), 22.

17. Darren Yourk, "Religious University Wins Pledge Battle," *Globe and Mail*, 17 May 2001.

18. Erwin W. Lutzer, *Hitler's Cross: The Revealing Story of How the Cross of Christ Was Used as a Symbol of the Nazi Agenda* (Chicago: Moody, 1995), 115.

19. Berenbaum, *The World Must Know*, 35–36.

20. Advertisement, *Village Voice*, 7 February 1998, 147.

21. Quoted in Janet L. Folger, *True to Life: The Incredible Story of a Young Woman Who Spoke up for the Unborn and Found Herself in the National Spotlight* (Sisters, OR: Multnomah, 2000), 26.

22. Richard Dawkins, "Is Science a Religion?" *The Humanist*, January/February 1997.

23. Reggie Rivers, *Rocky Mountain Times*, 4 August 1998, A-6.

24. Berenbaum, *The World Must Know*, 35.

25. "Contractors with State of California Must Offer Equal Benefits for Domestic Partners," The Segal Company, Abstract of February 2004 *Bulletin*, February 2004. http://www.segalco.com/corporate/ pub-corporate.cfm?ID=484.

26. Bruce Crumley, "Faith and Fury," *Time Europe*, 10 November 2003. http://www.time.com/time/europe/magazine/article/ 0,13005,901031110-536181-2,00.html.

27. Berenbaum, *The World Must Know*, 26–27.

28. Joel Johannesen, "Canada Keeps Censoring Fox but OKs Al-Jazeera," *NewsMax*, 19 July 2004.

29. Marni Soupcoff, "If You Like Fox News, You'll Hate Canada," The American Enterprise Online—Hot Flash Daily News and Commentary, 24 August, 2004. http://www.taemag.com/issues/articleID.17691/ article_detail.asp.

30. Berenbaum, *The World Must Know*, 39.

31. Linda Harvey "West Virginia Attorney General Uses Students as Informants on 'Homophobic' Speech," Concerned Women for America, 17 July 2002. http://www.cultureandfamily.org/articledisplay.asp? id=696&department=CFI&categoryid=cfreport.

32. Berenbaum, *The World Must Know,* 40.

33. Jack Nelson, *Terror in the Night* (New York: Simon & Schuster, 1993), 9.

34. "Classic Reagan Quotes" Annual Meeting of the 30 March 1961 Phoenix Chamber of Commerce, Geocities Web site, 26 August 2004. http://www.geocities.com/Pacific_Future/quotes_reag.html.

35. "President Delivers 'State of the Union,'" White House, U.S. Capitol, 28 January 2004. http://www.whitehouse.gov/news/releases/2003/01/20030128-19.html.

36. "Fifteenth Anniversary of the Tiananmen Square Massacre," *WorldPressReview,* Hong Kong, June 2004.

37. Paul Risenhoover, "A Midsummer's Night in Taipei County: Self-Esteem in Taiwan Rising!" *China Support Network,* 16 June 2004. http://www.chinasupport.net/buzz82.htm.

Chapter 11

1. "'You Ain't Seen Nothing Yet': City Hears of Even Better Times Ahead," (Cleveland) *Plain Dealer,* 3 November 1984.

2. "Classic Reagan Quotes," Annual Meeting of the 30 March 1961 Phoenix Chamber of Commerce, Geocities Web site, 26 August 2004. http://www.geocities.com/Pacific_Future/quotes_reag.html.

3. Peter Schweizer, *Victory: The Reagan Administration's Secret Strategy that Hastened the Collapse of the Soviet Union* (New York: The Atlantic Monthly Press, 1994), xii.

4. Ibid, xi.

5. Peter Schweizer, *Reagan's War: The Epic Story of His Forty-Year Struggle and Final Triumph Over Communism* (New York: Random House, 2003), 9.

6. Ibid., 10.

7. Ibid., 11.

8. Ibid., 12.

9. Ibid., 13.

10. Schweizer, *Victory,* xiv.

11. Schweizer, *Reagan's War,* 190.

12. Secretary of Defense Casper Weinberger, radio interview, *Faith2Action with Janet Folger,* 23 September 2004.

13. Schweizer, *Reagan's War,* 190;

14. Weinberger, *Faith2Action with Janet Folger,* 23 September, 2004.

15. Ibid.

16. Schweizer, *Reagan's War*, 190–91.

17. Ibid., 249.

18. Ibid., 251.

19. Ibid., 183.

20. Ibid., 185.

21. "Reagan in His Own Words," *Fox News*, 5 June 2004.

22. Peggy Noonan, *When Character Was King: A Story of Ronald Reagan* (New York: Penguin Books, 2001), 189.

23. "Classic Reagan Quotes."

24. Schweizer, *Reagan's War*, 183.

25. Adam Entous, "Cheney to Democrats: Weakness Invites Terror," Reuters, 27 July 2004.

26. Cheryl Wetzstein, "Gays to Gain in Kerry White House," *Washington Times*, 29 July 2004.

27. William Federer, *America's God and Country Encyclopedia of Quotations* (Coppell, TX: Fame Publishing Inc., 1994), 531.

28. Schweizer, *Reagan's War*, 19.

29. Joe Klein, "The Secrets of Reagan's Success, *Time* 163, no. 24 (14 June 2004), 21.

30. Ronald Wilson Reagan, Annual Conservative Political Action Conference Dinner, 26 February 1982. http://www.townhall.com/documents/victory.html.

31. "The Great Communicator," *World* 19, no. 24 (19 June 2004), 25.

32. George Otis, radio interview, *Faith2Action with Janet Folger*, 11 June 2004.

33. "Classic Reagan Quotes."

34. Stephen Mansfield, *The Faith of George W. Bush* (New York: Published jointly by Strang Communications and Penguin Group USA, 2003), 108–110.

35. Ibid.

Chapter 12

1. Peter Schweizer, *Reagan's War: The Epic Story of His Forty-Year Struggle and Final Triumph Over Communism* (New York, Random House, 2003), 129.

2. Charlie Peacock, "Cheer Up Church," *Kingdom Come,* © 1999 Sparrow Song/Andi Beat Goes On Music/BMI/Admin, by EMI Christian Music Publishing.

Chapter 14

1. Jeffrey Satinover, radio interview, *Faith2Action with Janet Folger,* 16 June, 2004.

2. Mark Cahill, radio interview, *Faith2Action with Janet Folger,* 27 October 2004.

3. Ibid.

4. Janet L. Folger, *:30 Seconds to Common Sense* (Ft. Lauderdale, FL: Coral Ridge Ministries, 2001), 231.

5. James Strong, "Greek Dictionary of the New Testament," *The New Strong's Expanded Exhaustive Concordance of the Bible* (Nashville, TN: Thomas Nelson, 2001), 234.

6. Ibid., 272.

7. Ibid., 234.

8. Diedtra Henderson, "FDA Approves Use of Chip in Patients," Associated Press, 13 October 2004. http://sfgate.com/cgi-bin/article.cgi?file=/news/a/2004/10/13/national0948EDT0497.DTL&type=printable.

9. "Hong Kong Airport Picks RFID Baggage Tracking," *SmartTravelNews.com,* 26 May 2004. http://www.smarttravelnews.com/news/2004/05/hong_kong_airpo.html.

10. "Reinventing Marine Corps Logistics," *Marine Corps News,* Camp Cintron, Haiti, 2 June 2004. http://www.usmc.mil/marinelink/mcn2000.nsf/0/35F73B2A5CD3CA6885256E890002E8AE?opendocument.

11. Gene J. Koprowski, "Wireless World: WiFi comes to Hospitals," United Press International, 30 April 2004. http://www.upi.com/view.cfm?StoryID=20040429-101218-5859r.

12. Jan Libbenga, "Munich Faces RFID-controlled Congestion Charge," *The Register,* 24 May 2004. http://www.theregister.co.uk/2004/05/24/munich_congestion_charge/?86e3c940.

13. Laurie Sullivan, "Loyal to RFID," *InformationWeek,* 19 May 2004. http://www.informationweek.com/story/showArticle.jhtml?articleID=20800056.

14. "Metro Group Cancels RFID Loyalty Cards under CASPIAN Pressure," *RFID News,* 1 March 2004. http://www.rfidnews.org/weblog/2004/03/01/metro-group-cancels-rfid-loyalty-cards-under-caspian-pressure/.

THE CRIMINALIZATION OF CHRISTIANITY

15. Will Weissert, "Microchips Implanted in Mexican Officials, Attorney General, Prosecutors Carry Security Pass under Their Skin," Associated Press/*MSNBC.com,* 14 July 2004. http://www.msnbc.msn.com/id/5439055/.

16. Ibid.

17. Declan McCullagh, "House Backs Major Shift to Electronic IDs," *CNetNews.com,* 10 February 2005. http://news.com.com/House+approves+electronic+ID+cards/2100-1028_3-5571898.html?part=rss&tag=5568415$subj=news.1028.5.

18. "Sudan Slave 'Crucified' by Master, but Christian Teen Rescued, Redeemed, Still Lives with Scars" *WorldNetDaily,* 7 April 2004. http://www.worldnetdaily.com/news/article.asp?ARTICLE_ID=37913.

19. "North Korea—Christian Persecution in North Korea, Religious Liberty in North Korea," *International Christian Concern,* 3 June, 2002. http://www.persecution.org/Countries/north_korea.html.

20. "Man Tortured for Preaching Christianity," *WorldNetDaily,* 15 June 2004. http://www.worldnetdaily.com/news/article.asp?ARTICLE_ID=38951.

21. "In Iraq, It's War on Christians," *WorldNetDaily,* 1 August 2004. http://www.worldnetdaily.com/news/article.asp?ARTICLE_ID=39742.

22. "India: Missionary Threatened with Death," *Voice of the Martyrs,* 21 October 2004. http://www.persecution.com.au/news/article.asp?artID={F7140339-D299-4D04-AF61-4393FCC20DF4}.

23. "Kazakhastan: Do Police and KNB Want to Catch Criminals?" *Voice of the Martyrs,* 13 October 2004. http://www.persecution.com.au/news/article.asp?artID={C93CB70E-F697-4FEC-9C23-1740B8FFA853}.

24. "Islamists Butcher New Christian," *WorldNetDaily,* 30 July 2003. http://www.worldnetdaily.com/news/article.asp?ARTICLE_ID=33819.

25. "Protests Help Release Chinese Christian," *WorldNetDaily,* 31 October 2003. http://www.worldnetdaily.com/news/article.asp?ARTICLE_ID=35363.

26. Ibid.

Chapter 15

1. Richard A. Vigueri and David Franke, *America's Right Turn: How Conservatives Used New and Alternative Media to take Power* (Chicago/Los Angeles: Bonus Books, 2004), 137–38.

2. Ibid., 139.

3. Rabbi Daniel Lapin, *America's Real War: An Orthodox Rabbi Insists That Judeo-Christian Values Are Vital for Our Nation's Survival* (Sisters, OR: Multnomah, 1999), 46.

4. Dick Meyer, "Moral Values Malarkey," *CBS News*, 5 November 2004. http://www.cbsnews.com/stories/2004/11/05/opinion/meyer/main653931.shtml.

5. Jeffrey M. Jones, "How Americans Voted, Bush Owes Victory to Support from Conservative-Leaning Groups," The Gallup Organization, 5 November 2004, http://www.gallup.com/poll/content/?ci=13957.

6. http://www.alliancealert.org/aa2004/2004_11_03.htm.

7. David Ahearn, "Woe to Those Who Call Evil Good," (Torquay) *Herald Express*, 23 March 2004, 9.

8. Ibid.

9. "Religion and the Presidential Vote: Bush's Gains Broad-Based," The Pew Research Center for the People and the Press, 6 December 2004. http://people-press.org/commentary/display.php3?AnalysisID=103.

10. Mel Gibson, *Braveheart*, Paramount Studio, 1995. Agencies, "Some of Film's Best Speeches," 21stCentury.com, 1 January, 2004. http://21stcentury.chinadaily.com.cn/article.php?sid=12046.

— ADDITIONAL RESOURCES —

Want to learn more?

Visit www.JanetFolger.net

If you want to be kept up-to-date on these hot current events, be sure to visit our website!

JanetFolger.net is your source for the most up-to-the-minute news stories that keep you informed about your world. On this timely website you may also find:

- Updates on stories and topics featured in the book
- Resources to make a difference in your community
- Exclusive articles by Janet Folger and other key experts
- Online forums for additional discussion and a place to obtain reader feedback

Join us today as we fight to win the cultural war.

Listen LIVE to Janet Folger! Janet hosts a daily radio program,
Faith2Action with Janet Folger *(from 2–3 p.m. EST) on*
www.f2a.org
syndicated in more than fifty markets and five countries.

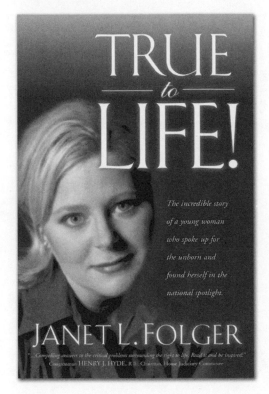

THE MAKING
of a
MESSENGER

The incredible story of a young woman who spoke up for the unborn and found herself in the national spotlight. As this desperate battle continues to rage, God has placed at its epicenter the most unlikely of persons: Janet Folger, who used to be afraid to speak, period—let alone to speak out on abortion. But there she was as a young single woman fighting for and winning passage of the nation's first ban on partial-birth abortion. In the midst of making you laugh, Janet will energize you with renewed hope and a creative action plan for success in the human rights movement of our time.

True to Life by Janet Folger
1-92912-523-2
US $9.99

Multnomah® Publishers